Introduction to
SCOTS CRIMINAL LAW

Introduction to
SCOTS CRIMINAL LAW

(2nd edition)

Dr Sarah Christie

Reader in Law, The Robert Gordon University, Aberdeen

DUNDEE UNIVERSITY PRESS
2009

First published in Great Britain in 2003 by Pearson Education Ltd

Second edition published in 2009 by
Dundee University Press
University of Dundee
Dundee DD1 4HN

www.dup.dundee.ac.uk

ISBN 978-1-84586-083-7

No natural forests were destroyed to make this product; only farmed timber was used and replanted.

British Library Cataloguing-in-Publication Data
A catalogue record for this book is available on request from the British Library.

Typeset by Waverley Typesetters, Fakenham
Printed and bound by Bell & Bain Ltd, Glasgow

CONTENTS

TABLE OF CASES

TABLE OF STATUTES

1 THE NATURE AND ADMINISTRATION OF SCOTS CRIMINAL LAW

THE NATURE OF SCOTS CRIMINAL LAW

All areas of law can be classified under broad descriptive headings, for example "European" or "international", but the great divide is between public and private law. *Private* law covers all areas of law that regulate the individual's rights and claims against other individuals. Thus, it includes property law, family law and contract law, to mention but a few. The other major classification is *public law*, which describes all those areas of law that involve the State or some organ of the State. It includes constitutional law, administrative law and, most importantly here, criminal law. Criminal law is treated as an aspect of public law because it involves the State in its capacity as prosecutor. Except in very rare cases where a private prosecution may be brought, the accused and his defence team face either the procurator fiscal, the Lord Advocate or one of his deputies, all of whom are representatives of the Crown. Prosecutions are thus run by the State, albeit for the benefit of society. It is this State involvement that characterises criminal law as public law.

The scope of the criminal law can be more difficult to justify, particularly at the boundaries of liability. It covers all criminal behaviour by any person over the age of 8,[1] but difficult theoretical issues are raised when an attempt is made to define criminal behaviour. At its most basic, criminal behaviour is simply that which legislation or case law prohibits, and to describe something as "criminal" adheres to some notion of proscribing immoral or unacceptable behaviour. The problem is this; who is to say what is immoral or unacceptable? One man's immorality may be another's pastime. However, those in charge of creating the criminal law have decided, and continue to decide, what is and is not criminal behaviour, and therefore the proper question is whether the accused has overstepped that line. If he has, he deserves punishment.

The question of the nature and purpose of punishment is a difficult one, on which there is a vast body of literature.[2] The classic divide in theories of punishment falls between retribution and rehabilitation. The retributive theory postulates that punishment is based on the State's duty to subject the criminal to such

---

[1] Note that the Scottish Law Commission has published proposals for reform of this area. See Scottish Law Commission, *Report on Age of Criminal Responsibility* (Scot Law Com No 185, 2002).

[2] Students who wish to read further should start with N Lacey, *State Punishment* (Routledge, London, 1988).

unpleasant consequences as the gravity of his offence requires. The oldest version of retribution in practice can be seen in the Biblical notion of "an eye for an eye". Other theories concentrate on the need for punishment to provide the offender with the opportunity to reform and rehabilitate or re-educate himself, or stress that its primary purpose is to deter the criminal from committing a similar, or indeed any other crime, in the future and thereby prevent or reduce re-offending.

THE MAIN SOURCES

Scots criminal law is unusual among its fellow systems in being based substantially on the common law. There are relatively few statutes, and most of them tend to relate to criminal procedure (that is, they relate to the handling of the criminal process of arrest, questioning, trial and sentence, rather than specify what amounts to a crime under Scots criminal law). However, the courts deal with statutory provisions on a regular basis, given that both road traffic offences and drug-related offences are governed by statute, and are among the most frequently prosecuted offences. There is, as yet, no such thing as a criminal code in Scotland, although these are favoured in many European systems, where the types of conduct that will be prosecutable are set out in one document.[3] As a result, most cases in the Scottish criminal courts are resolved on the basis of the doctrine of precedent, whereby previous established decisions from higher courts, usually the High Court of Justiciary as an appeal court, are used as authority and followed by lower courts in coming to a decision in the case in hand. The most noticeable result of this when examining Scots criminal law as a body of law is that the definitions of crimes tend to be broader and more generalised because they have developed from a series of authoritative decisions from previous years. The law in this area does not suffer from the stringencies of statutory definitions, which tend to be tighter and exclusive in nature. Common law definitions are more flexible and it is easier to adapt them to changing social circumstances and thereby retain the relevance of particular crimes over a longer period. However, this breadth of definition has become problematic following the incorporation of the European Convention on Human Rights into Scots law. Article 6 of the Convention requires that the accused be informed, in language which he understands and in detail, of the nature of the charge against him. Arguably, some of the more broadly defined crimes fall foul of this provision.[4]

---

[3] For example, the French *Code Pénal* or the American Model Penal Code. However, a proposed criminal code for Scotland has been submitted to the Scottish Executive and is available as *Scottish Law Commission Consultation on Draft Criminal Code for Scotland* (2003) at www.scotlawcom.gov.uk/downloads/cp_criminal_code.pdf.

[4] On this issue insofar as it relates to the crime of breach of the peace, see S Oliver, "Prosecutorial Precision and the European Convention on Human Rights" (2000) 2 *Scottish Law and Practice Quarterly* 111 and P Ferguson, "Breach of the Peace and the European Convention on Human Rights" (2001) 5 *Edin LR* 145.

There are several historical texts which are viewed as authoritative statements of Scots criminal law and used by modern courts on a regular basis.[5] The most important of these is Hume's work, originally published in 1797 as *Commentaries on the Law of Scotland Respecting Crimes*,[6] which, despite the fact that the edition used today dates from 1844, is still referred to in judgments and remains the main source for an initial definition of many crimes. The account given in this latest edition (based on Hume and updated after his death) is founded on principles that could be drawn from the decisions of the High Court prior to that date which Hume used as his sources.

USE OF LAW REPORTS

There are numerous series of law reports which reproduce the text of criminal cases. In modern times, it is fairly safe to say that no one series is more or less authoritative than another, although some are much more brief, providing only a summary,[7] while others reproduce the text with, for more notable cases, a short commentary.[8] The two main series of reports are the *Scots Law Times*[9] and the *Session Cases*. Each series is bound by year and covers civil as well as criminal cases. Each volume of the *Session Cases* is divided into three sections dedicated respectively to House of Lords cases, Justiciary cases and Session cases.[10] All criminal cases reported in the *Session Cases* are found in the Justiciary cases section.

USE OF LEGISLATION

Scots criminal law can be divided into two branches, comprising *substantive* issues, and *evidential and procedural* issues. Substantive criminal law covers the nature and extent of criminal responsibility and the description of offences. This is the subject-matter of this text. Evidential and procedural criminal law covers those rules regulating matters including the issue and use of search warrants, admissibility of evidence and the procedure for taking a case from charge to conviction and appeal. Evidential and procedural criminal law is not covered in this text, but it is the branch of criminal law that makes most use of statutes. Substantive criminal law is primarily based on common law (that is, law derived

---

[5] Beyond Hume's work, courts also make reference to Alison, *Principles and Practice of the Criminal Law of Scotland* (Edinburgh, 1833) and Macdonald, *A Practical Treatise on the Criminal Law of Scotland* (1867; 5th edn, Edinburgh, 1948).

[6] D Hume, *Commentaries on the Law of Scotland Respecting the Description and Punishment of Crimes* (1797; 4th edn, Bell (ed), Edinburgh, 1844; Butterworths, Edinburgh, 1987).

[7] For example, Greens Weekly Digest (GWD).

[8] See the Scottish Criminal Case Reports (SCCR).

[9] SLT.

[10] These are indexed respectively as SC (HL), JC and SC and each section starts at p 1.

from previous cases), although some areas are regulated by statute, such as the misuse of drugs and increasing aspects of the law on sexual offences. Statutes are published by year and are divided into sections. The bulk of these sections will detail the nature of the offence(s) in question and the appropriate penalties. Insofar as Scots criminal law has been made subject to statute, the rules on interpretation of those statutes apply as they do in other areas of law. The only difference is that any ambiguities are resolved in favour of the accused. Often the penalties will not be expressed in monetary terms, but rather as a fine of Level 1–5 on the standard scale. This refers to a scale of fines which are alterable at any time. With the advent of the Scottish Parliament, Holyrood has taken responsibility for passing much of the domestic legislation north of the border. This applies in all but the "reserved matters", which refers to the areas over which Westminster has retained the exclusive right to legislate. These reserved issues are laid out in Sch 5 to the Scotland Act 1998 and include firearms legislation, money laundering, drugs and terrorism. Thus, when looking for the applicable Scots law on an area covered by statute, it is now often necessary to investigate both UK and Scottish statutes in order to find the relevant provisions.[11]

THE DOCTRINE OF PRECEDENT

The doctrine of precedent requires lower courts to follow decisions of higher courts in cases dealing with the same area of law. These cases are said to be "in point". However, the doctrine of precedent is weaker in criminal law than it is in civil law. In the arena of criminal law, there is no possibility of appeal to the House of Lords, as it deals with Scottish appeals on civil matters only. Instead, the doctrine of precedent means that the Scottish criminal courts will follow decisions of the High Court of Justiciary, which sits as the most senior court within the jurisdiction. The High Court sitting as an appellate court binds the High Court sitting as a trial court, and the appeal court will follow its own prior decisions, although it is possible for a larger Bench to be convened in order to overrule an earlier appellate decision. However, a judge sitting in the High Court on his own is not bound by earlier decisions made by another sole judge. A sheriff will be bound by the High Court on appeal, and will usually also follow prior decisions by a sole judge in the High Court, or by a sheriff, although he is not bound to do so. Decisions retain their authoritative status until overruled.

Even if a judge is not bound to follow a prior decision, it can be treated as carrying some weight. It is known as persuasive, rather than binding, precedent.[12] Binding precedent can become even more authoritative if it has remained unchallenged,

---

[11] These are available at, respectively, http://www.opsi.gov.uk/acts.htm, and http://www.opsi.gov.uk/legislation/scotland/s-acts.htm, as well as on the Westlaw and LexisNexis databases.

[12] For example, this applies to the decisions of the supreme courts in other jurisdictions, such as America, Canada and Australia.

been cited with approval, and been followed by other courts for many years. Conversely, the weight of binding precedent can be diminished if the decision was by majority and the dissenting opinions were strong, or from a particularly respected judge. Once a case has been identified as binding, it is then necessary to isolate the part of the decision which is binding. Only the *ratio decidendi* is binding: that is, the underlying basis for the decision, which will be expressed as a general principle, without any of the specific details particular to the case from which it is derived.[13] Any statement which is *obiter dictum* is not binding. This applies to all statements made "by the way" and which are not necessary for, or strictly related to, the decision in hand.

THE DECLARATORY POWER OF THE HIGH COURT OF JUSTICIARY

The declaratory power is one of the most unusual features of the High Court of Justiciary. It was described by Hume as "an inherent power … to punish … every act which is obviously of a criminal nature".[14] This power allows the High Court to declare, as criminal, conduct which was not, at the time the act was committed, subject to a criminal sanction. In effect, the power allows the High Court retrospectively to declare the accused's conduct to be criminal. In determining what types of conduct would justify such retrospective criminalisation, older authorities suggest that the conduct should be so clearly and grossly immoral that it would be obvious to everyone and, crucially, would or should have been obvious to the accused, that it was criminal in nature. Indisputably, it is necessary for the common law to be able to adapt and move forward and, in order to do so, it is accepted that new types of criminal activity will be brought before the court and will lead to the gradual development of the definitions of existing crimes. The accused would be convicted of an existing crime because his act amounted to a new means of committing, for example, theft, fraud, or any other common law crime. However, the nature of the declaratory power is somewhat different: instead of allowing the new form of conduct to be assimilated into an existing crime, the High Court simply declares this conduct to be criminal in and of itself. Insofar as this power can be justified, it is found in the preservation of public confidence that entirely novel, but clearly grossly criminal, conduct will not go unpunished simply because it does not fit, even an adapted version of, the definition of a current crime.

The existence of the declaratory power has been recognised in a number of cases, beginning with the case of *Bernard Greenhuff*[15] which expressly states

---

[13] The *ratio* is not always actually expressed by the judge in his opinion, and often has to be deduced instead.

[14] Hume, i, 12, quoted in Gordon, *Criminal Law*, vol 1 (3rd edn, 2000), p 15.

[15] (1838) 2 Swin 236.

the existence of this power. More recent cases have acknowledged its existence, although they have not actually used it. These include *Khaliq* v *HM Advocate*[16] and *Grant* v *Allan*.[17] In *Grant*, the accused had been charged with unlawfully taking, detaining and offering to make available to another person confidential information belonging to his employer. It was argued that this was not a crime known to Scots law. The High Court on appeal was very cautious about using the declaratory power. Although it acknowledged Hume's statement that the power allowed the court to punish every obviously criminal act,[18] and that it would sometimes be appropriate to use such a power, it was also noted that any such exercise should be carried out with great care. Simply stating that conduct is immoral or reprehensible is not sufficient to make it criminal, but the court felt that it was properly for Parliament, and not the court itself, to declare new law.[19] If Parliament is not so minded, the courts are reluctant to step in.[20] The power is also subject to strong criticism to the extent that it offends against fundamental principles. It is axiomatic that there can be no crime without the existence of a law which makes that conduct criminal at the time of its commission. This is more often referred to by the Latin maxim *nullum crimen sine lege* or "no crime without a law". Thus, if the accused commits a particular act on a Monday, and legislation that criminalises such acts comes into effect on the Tuesday morning, he cannot be prosecuted as his act was legitimate at the time it was committed. It is irrelevant, under this principle, that it became criminal within a very short time of its commission. If the legislation had come into effect on the Tuesday, and the accused had carried out the act in question on the Wednesday, but in ignorance of the new law, he would be prosecuted for his acts because they were criminal at the time of their commission. It does not matter that he did not know they were criminal because ignorance of the law is not a defence.[21] The declaratory power also faces criticism from a different source, in that it offends against Art 7 of the European Convention on Human Rights, which enshrines the principle of non-retroactivity and prohibits any law from attaching liability to conduct that pre-dates the implementation of that law. Given its inconsistency with these core principles and the clear reluctance of the courts to use the power in modern times, it is safe to say that it is no longer a viable power of the High Court of Justiciary.

---

[16] 1984 SLT 137.

[17] 1988 SLT 11, although note *Clark* v *HM Advocate* 2008 SLT 787 where the extension of the law on shameless indecency set out in *Watt* v *Annan* 1978 JC 84 was viewed as an exercise of the power.

[18] 1988 SLT 11 at 14.

[19] *Idem.*

[20] As was famously stated in the English case of *Shaw* v *DPP* [1962] AC 220 at 275: "where Parliament fears to tread it is not for the courts to rush in"(per Lord Reid).

[21] More precisely, "ignorance of the law is no excuse", from the Latin maxim *ignorantia iuris neminem excusat.*

THE NATURE AND IMPACT OF THE EUROPEAN CONVENTION ON HUMAN RIGHTS

The Convention was incorporated into Scots law by virtue of s 57(2) of the Scotland Act 1998, which forbids the Scottish Executive[22] from acting in ways which are incompatible with the Convention and the rights it enshrines. Likewise, the same prohibition has been imposed on public authorities,[23] which are defined so as to include the courts.[24] Thus, even if the Scottish Parliament were to pass legislation which was Convention non-compliant, the courts could not lawfully enforce it. This has brought into Scots law a number of rights which are now explicitly identified.[25] Of particular note to the criminal law, these rights give an accused the right to a fair and timely trial and the right to be informed of the charge laid against him in detail.[26] This has already caused problems in relation to the charge of breach of the peace. The Human Rights Act 1998, s 3 further requires that all domestic legislation should be interpreted and given effect to in a way which is compatible with Convention rights. If legislation is not compatible with these rights, the court may make a declaration to that effect under s 4 of the 1998 Act. Section 6 requires that all public authorities act in ways which are likewise compatible, unless they are prevented from doing so by primary legislation (which would itself then fall foul of s 3).

The Convention sets out broad rights with little explanatory detail. Several articles impinge, to a greater or lesser extent, on the criminal law. Article 2 enshrines the right to life, but gives no guidance on issues such as when life begins and ends. Article 4 provides a right to liberty and security, unless those rights are compromised by a lawful detention or arrest. Article 6 is perhaps the most frequently used and comprehensive Convention right in a criminal law context. It gives the accused the right to a fair and public hearing within a reasonable time and before an impartial tribunal. It also encompasses the presumption of innocence and allows the accused to insist that he is informed promptly, in detail and in a language he understands, of the nature and cause of the charge against him. He is assured of adequate time and facilities to prepare his defence, and is given the right to choose to defend himself, hire a representative of his choice, and to apply for legal aid to cover the costs if he meets the financial criteria. Article 7 enshrines the principle of non-retroactivity, such that the accused can be charged with an offence only if his acts were criminal at the time they were committed. If an offence has been created after the date of the accused's acts, they cannot be penalised, as they did not constitute an offence at the relevant

---

[22] This refers to the First Minister, Ministers appointed by him, the Lord Advocate and the Solicitor General. See s 44(1) of the Scotland Act 1998.

[23] Human Rights Act 1998, s 6(1).

[24] *Ibid*, s 6(3)(a).

[25] Clearly, many of these Convention rights existed, at least implicitly, prior to 1998.

[26] See Art 6 of the Convention.

time. Articles 10 and 11 assure freedom of expression and assembly, and the Sixth Protocol, Art 1 outlaws the use of the death penalty unless re-introduced by the State in exceptional circumstances during wartime.

As part of the move to Scottish devolution, the role of the Lord Advocate as head of the prosecution system has been subject to scrutiny. The problem has been caused by his inclusion in the Scottish Executive which requires him to take account of Convention rights. For example, as head of the prosecution service, he had a core role in the appointment and re-appointment of sheriffs. The use of temporary, as well as full-time, sheriffs was deemed vital to the administration of the criminal justice system, in order to deal with the increasing workload of the sheriff court. However, the argument was put forward in *Starrs* v *Ruxton*[27] that, as their appointment and annual re-appointment followed recommendation by the Lord Advocate (and therefore by a member of the Executive), it was too closely connected to the Executive to be viewed as properly independent. It was alleged that this lack of an independent judge was an infringement of the Convention right to a fair trial before an impartial tribunal. The controversy caused by this ruling ultimately led to a change in appointment procedures such that, under the Bail, Judicial Appointments etc (Scotland) Act 2000, the office of temporary sheriff has been replaced with that of part-time sheriff with security of tenure for 5 years instead of 1 year and appointment is made by the Judicial Appointments Board for Scotland, thus ensuring the necessary degree of impartiality and independence. Difficulties have also been faced in relation to criminal procedure, and particularly the accused's right to a timely trial as enshrined in Art 6 of the Convention. However, in many of these cases the original conviction has been upheld as reasonable notwithstanding the delay. In *O'Brien* v *HM Advocate*,[28] 23 months had elapsed between the original charge and the trial. This was because of pressure of work on the forensic laboratory and the police. It was held that if this type of delay was a regular occurrence as the inevitable result of the limited resources available, it would amount to systematic under-funding by the State and therefore a failure to correct this inadequacy would be unreasonable in terms of Art 6. However, the appellant had failed to show that his case had suffered due to anything more than a temporary problem and his appeal was dismissed. In *Dyer* v *Watson*[29] the High Court had held that a delay of 27 months was too long in a case involving sexual offences committed by a 13 year old against younger relatives. The Crown had argued that, since the case was one requiring sensitivity and was to be dealt with by particular, specially trained personnel, it was inevitable that it would take longer. It was held that Art 6(1) did not lay down any precise time limits, but instead looked to provide an objective level of protection to all parties against procedural abuses. The test for establishing that a delay had been unreasonable is a stringent one, and it must be shown that

---

[27] 2000 SLT 42.
[28] 2001 SLT 1101.
[29] 2002 SLT 229 (PC).

the length of delay gives real cause for concern, on its face, before it is necessary to look into the details and require an explanation from the prosecution for the delay.

THE COURTS

There are a number of criminal courts in Scotland, and the decision as to which court is appropriate for a particular case depends on several factors.[30] First, there are geographical considerations; all the courts, with the exception of the High Court of Justiciary, hear those cases involving crimes committed in their own areas. The High Court of Justiciary is a peripatetic court, in that it can hear cases in its buildings in either Edinburgh or Glasgow or, for convenience, it can also move round the country, sitting in local sheriff court buildings in the area covering the crime scene. Second, the severity of the crime committed may also determine the type of court used, as each court has different maximum levels of sentencing powers and there is little point in prosecuting a serious assault before a court which can sentence the accused to only a short period of imprisonment. This decision is for the prosecutor in the individual case. Further, some offences must be heard before a particular court. The position of each type of court is discussed below, in ascending order of seniority.

The justice of the peace/district court

The district court is the lowest criminal court in Scotland, and, as part of the reforms undertaken in the Criminal Proceedings etc (Reform) (Scotland) Act 2007, these courts are gradually being replaced by justice of the peace courts.[31] The district court hears cases involving minor offences, such as breach of the peace and road traffic offences, committed in its locality. Cases are usually heard by a single lay justice of the peace, although there may be more than one, who is assisted by a legally qualified clerk. Prosecution is handled by the procurator fiscal and appeals are by way of the High Court of Justiciary sitting as an appeal court. Since it deals with only minor offences, the district court's sentencing powers are similarly restricted. The JP has the option of imposing a custodial sentence of up to 60 days, or a fine of up to £2,500.

The stipendiary magistrate's court

Again, the stipendiary magistrate's court is restricted to hearing cases involving offences committed in its area, but these courts operate only in Glasgow and are presided over by a legally qualified stipendiary magistrate. Prosecution is handled by procurators fiscal. The sentencing powers available to the stipendiary magistrate

---

[30] For example, a child under 16 who is thought to have committed an offence will usually be dealt with by the children's hearings system instead of the criminal courts.

[31] The aim is to have completed this process by the end of 2009.

are somewhat broader than those available to the JP. He can impose a sentence of up to 3 months' imprisonment (12 months' for a subsequent offence), or can fine the accused up to £10,000.

The sheriff court

Scotland is divided into six sheriffdoms, each of which has its own sheriff courts which hear cases from their own area. There are currently 49 sheriff courts, each presided over by a sheriff. Prosecutions are run by procurators fiscal or their deputes. Cases before the sheriff court can proceed under one of two different types of procedure, either *summary* or *solemn*. Summary procedure will be used in less serious cases and will involve the sheriff sitting alone as the judge. In more serious cases, solemn procedure will be used, and the sheriff will sit with a jury who decide the accused's guilt. The decision to use either summary or solemn procedure is taken by the procurator fiscal. In Scotland, a criminal jury comprises 15 adults chosen at random from the electoral roll. The jury is responsible for deciding all questions of fact on the basis of the evidence led before them, legal argument from the prosecution and defence, and the direction on the relevant law as given by the sheriff. The jury will then deliver, either unanimously or by majority,[32] one of three possible verdicts: "guilty", "not guilty" or "not proven".[33] The sheriff remains responsible for all questions of law. Thus, the sheriff can withdraw certain issues which have been raised during the hearing if he feels that they are legally inappropriate. However, bearing responsibility for all matters of law also means that the sheriff may misdirect the jury on the nature or application of the law, and so give rise to grounds for appeal.

The sheriff court is a more senior, although not the most senior, court and consequently enjoys wider sentencing powers. These extend to 3 months' imprisonment (6 months' imprisonment for a second or subsequent offence) or fines of up to £5,000. However, in more serious cases heard under solemn procedure, the sheriff can impose a 3-year sentence or an unlimited fine. Alternatively, if he feels that his own sentencing powers are insufficient, he can remit the case to the High Court of Justiciary for sentencing purposes, where unlimited sanctions can be imposed.

The High Court of Justiciary

The High Court (as it is commonly known) is the most senior criminal court in Scotland. It sits as a trial court for the most serious offences.[34] There are four

---

[32] A majority means a decision of eight or more members.

[33] The "not proven" verdict is controversial and unsuccessful moves have been made to abolish it. However, although stating that the case against the accused has not been adequately proved by the Crown rather than stating that the accused is acquitted of the charges he faces, the "not proven" verdict functions as an acquittal.

[34] This now also includes hearing prosecutions under the Corporate Manslaughter and Corporate Homicide Act 2007, s 1(7).

crimes which have historically been viewed as particularly offensive. These are: rape, murder, incest and treason and are technically known as the "pleas of the Crown". Thus, anyone accused of committing one of these crimes must be tried in the first instance before the High Court, as no lower court has jurisdiction to hear the case. Clearly, the first two (rape and murder), are the most common. As a trial court, the High Court sits with one judge and a jury of 15 members, although, if the case is complicated, a Bench of three judges can be convened. The principal judge in the High Court is the Lord Justice-General and prosecutions are run by the Lord Advocate or one of his deputies, known as Advocates-Depute. As a trial court, the High Court goes "on circuit" and sits, if necessary, in one of four areas[35] as business requires.

However, the High Court has another function. It also sits as an appeal court and hears appeals from all lower courts, including itself when sitting as a trial court. These appeals can stem from the accused who wishes to challenge his conviction or sentence, or from the procurator fiscal, alleging that the acquittal was unjustified. There is no opportunity to appeal a criminal case any further, as the High Court on appeal is the ultimate appeal court in Scotland. All such appeals are heard in Edinburgh. When sitting as an appeal court, the High Court will usually convene a larger Bench, often of three judges but sometimes of five or more. The decision taken by a majority of the High Court on appeal can take a number of forms. It can order that the accused should be acquitted of the charges on which he was originally convicted,[36] or it can confirm the decision of the lower court. If it chooses the latter option, it can further increase or reduce the original sentence if it feels it was inappropriate. Its final option is to remit (send the case back) to the original court for retrial. The High Court on appeal can also hear petitions from the Lord Advocate (Lord Advocate's references) in cases where some point of law has arisen that requires clarification. The court will deliver an opinion on the questions posed, but its opinions do not affect the outcome for the accused in question. Thus the effect of the court's opinion is for future reference only. As the ultimate court of appeal, its decision is final and cannot be appealed further. However, in cases where it is felt that there has been a miscarriage of justice, the accused can apply to the Scottish Criminal Cases Review Commission – a body of independent and appropriately qualified individuals – who will assess the case and may, if it feels it is necessary in the interests of justice, send the case back to the High Court for review.

Given the nature of the crimes heard by the High Court, its sentencing powers are extensive. It can impose unlimited sentences or fines and is therefore the only court which can impose a sentence of life imprisonment. Although used sparingly,

---

[35] Home (Edinburgh); North (Inverness, Aberdeen, Perth, Dundee); West (Glasgow, Stirling, Oban); and South (Dumfries, Ayr, Jedburgh).

[36] His conviction will be quashed and his criminal record wiped clean, so far as that conviction is concerned.

this level of sentence may be the only appropriate option given the severity of the cases commonly heard before the High Court.

PERSONNEL INVOLVED IN THE CRIMINAL COURT SYSTEM

The subject of a criminal trial is known as the "accused", although if he appeals against his conviction, he becomes known as the "appellant". He will be represented in court by his solicitor[37] who will handle his defence in the district (justice of the peace) or sheriff courts, in the face of prosecution by a procurator fiscal or one of the deputes. However, if the case goes to appeal in the High Court of Justiciary, the appellant will be represented by an advocate.[38] Advocates represent the arm of the profession who, unlike solicitors, are allowed to appear before the High Court.[39] In the High Court, prosecution is handled by the Lord Advocate (styled "Her Majesty's Advocate" or "HM Advocate") or one of his deputes.[40] The case will be heard by either a justice of the peace (or stipendiary magistrate), sheriff or by one or more judges in the High Court of Justiciary,[41] and may additionally be heard in the presence of a jury of 15 if the trial has progressed under solemn procedure.

TYPES OF SENTENCES AVAILABLE

Following conviction, it is for the judge to decide on the length and type of sentence to be served by the offender. There exists a tendency to assume that sentencing equates to imprisonment, but the truth is far from this. Despite the continued emergence of new alternatives to imprisonment, the fine remains the most common sanction. Prior to passing sentence, the judge will give the defence an opportunity to explain the offender's reasons for committing the crime[42] and to highlight any personal circumstances which may have a bearing on his actions. The judge will also take full account of any criminal record; the age of the offender (if under 21); the lack of any previous custodial sentence; the length of time spent in custody awaiting trial;[43] any prescribed minimum sentence; and any evidence of racial aggravation. The court also has the power to take account of the offender's plea of guilty and, crucially, it can also take due note of the time at which this was

---

[37] In the lower courts, the accused can be represented by a lay person.

[38] An advocate is a member of the Faculty of Advocates (or "Bar") and is known as "counsel".

[39] However, it is now possible for solicitors to gain rights of audience before the higher courts by becoming solicitor-advocates.

[40] It is technically possible to mount a private prosecution but this is extremely rare. It requires the agreement of the Lord Advocate, although the High Court may allow such a prosecution to proceed without his agreement.

[41] Judges are usually appointed from the ranks of senior advocates and, on taking up their appointment, become public officers and give up their private practice.

[42] At this point, the offender's motivation may become relevant.

[43] A practice referred to as "backdating" the sentence.

lodged. The effect of this is to reward offenders for pleading guilty at an early stage, by reflecting this fact in the sentence.[44]

The judge can then choose the sanction he feels is appropriate, from a wide variety of different disposals. The traditional sanction of imprisonment will vary widely, depending on the scope of the particular court's sentencing powers, the severity of the crime committed, and on any statutory minimum or maximum length of sentence. However, it is worth noting that imprisonment may not be imposed on an offender over the age of 21 who has no previous record of imprisonment, unless the court has decided that it is the only appropriate sanction in the circumstances.[45] In making this decision, the court is obliged to take account of information relating to the offender's circumstances, usually as evidenced by a social enquiry report. The court may also be required to decide whether to impose consecutive or concurrent sentences. This issue will arise where the offender has been convicted on several charges at the same time, or where he is convicted while already imprisoned for another offence. Imprisonment deprives the offender of any freedom he may otherwise exercise, but there is also a range of disposals that curtail, without completely removing, that freedom. A community service order requires that the accused is supervised by a social worker for a specified period[46] during which he undertakes unpaid work in the community. It is available where the offender would otherwise face a custodial sentence but where the court feels it is appropriate to use this alternative. It is not available if the offender has been convicted of murder. If such an order is breached, the court can either fine the offender or impose such sentence as would have been appropriate had the court opted for a custodial disposal at the original trial. However, it is not competent for the court to sentence the offender additionally for the act of breaching the order.[47] Further, if the offender is made subject to a community service order and is convicted of a further offence during the period of the order, a social enquiry report must be obtained before the court can proceed to sentencing.[48] A probation order[49] places the offender under the supervision of a probation officer for a set period of time,[50] and is used if, in all the circumstances, it is appropriate as an alternative to imprisonment. If the order is breached, the court may vary its terms or sentence the offender in accordance with the original charge. A supervised attendance order will apply where the offender has failed to pay a fine, and is supervised while carrying out between 10 and 100 hours of "constructive activities" such as unpaid work.

---

[44] Criminal Procedure (Scotland) Act 1995, s 196.

[45] *Ibid*, s 204(2).

[46] Between 80 and 300 hours.

[47] *Gilbert* v *Buchanan* 1998 SLT 303.

[48] The report should detail the circumstances of the offence and the character of the accused. On this, see *Townsley* v *McGlennan* 1998 SLT 104.

[49] Criminal Procedure (Scotland) Act 1995, s 228.

[50] Between 6 months and 3 years.

Beyond these sanctions depriving or curtailing the offender's liberty, there are also further options open to the court. The offender can be required to pay an amount by way of a fine. The actual amount imposed will depend again on the court and the offence, and can be paid in full immediately, at a specified later date, or under a schedule of instalments. If the fine is not paid, the court retains the option of sentencing the defaulter for non-payment.[51] The offender may find that he faces an order to pay compensation to the victim or the victim's family, either as the sole sanction or alongside a fine. The amount of compensation will take account of the offender's financial circumstances. The court can also require the offender to lodge money with the court for a period of time, which money will be forfeit if he engages in further criminal behaviour. There are also non-financial sanctions which can be imposed on the offender for more trivial offences. The offender can be admonished for his crime and warned of the consequences should he come before the courts again. Finally, the court may grant an absolute discharge where, in the circumstances, it is felt that punishment is not appropriate. However, this is not an exhaustive list of sanctions available to the court. There are a number of more offence-specific sanctions that can be imposed, such as endorsement of a driving licence or disqualification for road traffic offences. The court can also recommend deportation for those who should more properly be dealt with in their country of origin. This option is only available in the face of a serious offence committed by someone over the age of 17 who is not a British subject. The courts also have the power to order the confiscation of the proceeds of crime under the Proceeds of Crime Act 2002. The Act requires that the court has made some other disposal of the case, to which it then attaches a confiscation order, although, under s 92(2), an absolute discharge is sufficient. However, unless the offence which has been committed is drug related, the court must be satisfied that the offender has benefited from his crime.[52] The type of property that can be confiscated is extensive, and covers not only property of the offender but also such property as he may have given away in order to avoid its confiscation.

Somewhat more controversially, the courts can also impose restrictions on the offender's lifestyle or freedom of movement outwith the context of imprisonment, by way of electronic tagging orders, anti-social behaviour orders[53] and drug treatment and testing orders (DTTOs). The Crime and Disorder Act 1998[54] introduced this new form of order to provide a tailored alternative to the increasing number of imprisonments for drug-related crime. The order will be imposed only if there is evidence that the offender is either already an established, or likely to become, a drug user, is treatable and is willing to undergo such treatment as may be necessary. The order will last for between 6 months and 3 years. Once imposed,

---

[51] However, a supervised attendance order is also competent.

[52] Proceeds of Crime Act 2002, s 94. The Act sets out detailed rules which are too complex to discuss here.

[53] On which, see Chapter 11.

[54] Section 89 inserted a new s 234B into the Criminal Procedure (Scotland) Act 1995.

the court has the power, should the offender fail to comply with the order, to vary its terms or impose the appropriate custodial sentence. Electronic tagging is more properly known as a restriction of liberty order. This is provided for by s 5 of the Crime and Punishment (Scotland) Act 1997 which inserts a new s 245A into the Criminal Procedure (Scotland) Act 1995. Such an order is appropriate only where the offender is over 16 and has been convicted of an offence that does not have a fixed punishment, and it can be imposed for up to 12 months.[55] The order is flexible, to the extent that it can require the offender to be in a certain place for certain periods of time,[56] or to refrain from going to a particular location.[57] The most innovative aspect of electronic tagging comes in the provision allowing for remote monitoring of the offender. Under s 245C(2), the court can require the offender who is to be monitored from a distance, rather than in person, to wear an electronic device to enable those in charge to mark his whereabouts. Again, under s 245G(1), if the offender breaches the conditions of the restriction of liberty order, the court may dispose of the case in whatever way would have been competent at the time of conviction.

SUMMARY OF MAIN POINTS

Nature
- public versus private; civil versus criminal
- common law, based on precedent

Courts
JP/district court
- minor offences, heard by JP, max 60 days/£2,500

Stipendiary magistrate
- operates in Glasgow, heard by magistrate, max 3 months (12 months for subsequent offence)/£10,000

Sheriff court
- summary – sheriff sits alone, max 3/6 months/£5,000
- solemn – sheriff and jury of 15, max 3 yrs/unlimited fine
- or remit to High Court of Justiciary for sentencing

High Court of Justiciary
- trial – pleas of the Crown, judge and jury
- appeal – larger Bench, unlimited sanctions

---

[55] Section 245A(3).
[56] Up to a maximum of 12 hours in any one day.
[57] Section 245A(2).

THE CRIMINAL COURT STRUCTURE

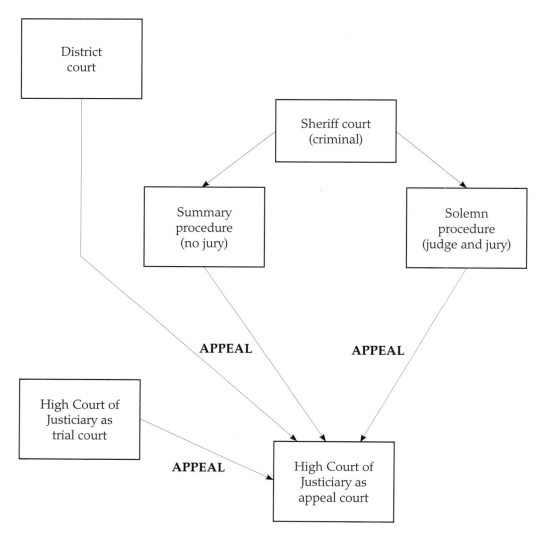

SELF-ASSESSMENT QUESTIONS (see Appendix for answers)

1 The accused is charged in connection with a traffic incident in Edinburgh. Where will his case be heard? Who will hear it? What is the maximum fine that can be imposed?

2 In the sheriff court, is a jury used in summary or solemn procedure? What is its function?

3 What are a sheriff's maximum sentencing powers? What can he do if he feels they are insufficient?

4 If the accused is charged with rape, which court will hear his case?

Further questions

1 Is there any argument that could justify the use of the declaratory power in modern times?

2 To what extent did the introduction of the European Convention on Human Rights affected the daily workings of the Scottish criminal courts?

Further reading

Jones and Christie, *Criminal Law* (4th edn), pp 1–51.

McCall Smith and Sheldon, *Scots Criminal Law* (2nd edn), pp 1–20.

Walker, The Scottish Legal System (8th edn), pp 321–331, 361–406, 433–442, 445–447 and 457–475.

2 THE *ACTUS REUS*

THE VOLUNTARY ACT REQUIREMENT

It is a fundamental requirement for liability under Scots criminal law that there is some form of voluntary act. As is often stated, there can be no conviction for a thought crime[1] alone, without a related criminal act. That act may amount to very little, for example an attempt to commit a crime that fails to come to fruition. Nonetheless, there has been some form of act that moves beyond preparation and shows the accused's criminal intent sufficiently to provide a basis for conviction. There are two main reasons for refusing to punish pure thought crimes. First, it is impossible for the prosecuting authorities to know what someone was thinking at a particular time, unless those thoughts were put into action. Second, even if those thoughts were evil, it is likewise impossible to predict whether they would necessarily lead to criminal actions. It is often stated that the legal system cannot justify interfering with a person's freedom simply because their thoughts are such that they might behave criminally in the future. What is required is an act that shows that the accused is capable of causing actual harm to society and that is prohibited under the criminal law. Thus, the combination of criminal act and criminal state of mind gives the legal system its justification for intervention.

There are two classifications of crimes, depending on the type and duration of the conduct involved. A crime which is encompassed within a single event is known as a *conduct* crime. For example, the law prohibits the possession of illegal substances under the Misuse of Drugs Act 1971. The mere fact of possession, which is an aspect of the accused's conduct, is sufficient for conviction. There is no need for a result to flow from that possession and thus it is termed a conduct crime. However, some crimes require a specific result to flow from conduct in order to make that conduct the subject of the particular crime and are thus called *result* crimes. The classic example is murder. If the accused commits murder, he is guilty. However, it is the unlawful result (the killing of the victim) that secures conviction. It does not matter what form of conduct the accused has engaged in order to achieve that result. He may have strangled, beaten or shot the victim, but the conviction will still be the same, because the crime of murder simply looks for a resultant unlawful killing by the accused.

---

[1] "Thought crimes" are instances where a person has had a criminal thought but has done nothing to put it into effect.

Although it is not possible to convict for a guilty mind without a criminal act, it is possible to convict someone on the basis of a criminal act without any intention. These are known as strict liability offences and will be dealt with later. However, once it is found that the accused has committed an act of some kind, it must be shown to amount to a *voluntary* act. This should not be confused with an act that the accused wanted to perform. For these purposes, a voluntary act is one over which the accused has exercised control, or one of which he is aware. There are established categories of voluntary and non-voluntary action.

CATEGORIES OF NON-VOLUNTARY ACTION

The unifying characteristic of non-voluntary action lies in the absence of both voluntariness and responsibility. The law does not impose criminal responsibility on those who have no control over their actions, unless their impaired state is self-inflicted. There are a number of categories of action which are classed as non-voluntary.

Reflex action

These actions are not under the control of the accused insofar as they are sudden, uncontrolled movements, often as a result of an instinctive response. Characteristically, the accused will have responded physically, instantly and without any thought, planning or deliberation. There are very few cases that illustrate the approach taken in these situations. Perhaps the fullest discussion of reflex action by the Scottish courts is to be found in *Jessop v Johnstone*.[2] A teacher was acquitted by the sheriff on a charge of assault after he repeatedly punched a pupil. He acted in response to the pupil suddenly and unexpectedly hitting him in the face with a rolled-up jotter. The sheriff found that the teacher had responded instinctively and spontaneously to a sudden attack, and had responded so immediately that he had no time to form any rational intention to assault the pupil. The Crown successfully appealed to the High Court of Justiciary. It was acknowledged that the teacher could have hit the pupil in a way that was compatible with the concept of reflex action (if he had turned round quickly in response to being hit and come into contact with the boy because he was right behind him). However, the court was not prepared to hold that such a situation applied in this case. The teacher had been sitting down when he was struck, and responded by jumping up and striking the boy repeatedly. It was clear that this conduct could not be classified as reflex action. The High Court allowed the appeal and remitted the case to the sheriff with a direction to convict for assault.

---

[2] 1991 SCCR 238.

Automatism

In these cases, the accused is held to be acting abnormally, but his state of mind is not to be equated with insanity. This category refers to actions which are performed automatically, that is to say in a state of unconsciousness or near unconsciousness. The rationale behind this is that the accused was not aware of what he was doing, and therefore is not to blame. The state of mind found in these situations is usually referred to as "temporary mental dissociation". This state can be caused in a number of ways: as a result of physical attack, emotional stress (psychogenic automatism), or disease (epilepsy or diabetic hypoglycaemia).

Mental dissociation was accepted in *HM Advocate* v *Ritchie*[3] as providing grounds for acquittal if the accused can prove to the court's satisfaction that he is "abnormal and irresponsible". However, one particular decision had a profound and limiting effect on the development of this concept. In *HM Advocate* v *Cunningham*,[4] the accused had been charged with a variety of road traffic offences including taking and driving away a vehicle. He pleaded not guilty and sought to raise a special defence of temporary dissociation caused by epilepsy. A special defence refers to a narrow class of defences which the accused cannot raise unless he gives prior notice to the court, or has good reason for failing to do so, and which, if made out, leads to a verdict of "not guilty". The High Court held that this situation was not one covered by the well-established categories of special defence and that the defence team was trying to extend those categories to cover a new type of situation. Alibi, incrimination, self-defence and insanity are all special defences, but the accused in *Cunningham* was attempting to introduce a new category where the state of mind of the accused fell somewhere short of actual insanity. The court was not prepared to entertain such an addition to the existing categories, expressing concerns about the public policy implications and public safety. It was held that temporary dissociation was not a special defence, but instead was relevant only to the issue of mitigating the sentence imposed.[5] The court in *Cunningham* also stated that the decision in *Ritchie* was incorrect. The only defence that the court was prepared to allow Cunningham to plead was full insanity, rather than simply temporary dissociation, thus leaving him to suffer the consequences of an acquittal under such a defence, namely detention in a mental hospital.

However, despite *Cunningham,* examples can be found of the Scottish courts' willingness to accept such arguments where they can find reasons to depart from its authority. In *Farrell* v *Stirling*,[6] the accused was involved in a series of road traffic incidents and was charged with driving without due care and attention. He argued that he was suffering from diabetic hypoglycaemia at the time and was unaware

---

[3] 1926 SLT 308 at 309.
[4] 1963 SLT 345.
[5] *Ibid* at 347.
[6] 1975 SLT 71.

of his actions. Expert evidence was sought as to the effect of hypoglycaemia and it was accepted that the result of an attack would lead the accused to pass rapidly into a state where he had no control over his actions and was unaware of their occurrence. The sheriff accepted that, although the accused was apparently in control of his car in that he was physically driving it, he was not exercising voluntary control over his actions as a result of his hypoglycaemic state.[7] He went on to consider the effect of *Cunningham* on this case. The Crown had put forward the argument, based on *Cunningham*, that a state of mind short of insanity did not establish a defence. The sheriff also noted that *Cunningham* was binding on him but that "it reaches a conclusion with which [he had] little sympathy".[8] However, he raised two points which allowed him to view *Cunningham* as irrelevant to the case before him. The first related to procedural issues, in that *Cunningham* involved the use of an alleged special defence, which is not appropriate procedure at summary level. He also felt that the decision in *Cunningham* was relevant only to cases where the intention of the accused had to be proved by the prosecution. The offence charged in this case (driving without due care and attention), did not require proof of any mental state on the part of the accused. In taking this stance, the sheriff departed from academic views but remained unpersuaded by them. In conclusion, he held that the accused was not to blame for his actions because he was not in conscious control of them and, having never experienced this state before, could not have been expected to recognise the symptoms of an attack. Thus, the accused was granted an absolute discharge. These final points do raise one further issue for comment. The accused's lack of experience of hypoglycaemic attacks acted in his favour. This then suggests that, if someone were well used to such attacks, they may not have received such a favourable hearing. They could reasonably be expected either to appreciate the risks of allowing a situation which might trigger an attack to develop, or to identify the early signs and take appropriate action to ensure they did not cause a danger to others while in the throes of an attack. This approach is shown in *MacLeod* v *Mathieson*,[9] where the accused, who had suffered from diabetes for around 20 years, was denied the plea of automatism precisely because he had sufficient experience to know how to manage his condition, and to know that it could come upon him without his appreciating the symptoms. He was thus able to foresee that he might suffer an attack, be unaware of the symptoms, and cause a danger to others and, as such, he failed to meet the criteria laid down for a successful plea.

The unsympathetic approach exemplified by *Cunningham* was subjected to intense scrutiny in *Ross* v *HM Advocate*.[10] The approaches taken in the two cases highlight an important distinction to be drawn in this area. This is the distinction

---

[7] 1975 SLT 71 at 72.
[8] *Ibid.*
[9] 1993 SCCR 488.
[10] 1991 SLT 564.

between the internal and external factor. Internal factors triggering a loss of conscious control are those factors which are to be found within the accused, and most often relate to mental or physical conditions, or illnesses from which he suffers. External factors are those causes of automatic action which are brought about by something outside the accused. Most often, these external factors are found in the consumption of intoxicating substances or concussing blows to the head. In *Cunningham*, the cause of the automatism was an internal factor (his diabetic condition) and was classified as insane automatism, whereas, in *Ross*, the cause was an external factor (consumption of drugs) which was not self-induced and was classified as non-insane automatism. This difference between the cases means that Ross does not overrule *Cunningham* wholesale, but rather provides a different outcome for cases where the automatism relates to an external factor and was not self-induced.[11] The legal issue involved was put succinctly by Lord McCluskey, who stated that the

> "appeal raises the general issue of the criminal responsibility … of an adult who has performed acts having all the characteristics of acts which the courts would normally treat as criminal but has done so in circumstances in which there is evidence that he would not have performed those acts at all but for the fact that at the material time he was acting under the influence of drugs administered to him without his knowledge".[12]

The facts of *Ross* present an extreme example of automatic behaviour. The accused had drunk a can of lager which had been adulterated with five or six temazepam tablets and some LSD. He then began screaming and attacking strangers with a knife. The defence argued that the combined effect of the mix of drugs he had unwittingly taken was to deprive him of his self-control to such an extent that he was not capable of forming the relevant *mens rea* for the offences with which he was charged and that he should therefore be acquitted. The Crown argued, following *Cunningham*, that the only appropriate defence in such circumstances was one of insanity, which had not been raised. The trial judge had felt himself bound to follow *Cunningham* and the doctrine of insane automatism, and had convicted Ross accordingly.

Ross's appeal was heard before a Bench of Five Judges which, as a larger court than was involved in *Cunningham*, had the authority to re-examine the earlier case. It was noted that there was no reason in principle why the special considerations that apply to insanity and allow for acquittal should not also apply in cases falling short of amounting to insanity but where it could not be said that the accused had formed the necessary *mens rea*.[13] The judges recognised that this case did not involve automatism arising from some internal physical cause such as epilepsy, as in

---

[11] G Laurie, "Automatism and Insanity in the Laws of England and Scotland" 1995 *JR* 253.
[12] 1991 SLT 564 at 572.
[13] *Ibid* at 566.

Cunningham. The court felt that *Cunningham* had been decided on policy grounds, with no discussion of the necessity for *mens rea* in order to convict.[14] However, the judges decided that these public policy considerations were not relevant in cases such as Ross's, where the issue was the accused's lack of *mens rea* on account of an external factor which was not foreseeable, not likely to be repeated and not within his control. They then went on further to distinguish cases where the automatism was self-induced, in which the accused could not be allowed to benefit from lenient treatment because he had knowingly taken a risk that he would be deprived of his self-control. However, they felt that situations such as Ross's, where the accused had no knowledge that he was taking, for example, drugs in his drink, were of a different quality and were such that responsibility could not be attributed to him. Therefore, such acts should not lead to conviction. The basis of his acquittal lay in the fact that, as a result of the drugs he had unwittingly taken, he was incapable of forming the necessary *mens rea* for the offences in question, and that, in such cases, the cause was both externally induced and unforeseeable. It was also held that, insofar as they conflicted with this decision, *Cunningham* and subsequent cases relying on it should be overruled. Thus, at least some of the severity of the traditional Scottish position, which has been described as an "extreme proposition",[15] has been diluted.

The approach taken in Ross has been followed in subsequent cases. In *Sorley v HM Advocate*,[16] the accused had been charged and convicted of breach of the peace and assault. He had drunk a can of lager which, unknown to him, contained two LSD tablets and three sleeping tablets and, although he had not had anything else to drink and was sober before he drank the lager, became violent, aggressive and appeared drunk. He gave evidence to the effect that he did not remember anything from that time until he woke up the following morning. He was convicted when the sheriff incorrectly instructed the jury following the line laid down in *Cunningham*, that mental abnormality short of insanity never operated as a defence, instead of adhering to Ross and allowing a defence of non-insane automatism in cases where the criteria were met. However, the defence was unable to lead any expert evidence to show that the drugs had caused the accused to lose control completely and it was felt that the causal link between the drugs and his behaviour could not be established without expert evidence to prove the accused's state of mind. The High Court held that, since the aim of such a defence was to show that the accused had no control over his actions, that defence had to be supported by a body of specific evidence pointing to that state. In the absence of any such satisfactory evidence in this case, his appeal against conviction was unsuccessful.[17] The decision outlines the modern test for a successful plea of

---

[14] 1991 SLT 564 at 569.

[15] Sheriff Noble in *Ebsworth* v *HM Advocate* 1992 SLT 1161 at 1162A.

[16] 1992 SLT 867.

[17] On this, see also *HM Advocate* v *Bennett* 1996 SLT 662, where absence of proof that his drink had been adulterated without his knowledge denied the accused the plea of automatism.

automatism where the argument is that the accused could not form the relevant *mens rea*. The automatism must be caused by an external factor rather than by a potentially recurring disease of the mind,[18] and the defence must further show that the external factor was not self-induced, was not foreseeable and caused a total alienation of reason amounting to a complete loss of self-control.[19]

A somewhat different aspect of automatism was raised in the subsequent case of *Ebsworth* v *HM Advocate*,[20] where the accused had been convicted of assault to severe injury and permanent disfigurement in an incident where he had attacked his victim with a bottle and a metal bar. A pre-existing injury caused him considerable pain and, in order to alleviate his suffering, the accused had knowingly taken 50 paracetamol and 10 black market diamorphine tablets without consulting his GP. He argued that the effect of the drugs he had taken was to prevent him from forming the necessary *mens rea* for the offences. The sheriff withdrew the defence of automatism from the jury who convicted him. On appeal, the High Court held that, if the accused had a legitimate (ie medical) reason for taking drugs, he would not automatically be prevented from arguing automatism simply because his state was self-induced to the extent that he had voluntarily taken the drugs. However, the court insisted that this would not apply if the accused had been reckless in his use of the drugs. In this case, it felt that the reasonable jury would have come to the conclusion that the accused's behaviour was indeed reckless, given the grossly excessive quantities of drugs consumed without any medical supervision. It confirmed that an accused who takes drugs solely for their intoxicating effects cannot benefit from any defence, but the issue in this case was slightly different in that the accused had given evidence to the effect that he had taken the drugs solely to relieve pain (a legitimate purpose). However, the view taken was that, since he had consumed an excessive amount without proper advice, his conduct was no different in terms of blame from the person who took drugs for an illegitimate purpose (intoxication). The court was content to assert that sufficient recklessness to preclude the defence of automatism could be found in taking powerful medication in contradiction of, or without medical advice.[21] This, added to the fact that the accused must have foreseen that such quantities of powerful drugs could have a detrimental effect on him, convinced the High Court to uphold the sheriff's original decision and refuse his appeal.

Many of the classic cases on automatism relate to violently aggressive conduct leading to serious charges such as attempted murder and assault. However, in *Cardle* v *Mulrainey*[22] the charges laid were road traffic offences and attempted theft. As is so often the case in these situations, the accused had unknowingly taken amphetamines that had been slipped into his drink. He argued that he had no

---

[18] This would instead raise the defence of insanity.
[19] 1992 SLT 867 at 868.
[20] 1992 SLT 1161.
[21] *Ibid* at 1166.
[22] 1992 SLT 1152.

mens rea because he had been acting under the influence of the drugs at the time, relying on the authority of Ross. However, the sheriff was convinced that although he had been able to form an intention at the relevant time, he was incapable of stopping himself, even though he knew what he was doing was wrong. On appeal by the Crown, it was held that the appellant knew both what he was doing and the nature and quality of his acts, and that therefore he could not be said to be suffering a total alienation of reason. The High Court asserted that "(n)ot every weakness or aberration induced by the external factor will provide the defence"[23] and stressed the need for a total alienation of reason as a absolute prerequisite of a successful defence. A similar charge was laid in *McLeod* v *Napier*,[24] where the accused was charged with driving without due care and attention while under the influence of alcohol, to which he raised the defence of automatism. He had been drinking and, while he was away from the table, his drink was adulterated with amphetamines. When he came back, he noticed that his drink tasted unusual but finished it nonetheless. He maintained that he had no memory of anything until the following morning. It was accepted at trial that the effect of the drugs had been to deprive him of his self-control and reason and he was acquitted on the basis of automatism. On appeal, the High Court reversed the sheriff's decision, rejected the finding that automatism was made out, and held that the sheriff had been incorrect in failing to apply the test from *Sorley*. In the latter case, it had been stated that such a defence required expert evidence to prove the link between the effects of the external factor and the accused's behaviour. In *McLeod* it was held that the sheriff had only heard evidence that the accused's behaviour was out of the ordinary. This was not sufficient to lead to the conclusion that he had been deprived of reason and self-control and he therefore had no proper basis on which to establish his finding of automatism.

Somnambulism

Somnambulism, or sleepwalking, has been recognised as an aspect of automatism. The accused will often perform complex actions while in a state of somnambulism, sometimes involving fatal assaults, and retain no memory on waking of his actions. It would seem therefore to be a classic example of non-voluntary conduct which should lead to a finding of not guilty. There is very little Scottish authority on this point. The only case prior to 2000 was *Simon Fraser*,[25] which is highly unusual in terms of the outcome. However, the concept of somnambulism has been explored more thoroughly in *Finegan* v *Heywood*,[26] where the accused was found guilty of a number of driving offences committed, he alleged, while sleepwalking. However, the court held that, in the circumstances of this case, the defence of automatism

---

[23] 1992 SLT 1152 at 1160.
[24] 1993 SCCR 303.
[25] (1878) 4 Coup 70.
[26] 2000 JC 444.

was not open to the accused. He was aware from previous occasions that the consumption of a certain amount of alcohol was likely to trigger an episode of sleepwalking. On the occasion in question, he had been out drinking to celebrate the birth of his son and therefore the court was able to hold that, since his sleepwalking was self-induced, he was guilty. The court specifically transferred the legal response to self-induced intoxication, which does not found a defence, into the arena of sleepwalking and stated that, because the accused had voluntarily consumed alcohol, knowing full well that it could cause him to sleepwalk, he was not entitled to a defence of automatism.[27]

OMISSIONS

It is, however, not necessary that the accused has *acted* in a criminal way; he may have failed to act in circumstances where the law requires him to act. Conviction for an omission can follow from a failure to act in any way, but only if the accused was under a legal duty to act.[28] As a general premise, legal systems tend to shy away from imposing wholesale liability for an omission or failure to act. The traditional justification for the lack of liability for omissions is that the accused has not *acted* in a reprehensible fashion. He has, instead, failed to act. The basic requirement is that the accused executes a *voluntary* act, which stems from a reluctance to widen the extent of the criminal law, and a recognition that the causal link between the omission and its consequences is not strong. Although it is straightforward to say that an omission can create a situation which allows harm to occur, it is argued that it is harder to say that the omission caused the harm. There are in fact two types of offence which can be committed by omission. First there are those offences relating to pure omissions. These are statutory provisions imposing automatic liability for specified failures. However, there is a further category of offences, often described as offences of "commission by omission", where the omission stands in place of an act for the purposes of satisfying the *actus reus* requirement.

Most systems will impose liability for an omission only in the face of a specific duty to act. Such duties can arise in a number of ways. There is no duty to prevent a crime from being committed. The Scottish authority on this is *HM Advocate v Kerr*,[29] where the accused had watched a rape but was acquitted of art and part liability in that crime since mere presence without any act was insufficient. However, liability can be imposed for mere presence, if the accused is aware that his passive presence at the scene of a crime amounts to encouragement of the protagonists. However, there is no Scottish case law on this point. A duty to act

---

[27] For more detailed comment, see S Christie, "Unconscious Acts, Guilty Minds: Placing Limits on the defence of Automatism" 2001 *JR* 147.

[28] It is necessary to distinguish the legal duty to act from the moral duty to act. It may have been morally imperative that the accused acted, but if he was not under a specific legal duty to do so, he will not be liable for his omission.

[29] (1871) 2 Coup 334.

can also be imposed through contractual relationships (for example, a nanny's contractual duty to ensure that no harm comes to children in her care) and duties derived from the status of the individual, for example on-duty policemen. Liability will also apply if the failure to act takes place within the context of a close personal relationship. There is some debate as to how far this duty extends, but it certainly applies within close family relationships. It is also possible to impose a duty to act where the accused has created a prior dangerous situation and failed to avert that danger. The courts will look for reckless indifference on the part of the accused. Authority here is found in *MacPhail* v *Clark*.[30] The accused, a farmer, had set fire to part of his field and had left it unattended. The fire spread to the embankment running alongside the adjacent road and smoke caused a car to stop on the road. A petrol tanker crashed into the car, running it off the road and injuring the passengers. The farmer was convicted because he had failed to control the fire and it was foreseeable that his actions would reduce visibility on the road and thereby endanger the public.

CAUSATION

It is vital, in order to secure a conviction, that the act of the accused was the cause of the criminal result. The accused's act must have contributed to the *actus reus* of the crime in question in some legally relevant way. The more remote the connection between the accused's act and the crime committed, the less it is legally relevant. If there is no causal connection, or if the accused's act did not bring about the criminal result, then there can be no conviction. Thus, the concern of the criminal law is to identify the operative cause of the criminal result. In doing this, it is often useful to employ the "but for" test. The question becomes: "but for this act, would the criminal result have occurred?". To put it another way, could the criminal result have occurred without the accused's act? However, it is also necessary to distinguish the factual and the legal cause of the criminal event. Factual causation looks for a causal link, which exists in the physical world, between the act and the result. But for the action of the accused, could the physical result have occurred as it did? If the answer to this question is "no", then factual causation has been established, and the focus shifts to matters of legal causation. There will often be a number of factual results that flow from the accused's original action and that are attributable to him by virtue of factual causation. However, not all of these will be brought within the ambit of legal causation. In legal terms, the accused will have caused those results which are reasonably foreseeable. Thus, the question becomes "was the criminal result a reasonably foreseeable consequence of the accused's original act?". This provides the criminal law with a means of drawing the line and restricting those consequences for which the accused is legally responsible from the potentially never-ending list of consequences that are factually attributable to his act. Some

---

[30] 1983 SCCR 395.

of those consequences will be judged too remote from the accused's original act to be attributable to him.

In most cases, the issue of causation will be satisfied relatively easily. There are, however, a number of points to note in relation to the operation of the concept of causation. First, if the victim has some pre-existing medical condition that makes him more vulnerable, the accused cannot use this as a ground for exculpation. The phrase commonly used is that "you take your victim as you find him". In *Fyfe* v *HM Advocate*,[31] the accused had severely beaten his victim, who was found semi-conscious and died a short time later. The victim had died as a result of inhaling stomach contents after suffering a subdural haemorrhage. Expert evidence was used to show that even mild injury often caused haemorrhages in chronic alcoholics such as the victim. It was clear that the accused had seriously assaulted his victim but it was not clear whether something else, such as a fall, had caused the haemorrhage. However, the High Court of Justiciary concluded that there was plenty of evidence to show that the victim had been beaten severely and had collapsed and died within a short period of time thereafter. Fyfe's appeal failed because the victim's particular susceptibility to such a haemorrhage was irrelevant. This rule is also referred to as the "thin skull" rule and states that any pre-existing abnormality of the victim making the consequences of the accused's criminal act unusually serious is ignored. Thus, the criminal who robs and badly frightens a young man who appears strong and healthy would still be liable if his victim had a serious heart condition and suffered a heart attack as a result. The conviction will stand despite the fact that the victim looks perfectly fit and able to withstand the shock of being robbed. The fact that the accused cannot see his infirmity is irrelevant.

Breaking the chain of causation

A result which would otherwise have been causally connected to the accused's act will be disregarded if the chain of causation from the act to that result has been broken. Thus, the accused can escape liability if something significant has happened to interrupt the causal link leading back to his act. Such an intervening act is referred to as a *novus actus interveniens* (that is, a new and intervening act) and can come in one of three guises. The intervening act can be described as an act of God; or it can originate from the victim himself; or a third party. Acts of God are rare and are limited to events in nature that are entirely unpredictable, such as freak weather conditions. The other two categories are more common. The victim may act in such a way as to interrupt the chain of causation leading from the accused's act to the resultant harm to the victim. Until recently, the approach taken here followed *Lord Advocate's Reference (No 1 of 1994)*,[32] where the accused had

---

[31] 1998 SLT 195.
[32] 1995 SLT 248.

been charged with culpable homicide for supplying a lethal dose of amphetamine to a user who had subsequently died. He did not suggest that she should take the drug, or encourage her to do so. Instead, she voluntarily decided to take the drug provided by the accused. At trial, this was held to be sufficient to break the chain of causation, since there was evidence of an intervening act, namely the victim's taking the drug herself. However, the High Court of Justiciary held that the chain had not been broken by the user's voluntary act of taking the drug. The harm that occurred to the victim required an act on her part, but the existence of this act was not sufficient to absolve the accused from liability for the harm. It did not amount to a *novus actus interveniens* sufficient to break the chain of causation leading back to the accused. Although the court recognised that the level of harm caused by the drug would depend on the amount the user chose to take, it felt that this was not relevant to the issue of causation once the accused had supplied a drug which was clearly intended to be used. This case follows the reasoning established in *Khaliq v HM Advocate*[33] and *Ulhaq v HM Advocate*[34] both of which involved the supply of solvents to, respectively, children and adults. In holding that the voluntary consumption of proffered drugs by the victim does not amount to a *novus actus interveniens*, Scots law was at odds with English cases, most particularly *R v Kennedy (No 2)*,[35] where the court held that, since the victim had voluntarily taken the proffered drugs, in full knowledge of their identity and likely effects, the accused could not be convicted of causing the drug to be administered to the victim. The cause of the administration of the drug was the victim's voluntary act, for which he alone was responsible. The House of Lords held that, if the victim administered the drugs to himself and was a responsible and fully informed adult, the act of administration could not be attributed back to the supplier. Thus, the act of the victim had broken the chain of causation. In *MacAngus v HM Advocate*,[36] the Scottish position was brought more into line with the approach in *Kennedy*, although *MacAngus* does not overrule *Lord Advocate's Reference (No 1 of 1994)*. Instead it finds that, if the victim is adult and fully informed, and therefore takes a decision to ingest the drugs recklessly proffered by another, then the adult victim may well carry responsibility for his actions and for the cause of his death, rather than the supplier. It will depend on the facts of the particular case, and there will be cases where the deliberate decision of the victim to ingest the drugs will not break the chain of causation.

Scots law also disregards an act of the victim that is designed as an attempt to escape from the accused. This will not be classified as a *novus actus*, as it will generally be entirely foreseeable that the victim will try to escape, and that, in doing so, may harm himself. Thus the accused will remain liable for the additional

---

[33] 1984 SLT 137.
[34] 1991 SLT 614.
[35] [2008] 1 AC 269.
[36] [2009] GWD 4-61.
[37] 2007 SCCR 10.

harm created by the attempt to escape. In *McDonald* v *HM Advocate*,[37] the accused assaulted their victim and left them locked in a flat, from which the victim then tried to escape, falling to their death from a window. It was held that this did not establish a break in the chain of causation. The chain of causation can also be broken by the voluntary acts of a third party. If the third party intervenes following the accused's act and goes on to commit a crime, the crime cannot causally be linked back to the original accused. The voluntary act of the third party has broken the link. Although there is little authority on this point, an example can be found in cases of malregimen (subsequent and unorthodox medical treatment which makes the condition of the victim substantially worse). There is English authority to the effect that the accused can escape liability for murder if he has inflicted a fatal wound on a victim who is then incorrectly treated such that he dies immediately, say from an injection of the wrong drug.[38] However, in these cases, the fatal medical treatment must wholly eclipse the original harm caused by the accused.

SUMMARY OF MAIN POINTS

Voluntary act
- must have an *actus reus*
- voluntary action is that over which the accused has control, or of which he is aware

Non-voluntary action

Reflex action
- sudden, uncontrolled movements
- instinctive, spontaneous response

Automatism
- does not amount to insanity
- unconscious or semi-unconscious state, temporary mental dissociation, no evidence of recurring disease of the mind
- cause can be internal to the accused (eg diabetes) or external (eg knowingly or unknowingly ingesting drugs)
- self-induced states will not lead to acquittal, whereas uninduced states may do so (*Ross*)

Somnambulism
- self-induced sleepwalking does not provide a defence

---

[38] On this, see *R* v *Smith* [1959] 2 QB 35.

Omissions

- can be liable for a failure to act
- must establish a duty to act based on contractual relationship, close family relationship, status (eg policemen), creation of prior danger

Causation

- *actus reus* must be causally linked to criminal result
- no causal connection, no conviction
- if the criminal act is the cause of the criminal result because of some particular frailty of the accused, then you take your victim as you find him
- a *novus actus interveniens* breaks this chain of causation

VOLUNTARY ACTION

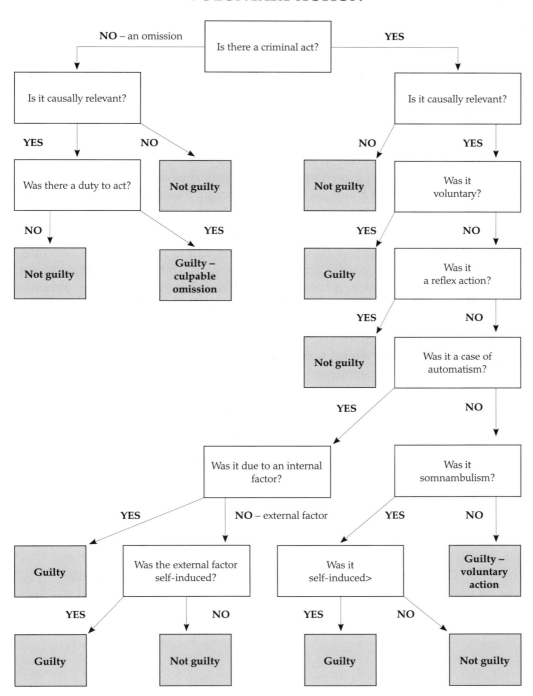

Note: Use of the world "guilty" is a convenient shorthand. There may be other issues to consider before the accused is convicted.

SELF-ASSESSMENT QUESTIONS (see Appendix for answers)

1 X has been arrested by the police following an incident during which he was aggressive, violent and abusive, destroyed property and caused some injury to passers by. He has led evidence during his trial to establish that, shortly before the incident, he had been drinking with a friend. He had left the table for a while and when he came back, his pint of lager tasted slightly odd. He thought nothing of it at the time, but remembers nothing further from the point of leaving the pub until he became aware that he was in the back of a police van. It transpires that he had considerable quantities of amphetamines in his bloodstream on his arrest. Would you expect X to be convicted of the several offences with which he is charged? Would your expectations be altered in the light of evidence that X and his friend had though it would be fun to swill down a handful of amphetamines with their lager to see what happened?

2 X and Y are involved in a heated argument that becomes violent. X picks up a kitchen knife and stabs Y, although his aim is not good and Y receives only a knife wound to the arm. Y is taken to hospital where his condition progressively worsens and he eventually dies. It becomes clear that, although the wound was slight, the knife had been used to cut raw meat which was infected and the bacteria had passed into Y's bloodstream. Unknown to X, Y had recently undergone transplant surgery and was on a high dosage of immuno-suppressants to prevent his body from rejecting the new organ. As a result, Y's immune system was significantly compromised, and was unable to fight off the infection from the contaminated knife. Is X liable for murder?

Further questions

1 How far should liability for omissions in the context of close personal relationships extend?

2 How can the causal chain be broken?

Further reading

Jones and Christie, *Criminal Law* (4th edn), pp 52–59, 73–110 and 113–128.
McCall Smith and Sheldon, *Scots Criminal Law* (2nd edn), pp 21–35 and 63–76.
Gordon, *Criminal Law* (3rd edn), vol 1, pp 57–94 and 115–143.

3 MENS REA

Mens rea refers to the accused's state of mind, specifically to the guilty state of mind which is required for criminal liability. He must be shown to have one of the relevant criminal states of mind. Once it has been established that the accused has committed the *actus reus* of the offence, it still remains for the prosecution to prove that he had the necessary *mens rea* before it can achieve a conviction.[1] It is not possible to convict an accused for committing a criminal act without some criminal state of mind, except in cases of strict liability.[2] The necessary *mens rea* must be proved in respect of those elements of the crime that are included within the definition of, but not those circumstances that lie outside, the *actus reus*. For example, in reset, it is necessary that the accused take possession of stolen goods, but also that he knows the goods to be stolen. Thus, the *mens rea* is not simply an intention to take possession of stolen goods, but the said intention while also being aware of the surrounding circumstances – that the goods are stolen. Thus, establishing the necessary *mens rea* requires careful consideration of the exact description of the *actus reus*.[3] This becomes particularly important in those crimes which include surrounding circumstances as part of the *actus reus*. There is, however, more than one criminal state of mind and each crime will have its own *mens rea* specified either in terms of a single required mental state, or (as in murder) requiring one of two possible alternative states. There are three possible states of mind: intention; recklessness; and negligence. Of these, intention is the most common and the most morally culpable. Some confusion has been caused by the use of the term "dole". Dole, as used in much earlier times, referred to an evil disposition rather than to a state of mind that might render the actor liable. Thus the modern trend is to avoid using the term "dole" and talk instead of "*mens rea*" when referring to the guilty states of mind (intention, recklessness and negligence). The concern of the criminal law is to ascertain that the accused committed a particular prohibited act with the particular state of mind required for prosecution.

A crime requiring intention will be identifiable by the precise language used in its description. There is no set phrase which should be used, but words such as "wilfully", "knowingly" and other such synonyms will indicate a *mens rea* of intention. "Wickedly" is also used sometimes. Intention can be required as the

---

[1] The Latin maxim frequently encountered here is *actus non facit reum nisi mens sit rea*.
[2] See Ch 4 on statutory offences.
[3] Gordon, *The Criminal Law of Scotland* (3rd edn, W. Green/SULI, Edinburgh, 2000), vol 1, pp 251–252.

only acceptable form of *mens rea* for the crime in question, or it can appear as an acceptable mental state along with a lesser state. The classic example here is murder, which requires that the accused intended the death of his victim or was wickedly reckless. When requiring that the accused intended to commit a criminal act, his intention will usually have to be shown not only in regard to the act, but also with regard to any other material and definitional aspects of the offence.

MOTIVE VERSUS INTENTION

The accused's reasons and motivation for acting as he did are viewed as irrelevant. In *HM Advocate v Rutherford* it was stated that "(w)hat the law looks for is, not the motive at the back of a man's head, but the intention, the intent with which he acts".[4] More problematic decisions have arisen in cases where the accused's "defence" is that he was playing a joke on the victim, never meant to be taken seriously and therefore never intended any criminal consequence. Such a case is exemplified by *Lord Advocate's Reference (No 2 of 1992)*.[5] The accused had entered a shop, holding an imitation gun, and demanded money from the till. He left the shop when another member of staff appeared and, although he accepted that the staff in the shop had been alarmed by his actions, he maintained that it had all been a joke. At trial, it was held that, in order to be found guilty of assault, the accused must have shown evil intent. Since his conduct had been meant as a joke, the trial judge concluded that he had no such intent and therefore should be acquitted. The Lord Advocate appealed successfully, arguing that he had deliberately committed the relevant acts and that therefore his intent to assault the victims could be inferred. The appeal court held that his desire to play a joke amounted only to his motive for acting and that it did not negate his intention to commit the crime. This case was applied in *Quinn v Lees*,[6] where the accused had set his dog on some young boys. He argued in his defence that he had not intended to assault the boys and that it had been meant as a joke. As was rightly observed by the court on appeal, it could not be suggested that the dog would be able to distinguish between a joke and a command. It was held that the accused's actions were entirely deliberate, the consequences predictable, and he was convicted accordingly. This same issue has also arisen in the context of incitement to commit murder. In *Baxter v HM Advocate*,[7] the accused had incited a third party to kill his neighbour, with whom he had a dispute. Baxter had explained his motivation, the proposed timescale and the cost of hiring an assassin and yet still argued, in part, that it had all been meant as a joke. However, it was clear that he had intended that he should be taken seriously by the third party, at least in part due to the tone of his voice and the tenor of the conversation which had been taped. Thus, if the accused's conduct clearly shows

---

[4] 1947 SLT 3 at 4.
[5] 1993 SLT 460.
[6] 1994 SCCR 159. See also *Gilmour v McGlennan* 1993 SCCR 837.
[7] 1998 SLT 414.

an intention to commit a crime, he cannot raise a successful defence by asserting that he was joking.

INTENTION

One of the classic definitions of what is meant by "intention" comes from the English case of *Cunliffe* v *Goodman*,[8] where it was described as a state of affairs beyond contemplation of a particular act.

> "(I)t connotes a state of affairs which … he decides, so far as in him lies, to bring about, and which, in point of possibility, he has a reasonable prospect of being able to bring about, by his own act of volition."[9]

The accused who acts intentionally does so in order to bring about a desired state of affairs. He acts purposely in relation to a particular result. His intention will not necessarily be something about which he has consciously deliberated; many everyday activities are done intentionally, with a deliberate purpose to achieve a particular result, but yet are so mundane and unexceptional that the actor will have carried them out without any real conscious thought about the nature of his intention and the best means of effecting that intention. The accused can either intend to commit an act, or he can intend to cause a particular consequence as a result of his actions. Any act which he brings about as the result of an accident will not be considered as intentional action as he will not have *decided* to bring it about. Intended action also does not equate with action or consequences which are wanted by the accused. A consequence can be undesired, or even regretted, but still brought about intentionally. Intention is notoriously difficult to identify. It has been said time and time again that it is, of course, impossible to examine the inner workings of a man's mind in order to see what his intention might be. The only means of verifying that intention, and therefore determining his guilt, is to infer his intention from his actions. As was said in *HM Advocate* v *Rutherford*, "… intent must always be a matter of inference – inference mainly from what the person does, but partly also from the whole surrounding circumstances of the case."[10] Thus, it can be said that intention has a subjective element, in that it is internal to the accused, but that it is assessed objectively, that is by reference to a reasonable person's assessment of the accused's actions.[11]

However, intention does not necessarily go hand in hand with knowledge. If the accused intends to achieve a particular goal and acts in a particular way, believing or hoping that he is thereby achieving the said goal, then his intention

---

[8] [1950] 2 KB 237 at 253.

[9] *Idem*. Note that, in Gordon, p 254, the phrase "in point of possibility" is queried, and it is suggested that it should be replaced with "which he thinks".

[10] 1947 SLT 3 at 4.

[11] In taking an objective stance, the law here follows the traditional Scottish approach, although subjective assessments have become more accepted, for example in provocation. See Ch 8.

can fill the gap left by his lack of actual knowledge. Thus, if the accused intends to import cocaine, and does in fact import a white substance which he fervently hopes and believes is cocaine, he can be found guilty under s 3(1) of the Misuse of Drugs Act 1971. His intention to import cocaine, and the fact that he actually did import cocaine, will convict him even though he did not definitively *know* that he was importing cocaine. His intention to do so stands in the place of his absent knowledge of the nature of his actions. The offence of importing drugs under s 3(1) is not phrased so as to require that the accused "knowingly" imports drugs, and thus his intention can be substituted for actual knowledge in this way. Most crimes follow this pattern and do not specifically require knowledge. However, had the accused been charged under the related provision of being knowingly concerned in the fraudulent evasion of a prohibition on importation,[12] his lack of actual knowledge of the nature of his actions would preclude conviction.

Further problems may also be caused by the precise type of offence in question. If the offence involves some kind of knowledge as a prerequisite, then the accused cannot have intended that offence if he did not know that piece of information. For example, if the offence requires that the victim is a police officer and the accused does not know this, then he cannot be said to have intended the offence. However, if the accused should have known a particular fact and exhibited deliberate and wilful blindness in relation to it, then that will amount to knowledge and the accused can be convicted. Wilful blindness arises where the accused may have suspected something but deliberately did nothing to ascertain the truth, preferring instead to remain ignorant. However, simply failing to find out the truth of a particular situation is not wilful blindness. It requires more, because the effect of a finding of wilful blindness is to hold the accused responsible as if he had full intention. The wilfully blind accused is more than tenuously suspicious of a situation; he has strong suspicions in a particular direction, recognises that there are means available to him to ascertain the truth and deliberately does not avail himself of those means because he does not want to confirm the truth. Some offences are phrased in such a way that the accused must intend some further crime. He may face a charge such as opening lockfast places with intent to steal. Again, he cannot be convicted under this charge if it cannot be shown that, as well as opening a lockfast place, he also intended further criminal activity, namely to steal. However, once the accused intends to bring about a particular act, he is also liable for intending to bring about all those acts necessary to bring about that particular act: "he who wills the end wills the means".[13] Thus, if the accused intends to steal a laptop that has been left on the back seat of a locked car, he must also intend to break into the car in order to steal the item. A further problem is caused when the accused's intended act comes hand in hand with another act which he may argue he did not intend, but which is so obviously a consequence of his intended act that he is made liable for

---

[12] Customs and Excise Management Act 1979, s 170(2).
[13] Gordon, vol 1, p 256.

it. Here, the consequence is foreseeable as a certainty. The classic example used in academic literature to illustrate this problem is that of an accused who plants a bomb on a plane in order to claim the insurance money. Since the death of some or all of the passengers on that plane is foreseeable with certainty (indeed, it goes hand in hand with destroying the plane), the argument holds that he should be guilty of intending their deaths as well as intending destruction of the aircraft.[14] Some commentators view foresight of certainty, at least when the consequence can be foreseen as a virtual certainty, as an equivalent of intention.[15] However, this does raise its own problems when trying to define concepts such as "virtual certainty".

A further cloud of controversy surrounds the concept of transferred intention. The circumstances surrounding the accused's criminal act may be such that, although he forms the intention to, for example, assault that particular victim, and takes steps to carry out his intention, he may instead mistakenly assault someone else. The classic example is that of the *aberratio ictus* – the blow that lands astray. If the accused has intended to punch a particular person, he has the *mens rea* for assault and, when he strikes that person, he has committed the *actus reus*. However the victim may, whether through good fortune or quick reflexes, avoid the blow and it may fall instead on an innocent by-stander. This raises a problem, as the accused has the *mens rea* so far as his original victim is concerned, but has not carried out the *actus reus*. Conversely, he has committed the *actus reus* so far as his actual victim is concerned, but had never formed any relevant *mens rea* with regard to that person. The answer is fairly straightforward, although not without its criticisms. The concept of transferred intention takes the *mens rea* that was present with respect to the intended victim and transfers it to the situation which develops regarding the actual victim. For example, X is involved in a brawl, during which he intends to punch, and takes aim at A. A is fortunate that X has been drinking heavily and his aim is poor. Instead of punching A, X actually punches B. The approach adopted by Scots law takes the intention exhibited by X to assault A and transfers it, with the result that, in legal terms, X has physically assaulted B (*actus reus*), and is deemed to have done so with the evil intent he had formed against A (*mens rea*). This then secures conviction for the undoubted assault, while avoiding the problem of convicting for the assault on B without evidence of *mens rea* in respect of B. Clearly, this will be possible only if the crime intended to be committed against A, and the crime actually committed against B, are one and the same. This has been criticised for allowing conviction for a crime requiring intention when there is very clearly no intention present for the crime which was actually committed. It has been noted that, at least in the context of assault, the better option would be

---

[14] Gordon, vol 1, p 256.

[15] See *R v Woollin* [1998] 3 WLR 382 in Gordon, vol 1, pp 256–257. The problem of foresight of certainty can be more difficult in England, in cases of murder, where the *mens rea* is restricted to intention. In Scotland, where it includes wicked recklessness, there is no need to extend the concept of intention to cover consequences foreseen as a certainty, as there would certainly be wicked recklessness.

to charge the accused (X) with recklessly causing injury to B, thereby avoiding the need to consider the extent of X's intention to assault B.[16]

RECKLESSNESS

Recklessness will not satisfy the *mens rea* requirement of all crimes. Some crimes can only be committed intentionally,[17] whereas the description of others makes it clear that recklessness is a definitional component,[18] and other crimes can be committed either intentionally or recklessly. The essence of reckless conduct is that the accused, while not intending his actions, has acted carelessly and with complete disregard for the consequences of those actions.[19] The accused will have been consciously aware of the risk that his conduct would be classified as criminal, but is indifferent to this fact. The carelessness required here is objective carelessness, that is, conduct that the objective observer would classify as careless,[20] and will vary depending on the circumstances.[21] Thus, recklessness is determined by reference to the conduct that would be exhibited by a reasonable, prudent man in the same position as the accused. The question posed is whether the ordinary man in the same position would have been aware that a particular consequence would follow from particular actions. Thus, it does not matter whether the accused was actually aware of the particular consequence of his actions. The pertinent issue is whether the reasonable man in his position would have been so aware and, therefore, whether the accused should also have been aware. This is shown in *Gizzi* v *Tudhope*.[22] Here, the two accused were convicted of recklessly discharging a firearm. On appeal against conviction, the High Court affirmed the sheriff's decision, noting that the appellants had begun to shoot in an area with a line of trees which obscured their view of the land beyond. However, the land beyond the trees was within the range of the guns, and thus they were literally firing blind. It was reasonable to expect that people could have been within the range of the guns and it was clear that the appellants had done nothing to ensure that there was no one within their line of fire before commencing. The reasonable man in that position would not have started firing without at least checking the area

---

[16] McCall Smith and Sheldon, *Scots Criminal Law* (2nd edn, Butterworths, Edinburgh, 1997), p 159, citing *HM Advocate* v *Harris* 1993 SLT 963.

[17] For example, assault.

[18] Such as culpably and recklessly causing injury.

[19] See *Quinn* v *Cunningham* 1956 SLT 55, defining recklessness in two ways; as an utter disregard for the consequences of one's acts so far as the public are concerned, and as indifference as to the consequences for the public. This is further endorsed in *Cameron* v *Maguire* 1999 JC 63.

[20] See Gordon, vol 1, p 269, citing *Crowe* v *HM Advocate* 1989 SCCR 681.

[21] Something that may only be slightly careless in some circumstances may be made grossly careless if the circumstances surrounding the act are different. For example, driving in excess of the speed limit is of a different quality if the speeding takes places outside a primary school as compared with speeding on the open road.

[22] 1983 SLT 214.

and thus they showed sufficient recklessness for the High Court to uphold their convictions.

Although considerations of recklessness are based on assessments of the degree of risk taken by the accused, some risks are accepted as non-criminal. If the level of risk involved in a course of conduct is so small that the reasonable man would have recognised but disregarded it, then the criminal law will take no account of it. However, it may be that the accused has taken a substantial risk, and yet will not be liable for it. These cases are classified as ones involving justifiable risks, such as the risk taken by a doctor performing a dangerous operation. The risk of the patient's death may be very high, but yet it may be the best course of action. Similarly, those involved in emergency situations or dangerous rescues may take grave risks which are nonetheless justifiable in the context.[23] A further issue in relation to recklessness arises when a distinction is drawn between recklessness as to consequences and recklessness as to circumstances. The most obvious form of recklessness arises when the accused is careless and indifferent as to the consequences of his actions. However, he may equally have exhibited carelessness about a circumstantial aspect of the offence. He will have been reckless as to whether a particular fact applies in a given situation. Again, the standard used is that of the reasonable man and thus, if such a man would have ascertained whether a particular circumstance applied in his situation, the accused will be held to be reckless if he has failed to ascertain this.

NEGLIGENCE

Negligent behaviour, like reckless behaviour, involves careless conduct. The crucial distinction between the two states of mind is found in the level of awareness exhibited by the accused. Reckless behaviour is more serious because the accused has acknowledged the existence of the risk and deliberately disregarded it. This behaviour is advertent; that is, the accused has turned his mind to the risk involved and has foreseen the likelihood of harm. Negligent conduct is less blameworthy as it involves inadvertence; that is, a failure to appreciate the risk involved, or to consider the nature of the situation in hand. Negligence is assessed objectively and so requires proof that the accused was careless in failing to appreciate something which would have been appreciated by the reasonable man. However, negligence as a basis for criminal liability has fallen out of favour to some extent, and is most often charged in the context of statutory offences involving carelessness,[24] or at common law, in the guise of gross negligence which can be viewed as a form of recklessness.[25]

---

[23] On this, see Gordon, vol 1, p 272.
[24] For example, careless driving.
[25] On this, see Gordon, vol 1, pp 301–303.

SUMMARY OF MAIN POINTS

Mens rea
- guilty state of mind
- intention, recklessness or negligence
- motive differs from intention and is irrelevant
- saying that it was a joke will not succeed

Intention
- decision to bring about a state of affairs
- intention is inferred from actions
- if the accused is wilfully blind about an aspect of the offence, he can still be convicted
- his intention will cover his goal, but also the acts needed to bring about the goal
- it will also cover consequences which are foreseeable as a certainty
- transferred intent – if an intended assault misses its victim and harms another, the intention attributable to the intended victim can be transferred to the actual victim

Recklessness
- acting carelessly/taking unjustified risks with complete disregard for the consequences
- advertent carelessness
- objective test, using the "reasonable man" standard
- some risks are justifiable

Negligence
- inadvertent carelessness
- less blameworthy
- assessed objectively

GENERAL CRIMINAL LIABILITY

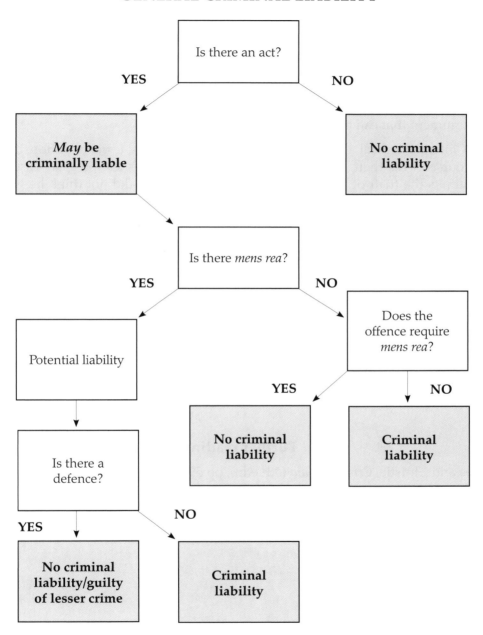

Note: Use of the phrase "criminal liability" is a convenient shorthand. There may be other issues to consider before the accused is convicted.

SELF-ASSESSMENT QUESTIONS (see Appendix for answers)

1   X has been charged with aggravated assault, following an incident in a shop. He had entered the shop behaving suspiciously and had suddenly leapt over the counter at the two assistants, waving a toy gun and shouting at them to empty the till. A passing policeman witnessed the incident through the shop window and immediately arrested the accused, who was dragged away while protesting that it had been a joke and that the gun was not real. Is there any argument that can be raised in X's defence?

2   X intends to steal a quantity of diamonds from a local jeweller's shop. In the course of his theft, he forces a locked door and smashes a display case. He admits the theft of the diamonds, but argues that he did not think he would need to force the door or cause any other damage, and so objects to the charges of opening lockfast places and damage to property. Can he be held liable for these other offences, given his assertions that he lacked the necessary *mens rea*?

Further questions

1   Does the concept of transferred intention amount to an impermissible conviction on the basis of the *actus reus* alone?

2   Should negligent behaviour be subject to the criminal law?

Further reading

Jones and Christie, *Criminal Law* (4th edn), pp 59–72.
McCall Smith and Sheldon, *Scots Criminal Law* (2nd edn), pp 35–46.
Gordon, *Criminal Law* (3rd edn), vol 1, pp 245–310.

4 STATUTORY OFFENCES AND CORPORATE LIABILITY

Scots law relies in large part on the common law to define and punish criminal conduct. In this respect it differs from many other jurisdictions which tend towards the use of criminal codes to provide an exhaustive list of prohibited conduct. However, that is not to say that substantive criminal law in Scotland is never found in statutes.[1] Although statutory offences would appear to be more straightforward, defined as they are by the wording of the section, they are beset with their own problems of interpretation and, in particular, with problems in relation to the appropriate *mens rea* requirement. Most statutory provisions are phrased specifically to include some form of *mens rea*, whether intention, recklessness or negligence. However, this is not always the case.

STRICT LIABILITY OFFENCES

One of the most fundamental tenets of the criminal law is that the accused must be shown to have committed the *actus reus* of the offence with the required *mens rea*. Without a criminal act, the accused cannot be convicted simply for his criminal thoughts. However, although the converse usually holds, there are instances where the accused can be convicted simply on the basis of his criminal acts without the need for the prosecution to prove any particular criminal state of mind. These instances comprise strict liability offences. Removing the need for proof of *mens rea* is, however, very much the exception rather than the rule and is found only in statutory offences.

The justification for these offences is grounded in policy. Some arise in areas where the sheer number of prosecutions would make it intolerable to expect the authorities to establish *mens rea* as well as the guilty act in every case. Others relate to areas where the scale and nature of the industry involved would make it very easy to argue a lack of knowledge that an offence was being committed. If the section makes no mention of *mens rea*, it is still necessary to consider the surrounding circumstances to ensure that Parliament intended strict liability, and it cannot simply be assumed that if every other section requires *mens rea* and the section in question does not, that it is therefore a strict liability offence. There is a presumption that, in the drafting of legislation, Parliament does not intend to

---

[1] Statutes are, however, mainly found in the areas of road traffic offences, drugs and regulatory matters such as environmental offences, licensing and food regulation.

make people liable without proof of *mens rea* and thus words implying *mens rea* will be read into statutes that are otherwise silent.[2] However, this presumption can be rebutted if, without a *mens rea* requirement, the statute will more effectively protect public safety.[3]

Statute implies *mens rea*

Several words commonly used in statutes are taken to imply that some mental state should be present, even if there is no explicit reference to intention, recklessness or negligence. These include "knowingly" , "wilfully", "fraudulently" and "maliciously".

No mention of *mens rea*

If the statute does not use words that imply *mens rea*, the courts may decide to rebut the presumption in favour of *mens rea*. Several factors will be taken into account in deciding whether the statute requires *mens rea* or not, of which at least two are consistently applied. Strict liability will be justified in statutes where the offence is purely regulatory and is designed and necessary for the protection of society.[4] If the provision is drafted in such a way that it cannot be applied effectively unless the *mens rea* element is removed, then the courts will apply it as a strict liability offence.

Defences

Since there is no *mens rea* element in a strict liability offence, any of the defences that are normally available but which relate to the *mens rea* element of the offence will not be open to the accused. Thus, error which relates wholly to the *mens rea* of the accused is not an available defence, but it is thought that insanity and automatism will be available.[5] Necessity has been accepted as a defence to strict liability offences under road traffic legislation[6] and some statutes provide a specific defence for the accused. This will usually be based on the notion that the accused had exercised all due diligence or care to ensure that the criminal act in question did not occur.[7]

"CAUSING AND PERMITTING" OFFENCES

Some statutes make it criminal to cause or permit something to happen. It has been established that liability for causing something to happen or for permitting

---

[2] *Sweet* v *Parsley* [1970] AC 132. See also *Salmon* v *HM Advocate*; and *Moore* v *HM Advocate* 1999 SLT 169 at p 186.

[3] See *Lockhart* v *National Coal Board* 1981 SLT 161.

[4] *Alphacell* v *Woodward* [1972] AC 824.

[5] For general defences, see Chapter 7 and, for automatism, see Chapter 2.

[6] *Tudhope* v *Grubb* 1983 SCCR 350.

[7] See below.

something requires knowledge on the part of the accused.[8] There are numerous such offences, for example driving without insurance,[9] which is phrased in terms of causing or permitting another person to use one's car while there is no valid insurance policy in force covering that other driver. In *MacDonald* v *Howdle*[10] the accused had arranged for a friend to drive her car to the garage for repair, and had discussed the issue of insurance cover. Her friend had wrongly told her that he would be covered. It was found that the accused would not have let him drive had she known that he was not insured. Following conviction, she appealed and it was held in the High Court that, since her permission was given conditionally, she had not committed an offence. She had placed a condition on her permission, namely that he should be insured to drive her car, and that condition had not been satisfied. Thus, she had not committed the offence of causing or permitting someone to drive without insurance. In effect, the friend drove the accused's car without her permission and therefore she could not be guilty of a "causing or permitting" offence. This follows the approach taken in *Newbury* v *Davies*[11] and the court took the opportunity to distinguish the case from the previous Scottish decision of *Smith of Maddiston Ltd* v *MacNab*[12] which insisted on conviction in similar circumstances, but under an older and differently worded statutory provision.

Under the same section, giving permission to one person may, in the circumstances, amount to giving permission to others. In *Elsby* v *McFadyen*[13] the accused had given permission to one of three youths to drive her car. All three had then set off, with the permitted driver at the wheel. However, by the time the police stopped the car, one of the other youths, who did not have a driving licence, was driving. The accused admitted initially that she knew this youth had no licence, but then withdrew that admission. The sheriff refused to accept that withdrawal and convicted her. The High Court upheld the conviction as, given the circumstances, it was reasonable to imply that permission had been granted to all three, and that this was confirmed by her initial admission.

An area that gives rise to particular difficulties in "causing and permitting" offences is that of knowledge on the part of the accused. For example, in *Brown* v *W Burns Tractors Ltd*,[14] the employer was accused of causing and permitting employees to drive in contravention of regulations governing hours of work and hours of rest. However, the drivers were actually supervised by a clerical assistant who was then responsible to one of the directors. The assistant did not provide

---

[8] If, however, the offence is described as "causing or knowingly permitting", then *Lockhart* v *National Coal Board* 1981 SLT 161, which cites *Alphacell*, decided that the specific reference to "knowingly permitting" implied the need for *mens rea* in respect of "permitting" only. It therefore excluded knowledge as a criterion for "causing", leaving these cases as instances of strict liability.

[9] Road Traffic Act 1988 s 143(1) and (2).

[10] 1995 SLT 779.

[11] [1974] RTR 367.

[12] 1975 SLT 86.

[13] 2000 SCCR 97.

[14] 1986 SCCR 146.

the director with adequate information, and the director did not carry out checks on the assistant's supervision of the drivers. On appeal it was held that there was sufficient evidence to deduce knowledge on the part of the company and the case was remitted to the sheriff with a direction to convict. The courts have been prepared to uphold convictions in this area on the basis of constructive knowledge. This will apply where the employer does not know a particular fact, but should have known it had he instituted proper procedures and checks.

In *MacPhail* v *Allan and Dey Ltd*[15] the company was charged with causing and permitting an employee to drive without the necessary heavy goods licence. The employee had completed a form which gave the transport manager reason to believe that the driver had the required licence and, 2 weeks prior to the incident, the driver said that he had been inspected by the traffic commissioners who were satisfied. This gave the transport manager sufficient faith in his perception of the situation that he failed to check on the actual existence of the licence in question. However, the court held that, since the transport manager had no system for checking the existence and validity of the drivers' licences, he (and therefore the company) should be held to have constructive knowledge that, at the time in question, the driver did not hold a valid HGV licence.

CORPORATE CRIME

An increasing amount of crime can be committed by companies. This often, but not exclusively, arises in the context of environmental offences such as pollution and the disposal of toxic waste, and in regulatory offences such as vehicle licensing requirements. The idea behind corporate liability is that the company involved can be identified and in some circumstances it may be both possible and appropriate to criminalise such conduct at the company level. It is often argued that such an exercise is pointless in that criminal sanctions do not have any significant deterrent effect on a company. However, although the company itself clearly cannot be imprisoned, responsible individuals within it can, and the option of a fine will have a significant effect on a company if set at an appropriate level. It is also worth noting the adverse effect on the company of the publicity and stigma surrounding a trial and, even more so, a conviction. A number of theories have been used to explain the basis of corporate liability, the dominant theory being that of the "controlling mind"which was derived from the English case of *Tesco Supermarkets Ltd* v *Natrass*,[16] brought into Scots law by *Purcell Meats (Scotland) Ltd* v *McLeod*[17] and affirmed in *Transco plc* v *HM Advocate (No 1)*.[18] However, this theory was prone to its own difficulties, most notably that of identifying an individual within the company who

---

[15] 1980 SLT (Sh Ct) 136.
[16] [1972] AC 153.
[17] 1987 SLT 528.
[18] 2004 JC 29.

took the decision and was at a sufficiently senior level to be viewed as the, or part of the, "controlling mind" of the company. As a result of sustained criticism and public disquiet at the lack of accountability in this area in respect of corporate acts leading to deaths, the Corporate Manslaughter and Corporate Homicide Act 2007 has replaced the common law with a statutory regime for those specific cases.

Corporate Manslaughter and Corporate Homicide Act 2007

In imposing liability for the offence of corporate homicide, the statute focuses on whether the victim's death was caused by the way in which an organisation's activities are managed or organised. The organisation[19] will bear liability if the senior management made a substantial contribution to the way those activities were managed, and where the organisation committed a gross breach of its duty of care to the victim.[20] Section 1(4)(c) defines "senior management" as someone with a significant role in decisions about how the whole or a significant part of the organisation's activities are managed, or in the actual managing of the same. The relevant duty of care to the victim will be found in the law of negligence and includes duties towards its employees and others working for the organisation, and duties owed by virtue of being the occupier of premises. Limitations on liability based on a finding of a duty of care are found in ss 3–7 relating to, for example, the police, military, emergencies and public policy decisions. Section 1(6) imposes as the penalty an unlimited fine, although it will be interesting to see how successful prosecutions brought under this statute deal with the issue of the appropriate level of fine, as this has historically been a source of dissatisfaction in corporate criminal accountability cases. The court also has the option of imposing a remedial order under s 9, requiring the organisation to correct any deficiencies in its procedures that caused the death in question, and subjecting the organisation to an unlimited fine for failure to comply with such an order. However, s 10 presents perhaps the most interesting aspect of the available sanctions. It allows for a publicity order to be imposed on the organisation, requiring it to publicise its conviction and the details thereof, the amount of the fine imposed on it, and the terms of any remedial order. This is clearly designed to provide an additional, and arguably more powerful, form of deterrent to organisations, since it puts their reputation and place in the market in jeopardy.

Corporate liability outwith homicide cases

A company can be held vicariously liable for an offence committed by an employee who was acting in the course and scope of his employment. However, the employer can argue that the employee has acted such as to remove them from the scope of

---

[19] This is defined more widely than simply a company and includes, among others, public bodies, police forces and partnerships.

[20] Section 1(1) and (3).

their employment. Thus in *Auld* v *Herriot*[21] the illegal dispatch of whisky from a public house by an employee was not held to be the responsibility of the employer, as the employee had acted surreptitiously and concealed the nature of his actions from his employer. Thus he was acting outwith the scope of his employment. In contrast, in *Simpson* v *Gifford*,[22] illegal sale of alcohol by an employee was held to be within the scope of her employment even though she had been instructed not to do so. It was held that it was for the employer to prove that the employee had acted outwith the scope of their employment and, in this case, the court was not satisfied that this had been proved. However, this imposes liability on the company as employer because of the crime committed by an employee. It does not impose criminal liability specifically on the company itself.

In order to attribute criminal liability to the company itself, where the offence involved is a statutory offence requiring *mens rea*, the prosecution must prove to the court that an individual within the company satisfied the *mens rea* requirement, and that this *mens rea* can be transferred to the company in order to make it liable. This has been established in a variety of cases as the "controlling mind" theory.[23] It is, however, necessary that the employee who has such knowledge has acquired it as part of their duties or role within the company. In *Brown* v *W Burns Tractors Ltd*[24] a clerical assistant responsible for the area of operations in question knew that employees of the company were committing illegal acts and this knowledge was then transferable to the company.

It is well established that a company can be held liable at common law for all crimes which do not conceptually require to be committed by a human being. As such, crimes like rape and murder are clearly excluded. In *Dean* v *John Menzies (Holdings) Ltd*[25] the company was charged with shameless indecency for selling, exposing for sale and having for sale pornographic magazines. The sheriff dismissed the charge as incompetent and this was upheld on appeal. The High Court agreed that, as a common law crime, it could not be charged against a company since the company could not form the necessary *mens rea*. However, the decision was not unanimous and Lord Cameron felt that a company could be charged with a common law crime where the company had undertaken an act which was within its powers and which would have amounted to an offence if committed by an individual. Thus in *Purcell Meats (Scotland) Ltd* v *McLeod*[26] it was competent to charge a company with attempted fraud. The company had argued that it was impossible to charge it with a crime that required *mens rea*, particularly when the Crown could not identify in the charge the exact persons within the company who had allegedly committed the crime. Its argument failed.

---

[21] 1917 2 SLT 178.
[22] 1954 SLT 39.
[23] See above.
[24] 1986 SCCR 146.
[25] 1981 SLT 50.
[26] 1987 SLT 528.

DUE DILIGENCE DEFENCE

It is possible that the statutory offence may provide a defence for the accused. In *Ahmed* v *MacDonald*[27] the accused was a licensee who was charged with admitting under-age persons, contrary to the Licensing (Scotland) Act 1976, s 67(2). Under the section, the licensee can be prosecuted if an employee commits an offence for which the employer is vicariously liable. However, the accused can argue that he did not know that the offence was being committed and that he had taken all possible steps to prevent it. Ahmed had regularly instructed the doorman to keep under-age patrons out of the premises, but a 16-year-old girl had gained admittance without being questioned as to her age. On appeal, the High Court held that the systems in place were sufficient to satisfy the due diligence test and quashed the conviction. It was satisfied that the system would work under normal conditions and that the doorman was suitably instructed to carry out this system. While it may have been preferable to institute a second check at the ticket booth inside the door, the High Court was still persuaded that Ahmed had done everything necessary to establish the defence. In *First Quench Retailing Ltd* v *MacLeod*[28] it was found that a policy of selling alcohol only to those over the prescribed age was carried out on the basis of subjective assessments of age by staff at the point of sale, rather than on the basis of enforcing a company policy. An employer exercising due diligence would, it was held, both implement the policy and monitor it and, as the employer had not done so, it was properly convicted and the due diligence defence was denied.

SUMMARY OF MAIN POINTS

Strict liability
- conviction based on *actus reus* alone
- justified by reference to policy
- cannot assume strict liability on the basis that no *mens rea* is mentioned
- rebuttable presumption against strict liability
- implied *mens rea* – knowingly, wilfully, maliciously etc.
- defences available so long as they do not relate to the *mens rea* aspect of the offence

Causing and permitting
- requires knowledge

---

[27] 1995 SLT 1094.
[28] 2001 SLT 372.

Corporate crime

Controlling mind

- identify those within company who direct and control its activities
- if they have the *mens rea* for the crime, then it can be imputed to the company
- Corporate Manslaughter and Corporate Homicide Act 2007 – liable if victim's death was caused by the way in which an organisation's activities are managed or organised and senior management made a substantial contribution to the way those activities were managed, and where the organisation committed a gross breach of its duty of care to the victim

Due diligence defence

- the company must show that it exercised all due care and diligence to prevent the possibility of commission of the crime

CORPORATE CRIME

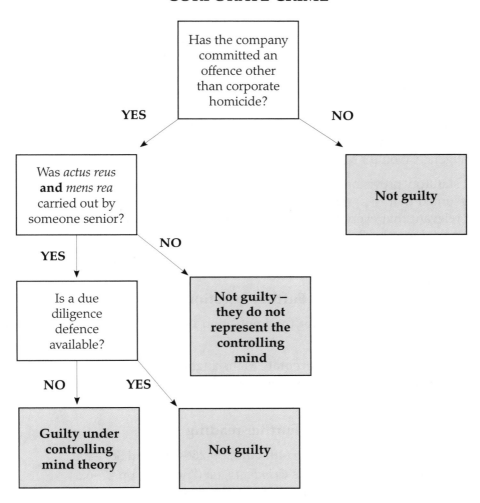

Note: Use of the word "guilty" is a convenient shorthand. There may be other issues to consider before the company is convicted.

SELF-ASSESSMENT QUESTIONS (see Appendix for answers)

1   X is a shop assistant in a branch of Y Ltd. Among other items, he regularly sells cigarettes. He has been told that he cannot sell cigarettes to those under 16 and has been told that there is a manual detailing company procedures for checking the age of customers. He has asked to see the manual, and has asked for training on identifying potentially under-age customers, but both requests have been ignored. Charges are later laid against Y Ltd for selling cigarettes to under-age customers. The company argues that it had put in place procedures in order to avoid such an eventuality, and that it had therefore exercised all due diligence. Would Y's argument succeed?

2   A statutory provision makes no mention of any *mens rea* requirement. Can it be assumed that this was Parliament's intention when drafting the provision? Is it relevant that every other section in the statute contains words denoting the required *mens rea*?

Further questions

1   What is the justification for the imposition of strict liability? Is it a sufficient justification?

2   To what extent does the Corporate Manslaughter and Corporate Homicide Act 2007 overcome the problems identified with the "controlling mind" theory?

Further reading

Jones and Christie, *Criminal Law* (4th edn), pp 266–267 and 387–400.

McCall Smith and Sheldon, *Scots Criminal Law* (2nd edn), pp 47–62.

Gordon, *Criminal Law* (3rd edn), vol 1, pp 311–394.

Ferguson, "Corporate Manslaughter and Corporate Homicide Act 2007" 2007 SLT (News) 251.

5 PARTIES TO AN OFFENCE

ART AND PART LIABILITY

The purpose of art and part liability is to criminalise those who participate, to one extent or another, in the commission of a crime. The doctrine of art and part liability exists both at common law and under statute. Section 293(1) of the Criminal Procedure (Scotland) Act 1995 states that any person can be convicted for a breach of any enactment, even if his liability is only art and part.[1] Although many incidents of crime are committed by a single individual acting on his own, this is not always the case. Criminal sanctions also apply to groups of people who act together to commit crimes, each of whom will have contributed their own part[2] in the overall scheme. These individual contributions to the scheme will differ considerably, and yet they will all be convicted art and part of the one overall crime that has been committed. Thus, someone who simply provides tools can find himself convicted of theft on an equal footing with the person who forced open the door and stole the property, even though he has not personally stolen any property. These people are often referred to as accomplices or those acting "in concert", although the technical term in Scots law is that they are liable "art and part" for the crime in question. This provides a means of extending criminal liability beyond the person who eventually commits the *actus reus* of the crime, and attaches liability to all those who have played some role in the planned crime, or carried out some aspect of, but not the whole, *actus reus*. They will all be held liable for the offence, even though they will not all have played an equal part in it. Although their conduct may fall short of the full *actus reus* of the crime,[3] it is not necessarily the case that their participation will be insignificant in the overall commission of the crime. Without someone to supply the necessary tools, or stand guard, the crime may be impossible to commit.

Occasionally, there are instances where the accused cannot be convicted of the full offence because of some narrowness in its definition, but can be liable art and part, as in the case of rape. A woman is physically incapable, under the common law definition, of committing rape, but may be liable art and part if she plays some role[4] along with the male accused. A conviction has also been upheld in the

---

[1] Thus, all statutory offences can be committed art and part.
[2] In the form of skills, physical abilities, knowledge etc.
[3] Indeed, their conduct may fall considerably short of the *actus reus* and so it may seem unfair to convict them for the full offence.
[4] Perhaps drugging or restraining the victim.

context of s 11(1) of the Criminal Law (Consolidation) (Scotland) Act 1995, which imposes penalties on men who knowingly live wholly or partly on the earnings of prostitution. In *Reid* v *HM Advocate*[5] the female accused had been charged with the above offence along with two male co-accused. At trial, it was argued that she could not competently be charged with this offence because it was gender specific. This argument was rejected by the sheriff, and also by the High Court, as it is clear that it is perfectly possible to convict someone art and part of an offence that they could not commit in full. The justification for art and part liability is based in policy and public safety and a recognition that those who play a part in an offence are as much of a social danger as those who actually carry out the final acts required. It may not be possible to carry out a particular robbery without someone to act as a getaway driver. The driver himself plays very little part in the *actus reus* of the robbery but, without him, the crime would never have been committed. In that respect, he is as vital a participant as the actual robber even though what he does is of a different quality and much less significant. However, it is possible for the courts to judge the level of criminality displayed by each accused and assess whether one of them is sufficiently less culpable than the other in order to justify a lesser sentence. In *Gray* v *HM Advocate*[6] the High Court held that it was quite proper for two of the accused to be convicted art and part of murder, while the other two were convicted art and part of culpable homicide on account of provocation. Thus, it is possible for the court to vary the sentence handed down to different members of the group or, if the area of law allows for it, vary the crime of which an individual is convicted to a lesser but related one.

In such cases of group criminal activity, it is possible to find instances where the prosecution has been unable to satisfy the jury that all of the accused took part in the crime. The question sometimes asked is whether, when the main accused has been acquitted, there is still scope to convict other members of the group art and part. In *Capuano* v *HM Advocate*[7] three accused had been charged with assault committed in concert, but the jury returned "not proven" verdicts against two of the three. The third, Capuano, appealed on the grounds that it was inconsistent to find him guilty on his own, when his fellow actors had not been convicted. The High Court rejected his appeal, holding that the jury was still entitled to find the evidence against Capuano sufficient to convict him. The crime had been committed by a group and, as the only identified member of that group, the jury was free to find him guilty while the other two walked free. Again, in *Johnston* v *HM Advocate*[8] it was held on appeal that the jury must be directed to weigh the evidence against each separately and, if the evidence so directs, it is perfectly competent to convict one of acting art and part while acquitting the other. It is possible to imagine a

---

[5] 1999 SLT 1275.
[6] 1994 SLT 1237.
[7] 1985 SLT 196.
[8] 1997 SCCR 568.

number of situations that would allow for acquittal of one of the accused: it could arise from a weakness in, or lack of, evidence against that particular accused; a procedural defect in the case against him that did not apply to the other accused; or a defence which he alone could raise, such as a defence relating to his state of mind (for example, insanity, non-insane automatism or coercion).

Different forms of art and part liability can be identified. Someone who holds the position of an official and who allows a breach of the law to take place is liable art and part in that offence. In *Bonar* v *McLeod*[9] a junior police officer had assaulted a prisoner in the presence of a more senior colleague. The senior colleague was found to be an official who had stood by and allowed a breach to take place and was therefore held liable for the assault art and part with the perpetrator. His guilt was further established by his giving assistance to his junior colleague after the assault had taken place. Someone may commit a crime in all innocence, unaware that they have been used as an agent by someone else. In these cases, the innocent agent will usually be acquitted while the other party is convicted art and part. An example can be drawn from English case law. In *R* v *Cogan and Leek*[10] Leek used Cogan as an innocent agent to carry out a rape. He forced his wife to have sexual intercourse with Cogan, but told Cogan that she was a willing party. Thus, Leek (who had not physically committed rape) was convicted of aiding and abetting rape (to use the English term), whereas Cogan (who had committed the *actus reus* of rape, but in all innocence) was acquitted as the innocent agent.

Cases of joint commission require that all the accused have jointly committed the *actus reus* of the offence in question. They may all have carried out the same acts, or each may have carried out different roles within the commission of the crime. They may all assault the victim at the same time or one may keep watch while others commit the crime. It may be possible to bring home a charge against one accused on the grounds of antecedent liability or prior concert. This is shown in *Spiers* v *HM Advocate*,[11] where the evidence that Spiers had been a party to the crime came from two others whose evidence the jury did not accept. These two witnesses gave evidence that Spiers was there when another accused, wielding a knife, called for others to join in. Since he did not participate in this attack, the only way he could have been liable art and part would be for this evidence to be accepted as evidence of prior concert between Spiers and the other accused. However, in the absence of any accepted evidence that he was a party to the main body of the offence (assault and attempted murder), his conviction at trial was quashed on appeal. The final way in which an accused can be made liable is via "associate liability". The accused must have associated himself with the main perpetrator of the offence in some way. Other examples of prior concert include those cases where the accused has

[9] 1983 SCCR 161.
[10] [1976] QB 217.
[11] 1980 JC 36.

counselled or instigated the crime at an earlier stage, but not proceeded to play a role in its actual commission.

A further issue that arises in art and part cases is that of the scope and extent of the accomplice's liability. Are they liable for incidental criminal activities carried out before they joined in the commission of the overall crime? In the context of assault, further problems can arise if the person offering assistance does so after the perpetrator has inflicted a fatal attack. Is he then liable for the homicide? The Scottish authority on this point is *McLaughlan* v *HM Advocate*,[12] where it was stated that the accused can only take joint responsibility for such criminal events as occur *after* the point when he joins in the criminal activity. The accused had joined her husband in an attack on another woman, but it was clear from the evidence that she had joined in at a later stage, after her husband had inflicted considerable serious injury on the victim. The wife was convicted of assault to severe injury along with her husband, following a direction to the jury that, when someone joins a criminal activity, they take on responsibility for the whole course of events, not just those occurring after they have joined. On appeal, this was held to be a misdirection, since there is no statement of Scots law to the effect that, on joining, the accused adopts all prior criminal activity. She was therefore responsible only for those injuries inflicted after she joined in the assault. The prosecution could not prove whether the life-threatening injury had taken place before or after such a point and therefore her conviction for assault to severe injury was quashed and replaced with one of assault to injury. This appears a deceptively simple solution to the problem but, as Gordon notes in his commentary following the report of the case, difficult cases will still arise where the victim has, for example, died of the combined effects of the assault both before and after the accused joined in.

FORMS OF LIABILITY

Several forms of art and part liability are recognised, depending, to a large extent, on the level of participation involved.

Mere presence

If someone simply happens to be present at the scene of a crime as a mere bystander and does nothing active to encourage or aid its commission, he will not be guilty art and part. Mere presence is insufficient for liability. This is shown in *Quinn* v *HM Advocate*.[13] The accused had been convicted art and part of indecent assault (against which conviction he did not appeal), and also art and part of rape (against which he did appeal). There was no corroboration of the victim's evidence of his actual participation in the rape and instead the prosecution relied on his presence

---

[12] 1991 SCCR 733.
[13] 1990 SCCR 254.

in the house at the time and awareness that some form of sexual incident was occurring. However, the High Court affirmed that mere presence, even if coupled with such awareness and with participation in an earlier indecent assault in the same premises, was not sufficient to found a charge of art and part liability. The accused's art and part conviction for rape was thus quashed.

However, there are situations where art and part liability can apply. Mere presence will create liability on those who have a duty to act when they witness a crime. In *Bonar v McLeod*[14] one police officer watched a junior officer commit an assault. He was held liable art and part in that assault because his presence put him under a duty to prevent the commission of the crime. Another situation where art and part liability will be imposed is in cases where the accused's presence amounts to encouragement of the crime. Although he has done nothing active, these cases will not be classified as true instances of "mere presence". He may do no more than be present at the scene but, depending on the circumstances, the very fact of his presence might actively encourage the perpetrator to commit the crime. Depending on the status and relationship between the bystander and the perpetrator, mere presence may strengthen the perpetrator's resolve or provide him with support and encouragement. If this is the case, then the bystander clearly does play some, although passive, part in the commission of the offence and should therefore be liable art and part. This is shown in *Stillie v HM Advocate*,[15] where the victim was robbed by one accused while another watched. Both then escaped together. Stillie (the bystander) argued that his involvement did not amount to more than mere presence and that therefore he could not be convicted art and part in the robbery. However, the High Court categorised his actions as more than mere presence; he was standing by, watching the execution of a crime, and therefore the jury was entitled to decide that he was there to provide assistance should it be necessary, and was not an innocent bystander who had been caught up in events. This interpretation was all the stronger given that Stillie made off with the other accused, which tends to suggest, if not indicate more strongly, that they were in some form of joint venture. However, it is possible to cite cases that appear fairly similar on the facts but where the result was quite different. In *Lawler v Neizer*[16] the accused had been present when a counterfeit banknote had been used and had left hurriedly with the co-accused who had passed the note. Lawler appealed on the ground that there was not sufficient evidence to convict him art and part of passing the counterfeit note, and his appeal was upheld. The High Court decided that his mere presence when the note was handed over was not sufficient on its own for liability, and that the other circumstances of the case were not sufficient to allow the sheriff to infer that he was a knowing participant in the offence.

---

[14] 1983 SCCR 161.
[15] 1992 SLT 279.
[16] 1993 SCCR 299.

Related to this point, it is important to distinguish true cases of mere presence, which will not lead to liability, from those where the accused's presence at a particular place infers guilt. This is shown in *White* v *MacPhail*,[17] where the accused was found hiding inside secured premises immediately after a window had been broken and an unidentified man seen leaving the premises. She would have found it difficult to enter the premises, and certainly had no legitimate reason to enter. It would be hard to imagine an innocent explanation for her presence. This placed her in a different category from someone who simply happened to be present at the crime scene, perhaps because they were walking down the same street, and, on appeal, the sheriff's inference of guilt from her presence at the scene was upheld. Similarly, an inference of guilt was found in the context of mobbing and rioting in *Coleman* v *HM Advocate*.[18] Here, the accused had been at a meeting where an agreement was reached to settle a dispute with the victim and weapons were distributed to the group. However, that accused had not been present throughout the whole meeting as he had been sent on an errand and, when he returned, he found that the others were preparing to leave. Although he had not formed part of the group that had agreed to confront the victim, he decided to go along with them. To this end, he was furnished with a baton and joined the rest of the group in verbally accosting several other youths whom they had met on the way and who refused to join them. In the course of the group's activities, the victim was stabbed to death. At trial, the judge did not direct the jury as to the effect of mere presence, but it was held on appeal that the evidence was sufficient for the jury to infer his agreement to the actions of the mob. Thus, the question of the effect of mere presence will be one requiring consideration, depending on the facts of each case.

Providing help

An art and part offender can be found liable on the basis that he has provided information or supplied materials to the perpetrator, unless their help has been entirely innocent. Thus, if a shopkeeper provides the perpetrator with some item which has an innocent use (say, a crowbar) and is completely unaware that it will be used to force open a window during a robbery, then that shopkeeper cannot be held art and part liable in the robbery. It would be grossly impractical to expect a shopkeeper in these circumstances to consider all the possible uses to which such a tool might be put, unless perhaps he had some other reason to be suspicious. It is unclear whether liability would attach if, in this example, the shopkeeper was suspicious of the perpetrator's motives but he would certainly become art and part liable if he knew that the perpetrator was going to commit a robbery or, arguably, that he was going to commit a crime even though he did not know precisely which one. A further question arises when considering whether the accused *should* have

---

[17] 1990 SCCR 578.
[18] 1999 SLT 1261.

had knowledge of the perpetrator's intention to commit a crime. If the accused was reckless and provided something to the perpetrator, knowing that it could help him to commit a crime but not caring, then he would probably still be liable art and part.

Assisting

Voluntary assistance in another's crime will render the assister art and part liable for that crime. However, art and part liability can also attach to the accused where he has not previously agreed with the perpetrator that he will assist in the commission of the crime. Such assistance may arise spontaneously. The effect of spontaneously joining the commission of the crime depends on whether the perpetrator welcomes the assistance. If the perpetrator is willing to be assisted by someone else, then both are liable for the crime. If, however, the perpetrator is unwilling to accept the assistance and terminates his role in the crime, then he will no longer be art and part liable. If he has reservations about accepting the assistance but continues with the crime nonetheless, then he will remain art and part liable.

Position of the victim

If the victim of the crime is truly a "victim" and was in no sense a willing participant, then he will bear no art and part liability. However, there are areas where the "victim" under the definition of the offence was in fact a consenting party. An under-age girl may have appeared to consent to sexual intercourse but, although there are no Scottish cases that can be cited, it would be sensible to assume that Scots law would follow the position taken in England and elsewhere. This would assert that, although the "victim" did indeed consent, that consent is irrelevant and would not render her liable for the appropriate offence because the purpose of that very offence was to protect her. This approach can be seen in the English case of *R v Whitehouse*,[19] where a father had incited his daughter to commit incest with him. There was no suggestion that the daughter could be prosecuted for the full offence, as the offence itself was aimed at her protection.

UNINTENDED CONSEQUENCES

The nature of art and part liability presupposes some type of group activity that unfolds according to a plan. Whether that plan has been explicitly formulated or not is irrelevant, but problems arise when one member of the group acts on his own initiative and behaves in a way which was not intended, or agreed to, in the original plan. Whether the other parties will be deemed to have acceded to his initiative and remain art and part liable for the consequences of this unintended

---

[19] [1977] 3 All ER 737.

action depends on whether they could have foreseen the unintended conduct. The parties may have agreed to commit an assault on a victim with their fists. If one of the parties is carrying a knife of which the others are unaware, and uses that knife in the course of the assault, then it may be possible for the other participants to argue that they had not foreseen its use and are therefore not art and part liable for the consequences attributable to that unforeseen conduct. They would, however, remain art and part liable for the aspects of the assault in which they had participated up to that point. They would only be able to remove themselves from continuing art and part liability for that assault if they stopped punching the victim as soon as the other participant started to use his knife. For example, in *Mathieson and Murray v HM Advocate*[20] a number of the accused had continued to kick the victim after one of their colleagues brought out a knife and stabbed him several times. The court was satisfied that they must have seen the knife and therefore been aware that the attack had become potentially fatal, and that therefore they were all art and part liable. Likewise, if the other participants had seen the knife prior to the commencement of the attack rather than during it, they could not then exclude themselves from liability for the stabbing because, by virtue of having seen the knife, they would again be able to foresee that it could have been used to fatal effect.

In *Coleman v HM Advocate*[21] the activities of a mob had begun with assault but had culminated in the fatal stabbing of their victim. Lord Cullen noted that, for all members of the mob to be guilty of the murder, the mob's intention must have been an intention to murder. However, the trial judge had given the jury the impression that membership of a mob brought with it liability for whatever criminal activities might come within its purpose as time went on. It was held that there was a distinction to be drawn in applying art and part guilt. If the consequence in question was one that occurred naturally in the course of the mob's activities, they would all remain liable. However, these could be distinguished from activities which were more properly the business of one or a few members of the group because they had formed a further intention which went beyond the original common purpose. It was necessary in such cases to identify the stages through which the mob's activities passed, and to attribute these individual stages either to the whole group or to some smaller part of it. If a number within the mob had progressed from the shared intention of assault, to a more detailed intention to murder, then, before applying art and part liability, it must be shown that any other member of the group had also taken upon himself that further murderous intention. This is further shown in *McKinnon v HM Advocate (No 2)*[22] where it was made clear that the art and part accused would only bear liability for murder where he had joined the common murderous purpose. If he had simply joined

---

[20] 1996 SCCR 388.
[21] 1999 SLT 1261.
[22] 2003 SLT 281.

in a less serious criminal act that resulted in the victim's death in circumstances where he could not have foreseen that death, he would instead be art and part liable in culpable homicide.

WITHDRAWAL FROM LIABILITY

Strict requirements must be satisfied before an accused can successfully argue that he withdrew from the criminal activity in question. It is clear that the accused cannot simply argue that he had dissociated himself from the perpetrator(s). This is clear from *MacNeill* v *HM Advocate*,[23] which involved a complex series of charges against a number of accused, one of whom was charged with art and part liability. He had been hired as an engineer on a voyage from Scotland to Africa. In Africa the vessel picked up a cargo of cannabis which the accused helped to hide in the fuel tank. He then left the ship at its next port of call and came home. He argued that he had not known of the nature of the cargo until after it had been stowed and, when he found out, he had dissociated himself from the venture and tried to persuade the rest of the crew to throw it overboard. However, on his return, he had tried to claim his wages for the voyage, which perhaps weakened his argument based on dissociation, and, in any event, the crime of importation had already begun by the time he left the ship. On appeal, the High Court agreed that evidence of dissociation would weigh in favour of the accused in deciding whether he had acted in concert with the other accused. However, the court was satisfied that the trial judge had properly put the relevant issues to the jury, and it upheld the conviction. As Gordon notes in his commentary, subsequent dissociation after the accused has played his part, or a portion thereof, will not generally justify acquittal, but may yet have a role in mitigation. It is unclear how much effort the accused must put in to preventing the offence. It would appear from other jurisdictions that the accused must cease to play a part in the crime because he has a change of heart and disapproves of the criminal conduct he has been involved with. He will not be successful if he merely takes fright or fears detection. It also seems clear that the accused should at least attempt to prevent commission of the crime at a point in time sufficiently early for it to be able to take effect. The need for the accused to take steps to prevent the completion of the criminal enterprise in clear from *Socratous* v *HM Advocate*.[24]

[23] 1986 SCCR 288.
[24] 1987 SLT 244.

SUMMARY OF MAIN POINTS

Art and part

- liability based on participation in the offence
- "accomplice liability", "acting in concert", "art and part liability"
- criminalise the accused for playing a part, but there is room for imposing a lesser sentence on less culpable parties
- the rest of the group can be convicted even if a main player has been acquitted
- public officials who allow crimes to be committed are liable for them art and part
- the accused will only be liable for offences committed after they joined
- mere presence will not be sufficient unless the accused had a duty to act or actually encouraged commission of the offence
- presence in a particular *locus* may infer guilt
- spontaneous assistance which is welcomed by the other accused leads to liability
- providing help is a form of art and part liability, unless it is done innocently
- the whole group will be liable for unintended consequences, unless they either withdraw from their part in the crime or could not have foreseen the consequences in question
- withdrawal from group crime requires considerable effort on the part of the withdrawer, probably including some attempt to prevent the commission of the crime

PARTIES TO AN OFFENCE

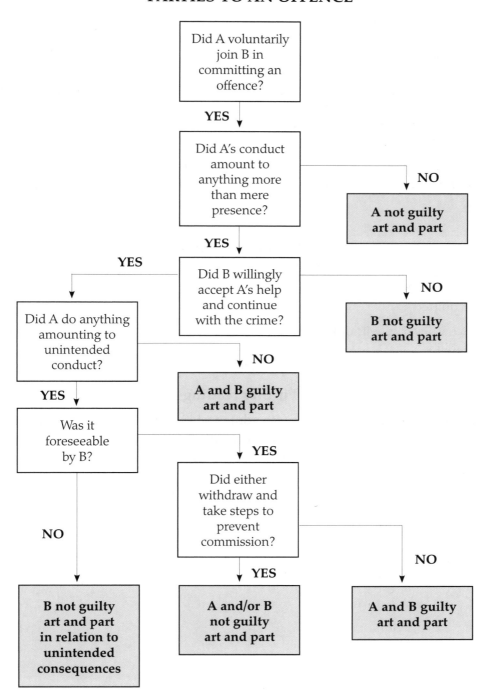

Note: Use of the word "guilty" is a convenient shorthand. There may be other issues to consider before the accused is convicted.

SELF-ASSESSMENT QUESTIONS (see Appendix for answers)

1   Three accused agree to assault their victim by beating him unconscious. In the course of the attack, one of them produces a knife and stabs the victim. This wound turns out to be fatal and all three are charged with murder. At trial, it emerges that one of the accused saw the knife and immediately stopped assaulting the victim as he had no wish to be involved in a stabbing. The other accused saw the knife but continued to punch the victim for several minutes after the fatal knife wound was inflicted. Will all three accused be convicted of the offence?

2   A police officer witnesses a colleague committing an offence. He plays no part in the offence himself. Is he liable to conviction?

Further questions

1   Is it justifiable that other members of a group who have played a lesser role may still be convicted art and part, even when the main accused has been acquitted?

2   What level of withdrawal should be required of the accused if he is to avoid liability?

Further reading

Jones and Christie, *Criminal Law* (4th edn), pp 143–158.

McCall Smith and Sheldon, *Scots Criminal Law* (2nd edn), pp 77–96.

Ferguson, *Crimes Against the Person*, pp 142–150.

Gordon, *Criminal Law* (3rd edn), vol 1, pp 145–186.

6 INCHOATE CRIMES: INCITEMENT, CONSPIRACY AND ATTEMPT

The three separate crimes of attempt, conspiracy and incitement form a category known as the inchoate crimes. Each of these crimes then comprises a huge variety of different types of behaviour because the accused can incite, conspire towards or attempt every offence known to the criminal law.[1] The term "inchoate" simply means that the crimes are unfinished or incomplete in some respect. In the case of incitement and conspiracy, this incompleteness is found either in the fact that the accused has encouraged another to commit the crime rather than commit it himself, or in the fact that a number of accused have agreed to carry out a crime, but as yet these plans have not been put into effect. In the case of attempted crimes, the incompleteness is found in the fact that the accused has tried to commit the crime, but has not succeeded in carrying it out fully.

The contentious issue with regard to these crimes lies in the fact that it is, in some respects, possible to argue that the accused has not caused any harm. It is then argued that, since there is no harm, there should be no conviction. However, this argument is theoretical as, in practice, every legal system recognises that, even though they have not reached the stage of committing the intended crime, these accused have caused some relevant harm. That harm may be restricted to causing a sense of social unease, or a more limited level of harm caused by the partial completion of the crime, or there may be some actual related harm caused in the process of carrying out the inchoate crime,[2] but nevertheless this harm is felt to be sufficient to justify punishment for the attempt. It is, however, recognised that this harm will inevitably be less than would have been caused had the crime been committed, and this is reflected in sentencing.

There are many stages during the process of committing a crime. If we imagine a robbery, the very first stage in its commission may be the thought in the mind of the accused. He may then decide to incite someone else to commit the crime, or conspire with a colleague, or he may decide to commit the crime himself. He may then go out to buy the necessary tools, drive round the building to familiarise

---

[1] Inchoate crimes are punishable not only at common law but also to some extent under statute. Section 293(2) of the Criminal Procedure (Scotland) Act 1995 criminalises incitement to commit any statutory offence, and s 294 renders criminal any attempt to commit a crime. Similarly, there are instances where it is possible to convict for conspiracy under statute.

[2] Clearly, if the accused has attempted to steal the victim's watch, has failed but in the process has assaulted the victim, he can be charged with the full crime of assault if *actus reus* and *mens rea* can be proved.

himself with it, make sketches, gather the equipment into his car, drive to the scene, force an entry and steal some property. The question is: if he is apprehended at some point during this lengthy process, is he liable to conviction and, if so, for what offence? A pure thought can never be punished, because there is no *actus reus* to attach to it, but once the accused starts to take some action, he may be liable to conviction. Incitement marks the earliest point of liability, followed by conspiracy, attempt and culminating in the full commission of the crime. As a result, liability increases as the accused reaches further into the commission of the planned crime.

Of the three crimes, an attempted crime is the most likely to be prosecuted. The reason for this is clear: an attempted crime involves a greater degree of action on the part of the accused and is therefore more likely to raise suspicion and lead to investigation by the authorities. In the case of incitement and conspiracy, prosecutions are less common. There are only two ways in which their existence can come to light. First, the person incited or a fellow conspirator can report the matter to the police. Second, the crime incited or conspired towards can be carried out, and the underlying incitement or conspiracy discovered in the course of investigations. As a result, there are few cases and, because modern examples are few and far between, cases used to illustrate aspects of these crimes are necessarily older and do not always cover all aspects of the crime in question.

INCITEMENT

The act required

The essence of incitement, broadly speaking, is that the inciter has encouraged the commission of a crime and should therefore be liable for his actions as a measure of crime prevention. Many different types of conduct are covered here: encouragement may take the form of persuasion, suggestion, request or inducement, but this is not an exhaustive list. Since what is required is encouragement, it seems clear that mere presence at the scene of a crime will not amount to incitement unless the inciter deliberately does something active to encourage the commission of the crime. There are very few Scottish cases on incitement and neither is there a statutory framework. However, a few aspects of the offence have been discussed. There is no requirement that the person incited actually responds to the incitement – they may go on to commit the crime but, equally, they may do nothing in response. This was shown in *HM Advocate* v *Tannahill and Neilson*,[3] where a contractor working for a government department had incited a subcontractor to pass non-government work to him in a way which meant that he could charge it to the department's account. As the incitee never

---

[3] 1943 JC 150.

responded to the incitement, the accused's intended aim had failed to proceed to commission but he was guilty of incitement nonetheless.

The extent and quality of the instruction given by the inciter to the incitee have been subject to discussion. The question posed was whether there could be incitement in the absence of any clear, definite instruction by the inciter. In *Baxter* v *HM Advocate*,[4] the accused had met the incitee and discussed the possibility of having someone killed. He explained his reasons and noted that it would be better if the plan were carried out while he was out of town and that it should look like an accident. The conversation was taped and, when charged, the accused argued that, although there had been detailed discussions, he had given no clear instruction to kill and was thus not guilty of incitement to murder. At trial, the jury was told that Baxter must have encouraged *and* instructed the commission of the crime. The inclusion of a requirement encompassing actual instruction was novel and there was no precedent on which to base it. On appeal, the High Court held that the sole requirement for the *actus reus* of incitement was encouragement.

The mental element

There is almost no detailed discussion of the mental element required for incitement in Scotland. From *Baxter* v *HM Advocate*[5] it is clear that an accused cannot deny that he intended the incitee to commit the crime simply by maintaining that it was a joke, if the circumstances show him to be serious. However, as the case does not discuss other aspects of the *mens rea* in any detail, the position common to other jurisdictions may serve as a helpful guide. In summary, other jurisdictions require evidence of an intention to encourage the commission of the crime. It is less clear whether recklessness would suffice. It is suggested that if the inciter is reckless about the consequences of his acts – if he does not care whether, as a result of his encouragement, the inciter acts or not – he is not guilty of incitement. The reasoning behind this restrictive requirement of intention is that incitement marks the earliest form of inchoate liability and therefore the interests of justice dictate that the accused show a clear intention to commit a crime. He has already been charged with a crime that sits at the earliest point of liability, and to convict him on the basis of reckless inadvertence, rather than actual intention, would widen the boundaries of the crime too far.

CONSPIRACY

The doctrine of conspiracy in Scots law is rather more developed than that of incitement and thus its progress can be traced through several definitions. Previously, a conspiracy would exist where two or more people agreed to do

---

[4] 1998 SLT 414.
[5] *Idem.*

something that would be unlawful if it were done by one of them. The agreement itself formed the *actus reus* and if intention could also be proved, those involved were guilty of conspiracy.[6] Two cases provide a clear picture of the development of the crime. The first of these is *Crofter Hand-Woven Tweed Co v Veitch*,[7] where it was held that conspiracy required two or more people to agree to do something that would be *unlawful* if one of them were to do it, whether or not their plan was actually carried out.[8] However, a later case further developed and narrowed one aspect of this definition. In *Maxwell v HM Advocate*[9] it was held that the crime of conspiracy required the accused to have agreed a course of conduct which had a *criminal*, rather than merely unlawful, objective.[10] The effect of this is to restrict the scope of the offence by confining it to those groups that truly intended to commit crimes. Thus, an agreement to commit an unlawful act, such as to breach a contract, will no longer form the basis of a charge of conspiracy. Historically, the more extensive scope of the *actus reus* of conspiracy was used as a means of outlawing, for example, trade union activity which was viewed as unlawful but was not actually criminal. Following *Maxwell*, this is no longer possible, and a charge of conspiracy requires that the accused has conspired to commit a *criminal* act.

It is clear that it is necessary to specify the means by which the unlawful purpose is to be achieved, following *Sayers v HM Advocate*.[11] The accused here had been charged with conspiring with others to further the aims of the Ulster Volunteer Force, by certain specified, and criminal, means. However, the jury convicted him of the conspiracy charge under deletion of these details and, as such, the High Court quashed his conviction on appeal. Minus these details, the charge did not disclose a crime known to the law of Scotland, as it envisaged liability for an agreement without proof of the criminal means to be employed.

The act requirement

The basis of liability for conspiracy is agreement and therefore it cannot be committed by a single individual. However, although there must be at least two parties, there is no upper limit. Indeed, in some areas, particularly drug importation, conspiracies can involve large numbers of individuals, each playing particular roles. It has been established abroad that, in large conspiracies, it is not necessary for each member to know of the existence of all other members of the conspiracy, so long as they are aware of those immediately above and below them. Some of those individuals may have joined the conspiracy later than others, provided that

---

[6] J MacDonald, *A Practical Treatise on the Criminal Law of Scotland* (1867) (5th edn, 1948, W Green & Son, Edinburgh), p 185.
[7] 1942 SC (HL) 1.
[8] *Ibid* at 5 per Viscount Simon.
[9] 1980 SLT 241
[10] *Ibid* at 243.
[11] 1982 JC 17.

they have agreed to the common purpose prior to its commission, but this will not affect the prosecution's case. However, it must be proved that the conspirators actually *agreed* to commit the crime and thus a mere suggestion that a crime be committed is not sufficient. The agreement will usually be proved by looking at the overt acts of the accused. This is shown in *West* v *HM Advocate*,[12] where the accused and another were charged with conspiracy to assault and rob. They argued that the agreement between them could not be proved from the evidence, but it was clear that they had loitered outside together for half an hour before entering the building, carrying a razor blade and scissors. Their agreement was established from these actions. It is also clear that, since actual agreement must be proved, spontaneous help from a passer-by will not show the necessary prior agreement to make him a conspirator.[13] This would cover situations where a passer-by stepped in to help the conspirators without any prior agreement.

Other aspects of the act requirement for conspiracy have not been discussed in Scottish cases, but a common consensus can be gleaned from other jurisdictions. Although the fundamental requirement is agreement, and therefore requires two or more participants, there are instances where only one of the two will be convicted. It seems clear that if one of the parties to the conspiracy is, for example, an undercover police officer, the other party can still be guilty of the crime on the basis of their agreement. In these cases, the police officer will clearly not truly agree to the commission of the offence; he will only pretend to do so in order to provide evidence of the conspiracy. However, from the point of view of the criminal, he and another party have reached a real agreement to commit the crime. Thus the criminal will be convicted on the basis of his willing agreement to commit a crime, even though, technically, he was alone in that agreement. Many other jurisdictions retain the rather outdated concept that a husband and wife cannot conspire because marital confidences are protected by law. In other areas, such as rape, it is now irrelevant that the parties are married[14] and it is questionable whether it should retain any relevance in conspiracy charges.

Another issue which has raised problems in other jurisdictions, but has not been dealt with in Scotland, is the acquittal of a co-conspirator. The general view abroad is that the acquittal of one party is irrelevant to the other's case. There may be many reasons why one party is acquitted; the weight of evidence may differ or there may be some relevant factor applying to only one of the accused. In these circumstances, the acquittal of one accused would have no bearing on the guilt of the other and therefore the latter's conviction should stand. The fact of agreement will make the conspirator liable and this cannot be diluted by some factor relating only to the other accused. This does not amount to convicting a sole individual of a conspiracy, but rather to convicting one party in circumstances where the other is affected by

---

[12] 1985 SCCR 248.
[13] *Burns* v *HM Advocate* 1983 SLT 38.
[14] *Stallard* v *HM Advocate* 1989 SLT 469.

some procedural consideration or has a legitimate defence. The parallels between this approach and that adopted by the Scottish courts in art and part cases suggest that this would also be adopted in relevant conspiracy cases.

The mental element

Again, there is no detailed discussion of the mental element required for conspiracy in Scots law. There is, however, a shared view across most other jurisdictions as to what is necessary and, in the absence of any contrary statements, it seems appropriate at least to consider this line. What is required is a shared common *intention* to commit a crime. It is very clear that these jurisdictions do not allow any place for recklessness as an alternative to intention. As was noted for incitement, this is perhaps the better option; it restricts the categories of individuals who will be liable, which is more appropriate when relatively little has been done towards the eventual commission of the crime.

Conspiring to achieve the impossible

The question of impossibility is a particularly vexed one in relation to inchoate crimes. Most discussion has focused on the appropriateness of conviction for attempted crimes which are impossible to commit, but the issue also arises in the realms of conspiracy. The crux of the issue is that the accused may have conspired to commit a crime he thought it would be possible to commit. In fact, for one reason or another, that crime may be impossible. He may have agreed to commit a crime using means which would be inadequate, for example a gang of robbers who conspired to steal property from a safe but envisaged using a quantity of explosive that would be inadequate to achieve that result. Impossibility can also arise in other situations: for example, in the case of *Maxwell* v *HM Advocate*,[15] where the conspirators had agreed to secure the transfer of a gaming licence by bribing a body which, unknown to the conspirators, no longer had the power to grant that licence. It is clear that the impossibility of success should not have been allowed to prevent their conviction, as the crime was committed when they reached agreement to bribe the board, regardless of the possibility of the result. It was merely fortuitous that their crime could not be carried to its conclusion and the impossibility in no way detracted from their guilt. Indeed, the accused's arguments were described as "startling" and it was stated that, if they were correct, "this would place criminal responsibility at the whim of extraneous events wholly divorced from the criminally directed actions of the participants themselves".[16] They had still agreed to commit the crime and exhibited the relevant intention, and therefore the impossibility of achieving the result was irrelevant. Conspiracy requires proof of an agreement to

---

[15] 1980 SLT 241.
[16] *Ibid* at 243.

achieve a criminal purpose; it does not specify any requirement in terms of the result flowing from that agreed purpose.

ATTEMPTS

The *actus reus*

In the course of attempting to commit a crime, the accused will have passed through a number of stages before he reaches the point of commission. The legal system has to determine a point at which to impose liability on the accused and the question becomes one of deciding how far he must have gone in order to present some identifiable level of harm that will justify punishment. It is possible to draw up a list of these stages[17] but there is little discussion of most of them in Scottish decisions. The "first stage" theory would convict an accused who has taken the first step towards commission of the intended crime. This is clearly unsuitable, as the first step towards something is inevitably ambiguous and it would be difficult to say at that stage whether his aim was criminal or innocent. Imagine someone wants to break into premises in order to steal property. The "first stage" theory might convict him when he goes out to buy a crowbar, although this could equally be intended for a DIY project. A more suitable stage is the preparation–perpetration stage, where the question asked is whether the accused has stepped over the line that divides preparatory conduct from something which can be classed as a part of the perpetration of the crime. If our accused was stopped while driving round the premises in order to familiarise himself with the layout, but with none of his equipment in the car, then this could be classed as preparatory conduct. However, if he had the crowbar, balaclava and perhaps a sketch map of the building with him, he could well be convicted for having moved into perpetration.

The "substantial step" theory looks for some significant move towards the commission of the crime, but this is a very subjective assessment and therefore perhaps not appropriate. A very similar test, known as the "proximity" test, seems to have found favour in American courts. This test requires that the accused has reached a stage in his course of conduct that can be described as "proximate" to the intended crime. Both the "substantial step" and "proximate conduct" tests could be illustrated by essentially the same behaviour. They would require our accused to have, for example, walked up to the building, balaclava on head and crowbar in hand. The final two tests are the "unequivocal step" test and the "last act" theory. Both of these are unsuitable; a test that looks for either an act unequivocally related to the crime (perhaps lodging the crowbar under a window frame and exerting pressure on it), or for the last act which the accused has to carry out (forcing the window open and climbing in), entail leaving liability so late

---

[17] First stage, preparation–perpetration, substantial step, unequivocal step and last act.

that the probability that the intended crime will be committed is very high. This does not accord with the overall aim of deterring the incidence of crime. From the illustrations provided, it seems clear that our accused should be made guilty at the preparation–perpetration stage, where he is stopped outside the premises with all the necessary equipment to hand. This would show sufficient determination and resolve to commit the crime, without having to wait until his conduct took him much closer – indeed dangerously close – to the commission of the crime. Commission is, after all, what the doctrine of liability for inchoate crime seeks to prevent.

It is clear from the cases that Scots law adopts the preparation–perpetration test where the accused's conduct is assessed to determine whether it amounts to a move towards perpetration of the crime, as shown in the above illustration. In *HM Advocate* v *Camerons*,[18] the two accused had gone a long way towards carrying out an insurance fraud (hiding the articles alleged to have been stolen, sending a letter to the insurers reporting the theft and making a claim on the policy) and were therefore convicted for having passed from preparation into the perpetration of the crime. In contrast, the accused was not liable for an attempt in *HM Advocate* v *McKenzie*,[19] where the act of copying out chemical recipes with the intent to sell them for profit was held to be an act of preparation only.[20] The preparation–perpetration test was also used in *Barrett* v *Allan*,[21] where the accused was arrested for attempting to enter a football stadium while drunk. He had only proceeded so far as to join the queue but it was held that he clearly intended to enter the stadium and had moved beyond preparatory conduct and into the actual perpetration. The judgment in *Guthrie* v *Friel*[22] also lends support to the preparation–perpetration test, where the accused was convicted of attempting to drive while under the influence of alcohol. He had been found asleep in his car with the engine and headlights on, although he had not actually gone so far as to release the handbrake. It was held that he had moved into perpetration of the crime, thereby reinforcing this as the accepted test in Scots law.

The mental element

If the accused has crossed into perpetration of his crime and it can be shown that he intended to commit that crime, then he will clearly be guilty of an attempt. The real question is whether the mental element will be satisfied by any lesser mental state. This arises particularly in relation to those offences where the full crime can be committed either intentionally or recklessly, the most obvious being

---

[18] (1911) 6 Adam 456.
[19] (1913) 7 Adam 189.
[20] Something else (perhaps being caught proffering the recipes for sale) would have been necessary in order to cross the line.
[21] 1986 SCCR 479.
[22] 1992 SCCR 932, although it is suggested that this case might be limited to its own facts.

murder. The Scottish position is found in *Cawthorne* v *HM Advocate*,[23] where the accused was charged with attempted murder for having fired several shots into a room in which he knew people were hiding. He was convicted on the basis that the crime of attempted murder has exactly the same *actus reus* and *mens rea* requirements as murder, the only difference being that the crime had not been successfully completed and the victim had not died. Thus, the mental element for attempted murder is either a wicked intention to kill or wicked recklessness as to the consequences of the accused's actions, these being the relevant forms of *mens rea* for murder. These views are given further weight by the subsequent case of *Brady* v *HM Advocate*,[24] where the accused was charged with attempted murder after an attack on his victim during which he repeatedly punched him, hit him with a bottle and struck him with a hammer. The instructions given to the jury made it perfectly clear that he was guilty of attempted murder if the jury was satisfied that he had acted with *either* a wicked intent to kill, *or* with wicked recklessness.

It seems clear, following *Cawthorne*, that Scots law will allow conviction for a reckless attempt where recklessness is part of the mental element of the full crime. This approach does not fit comfortably with the notion of what it means to attempt something. In ordinary language, to "attempt" connotes actively trying to bring about a result. This further tends to presuppose that the accused will have to intend that result in order to be said to be trying to bring it about. The accused who is reckless as to whether the crime is committed is not really trying to bring it about under the ordinary interpretation of the word. It is further asserted in foreign jurisdictions that an attempt is an independent crime and not a subsidiary crime which is to be formulated purely in terms of the definition of the full version of the crime. Judges abroad have gone to some lengths to insist that an attempted crime is a separate class of crime with its own requirements as to *actus reus* and *mens rea*, and is therefore not constrained to follow the rubric laid down for the associated full crime. However, Scots law seems resolute in its stance in relation to attempted murder. In the absence of any decided cases dealing with other crimes, it is unclear whether this approach will apply to other crimes with both intention and recklessness as possible *mentes reae*. However, it would be possible, relying on *Cawthorne*, for a Scottish court to convict of an attempt in any situation where the accused's mental state falls within the scope of the *mens rea* of the full crime.

Attempts to do the impossible

Situations have arisen where the accused has attempted to commit a crime that, for some reason, is impossible. There are a number of old cases that present a conflicting picture; in some, the impossibility had prevented conviction, while, in

---

[23] 1968 JC 33.
[24] 1986 JC 68 at 76.

others, convictions were upheld. Fortunately, the issue has now been resolved in the case of *Docherty* v *Brown*.[25] Here, the accused was convicted of attempting to possess Ecstasy tablets with intent to supply. In fact, the tablets did not contain the drug and, in refusing his appeal against conviction, the High Court of Justiciary took the opportunity to clarify the position. It is clear from the case that the accused was convicted of the attempted crime on the basis that he had satisfied the mental requirement and had also moved beyond the preparation of his crime, and thus the so-called defence of impossibility was disregarded. As noted in relation to conspiracy, this approach is justifiable on the basis that, were the attempter given a defence of impossibility, he would profit from a fortuitous event which had no bearing on his guilt. In his own mind, Docherty had possession with intent to supply a Class A drug. From a policy point of view, this was sufficient to make him a danger to society. Even though he could not supply a Class A drug on this occasion, if he was not punished, he could be more careful next time to ensure that he did acquire the correct drug. Thus, in this type of case, the criminal sanction is justified on the basis that, were the accused not apprehended for his subjectively criminal conduct this time, he could return better prepared and cause some real harm to society in the future.

SUMMARY OF MAIN POINTS

Incitement
- encouragement of another to commit a crime.
- no need for response from incitee.
- no need for a clear instruction to incitee.
- inciter must intend that the crime is committed

Conspiracy
- the agreement of two or more people to commit a crime.
- acquittal of co-conspirator is irrelevant.
- conspirators must share a common intention to commit the crime.
- impossibility is irrelevant.

Attempts
- liability is imposed when move from preparation to perpetration.
- attempter must intend to commit the crime, or be reckless as to the consequences of his actions if this is an alternative *mens rea* for the full version of the crime.
- impossibility is irrelevant.

---

[25] 1996 SLT 325.

INCITEMENT

```
          ┌─────────────────────┐
          │  Has the accused    │
          │  encouraged the     │
          │  commission of a    │
          │       crime?        │
          └─────────────────────┘
        YES                       NO

┌─────────────────────┐      ┌─────────────────────┐
│  Did he intend to?  │      │  No liability for   │
│                     │      │     incitement      │
└─────────────────────┘      └─────────────────────┘
   YES          NO

┌──────────┐    ┌──────────┐
│  Guilty  │    │ Not guilty│
└──────────┘    └──────────┘
```

Note: Use of the word "guilty" is a convenient shorthand. There may be other issues to consider before the accused is convicted.

CONSPIRACY

Have two or more agreed to commit a crime?

YES

NO

Not guilty of conspiracy

Are the parties spouses?

NO

YES

Not guilty of conspiracy

Did they intend to commit the crime?

YES

NO

Guilty

Not guilty of conspiracy

Note: Use of the word "guilty" is a convenient shorthand. There may be other issues to consider before the accused is convicted.

ATTEMPTED CRIMES

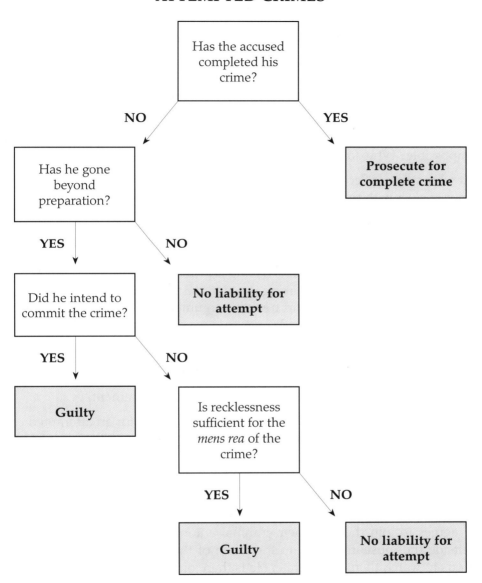

Note: Use of the word "guilty" is a convenient shorthand. There may be other issues to consider before the accused is convicted.

SELF-ASSESSMENT QUESTIONS (see Appendix for answers)

1   With reference to cases, outline the requirements for the *actus reus* of incitement.

2   The accused has been charged with inciting an illegal prize fight. His defence is that he was merely a spectator who took no active part in the proceedings. Will he be convicted of the offence?

3   How do the courts view a conspiracy to achieve something which is in fact impossible? Why do they take this stance?

4   At what stage do Scottish courts impose liability for attempted crimes? Illustrate your answer with reference to cases.

5   The accused was apprehended and searched by Customs officials at Edinburgh Airport. He was found to be carrying a bag containing a quantity of white powder but, before it could be identified, he confessed to attempting to import cocaine. In fact, the bag contains baking powder. His solicitor has argued that it is not an offence to import baking powder and therefore that his client should be released. How will the court treat this argument and what case will they rely on in coming to their decision?

Further questions

1   Should recklessness be included in the *mens rea* of incitement?

2   With reference to cases, explain the *mens rea* required for an attempted crime under Scots criminal law. Is the current position satisfactory?

3   A and B have agreed to break into the National Gallery in Edinburgh to steal their collection of Impressionist paintings. After some thought, it becomes clear to them that they do not have access to the necessary equipment, and therefore approach C, a builder, who owns crowbars and the like. A week later, C agrees to join them in their criminal enterprise. While they are standing outside the museum, trying to force one of the windows, D walks past and stops to watch them for a while. He is then joined by E who, seeing that they are having difficulty with the window, goes over to give them a hand. They are surprised – they do not know E and had not asked for his help – but are grateful nonetheless. E returns to stand and watch with D, as A and B lift C through the window. At this point, the police arrive, arrest everyone and all five of them are charged with conspiracy to steal the paintings. It emerges that the collection of paintings was actually on loan to another gallery at the time. Will they all be convicted of the conspiracy and, if so, why?

Further reading

Jones and Christie, *Criminal Law* (4th edn), pp 129–147 and 158–165.

McCall Smith and Sheldon, *Scots Criminal Law* (2nd edn), pp 97–116.

Gordon, *Criminal Law* (3rd edn), vol 1, pp 187–243.

Ferguson, P, "Criminal Incitement" 1997 JLSS 407–408.

Oliver, S, "Incitement, *mens rea* and mistake" 1999 SLPQ 293–299.

Sheldon, D, "Impossible Attempts and other oxymorons" 1997 Edin LR 250–260.

7 DEFENCES

DEFENCES AND MITIGATING PLEAS

Regardless of any apparent liability which potentially attaches to the accused, it may yet be possible for him either to escape liability by raising a successful defence, or to have the charge he faces reduced to one attracting a lesser sentence. If the charge against him is reduced, the accused will have benefited from a mitigating plea. Scots criminal law previously recognised two types of mitigating plea (diminished responsibility and provocation), both of which operate in the context of murder and, in the case of provocation, also assault. A plea of diminished responsibility acknowledges the fact that, although the accused's acts attract liability, he was not wholly responsible for them because he was suffering from some form of mental aberration falling short of insanity.[1] It is important to note that diminished responsibility does not affect the accused's criminal responsibility; he remains responsible but his sentence is reduced. A plea of provocation asserts that the accused responded instantly in the heat of the moment to behaviour by the victim which would have provoked even the reasonable man. It operates as a concession to human frailty. Prior to 2001, in the same way as diminished responsibility, provocation reduced the charge faced by the accused from murder to culpable homicide and was thus "mitigatory".[2] However, *Drury* v *HM Advocate*[3] clearly views provocation in murder cases as a failure to establish *mens rea*, rather than an instance of mitigation.

However, there are a number of instances where the accused can plead a full defence, thereby escaping all liability for his actions, rather than simply reducing the charge he faces. The defences recognised by Scots law are varied, ranging from the commonplace (intoxication) to the unusual (insanity, necessity), and including special defences, but the effect of all of them is essentially the same. The accused faces no criminal sanction for his conduct if his plea is successful: he will be acquitted and will acquire no criminal record in relation to that charge. Full defences can be categorised as either justifications or excuses. The distinction is clear: a justificatory defence takes proven criminal conduct and renders it lawful in the circumstances, the best example being self-defence. Those defences that

---

[1] Insanity operates as a defence rather than a mitigating plea.
[2] For both diminished responsibility and provocation, see Chapter 8.
[3] 2001 SLT 1013.

operate as excuses recognise that the conduct is criminal but deny that the accused was responsible for that conduct, for example in cases of involuntary intoxication.

SPECIAL DEFENCES

Special defences are a class of defence to which particular procedural rules are attached. A special defence must be notified to the court in writing; it must be intimated to the Crown Agent and lodged 7 days before the trial commences (if the case is to be heard in the High Court) or intimated to the procurator fiscal and lodged before or at the first diet (if the case is in the sheriff court).[4] The purpose of this is to allow the prosecution time to investigate whether the circumstances justify raising a special defence. A special defence must, logically, be raised before trial, as its purpose is to state that the accused is simply not guilty and therefore that the trial should not go ahead. If accepted by the prosecution, the effect of a special defence is to terminate the action against the accused before the case is due to come to court. However, it is always open to the Crown to proceed with the prosecution if it feels, on the basis of its investigations, that the special defence does not, or may not, apply in the circumstances of the case. There are four classes of special defence: insanity (both at the time of the offence and at the time of trial); self-defence; incrimination; and alibi. Coercion and automatism are treated as if they were special defences and therefore the notice requirement applies to them also.[5]

Insanity at the time of the offence

If the object of a criminal sanction is to prevent the accused from committing further offences in the future, then it must be acknowledged that there is little point in convicting someone who is insane. Insanity, in this context, is a legal consideration, rather than a medical or psychiatric one. This was made clear in *Brennan v HM Advocate*,[6] where it was stated that the question of what amounts to insanity is "a question which has been resolved by the law itself as a matter of legal policy in order to set, in the public interest, acceptable limits upon the circumstances in which any person may be able to relieve himself of criminal responsibility".[7] By raising a special defence of insanity, the accused admits that he committed the criminal act but asserts that his state of mind at the time of its commission was such as to relieve him of liability. If the defence is accepted, the accused will be found not guilty by reason of insanity, in recognition of the fact that, at the time of acting, he was not responsible for his actions. However, although the accused will be acquitted of the charge against him, the courts are

---

[4] Criminal Procedure (Scotland) Act 1995, s 78.
[5] Section 78(2). On automatism, see Chapter 2.
[6] 1977 JC 38.
[7] *Ibid* at 42–43.

not constrained to release him. He will be dealt with under the rubric of the Criminal Procedure (Scotland) Act 1995, s 54(6) which provides that, where the accused was insane at the time of the criminal act or omission, the court or jury shall acquit him by reason of insanity. It must then dispose of the case under s 57(2) by ordering him to be detained in a hospital, making him subject to the restrictions imposed under the Mental Health (Scotland) Act 1984, imposing a guardianship or supervision and treatment order, or making no order at all. However, the court must order him to be detained in hospital if the risk to the public of him being at liberty is too great.[8]

The test for insanity dates back to Hume who talks in terms of "a disorder (which) amount(s) to an absolute alienation of reason – such a disease as deprives the patient of the knowledge of the true aspect and position of things about him" and which prevents the accused from "distinguishing friend or foe".[9] This definition, or some paraphrase of it, has been used consistently by the Scottish courts, as can be shown through a number of illustrative cases. In *HM Advocate* v *Kidd*,[10] the accused had stabbed his wife to death. The issue in hand was whether he was able to plead insanity as a special defence to the charge of murder laid against him. In the charge to the members of the jury, the judge instructed them to determine first whether it had been proved that the accused had committed the acts in question, and then determine, broadly speaking, whether he was of sound or unsound mind at that time. If they found him to have been insane at the time, they were instructed that they could not hold him responsible for his actions and that he should be acquitted but detained in hospital. They were also informed that, for a special defence to succeed, the accused had to prove that, on the balance of probabilities, it applied to his case. The judge noted that it was difficult to find a definition of insanity, as cases were relatively uncommon. The reason for this is that, in most cases, the accused will remain insane from the time of the offence through to and including the time of trial. These cases will be dealt with on the basis that the accused was insane at the time of trial and unfit to instruct his own defence.[11] However, the judge defined insanity as unsoundness of mind, requiring an alienation of reason due to a mental defect which deprived the accused of his ability to reason and control his actions and reactions.[12] He also noted that the test for insanity in Scotland used to follow the English case of *McNaghten*,[13] where it was held that the accused was insane if he did not know the nature and quality of his act, or if he knew its nature and quality but did not know that the act was wrong. However, he made it clear to the jury that this had ceased to be the law in Scotland.

[8] Criminal Procedure (Scotland) Act 1995, s 57(3).
[9] Hume, *Commentaries*, i, 37.
[10] 1960 JC 61.
[11] See insanity in bar of trial.
[12] 1960 JC 61 at 70.
[13] (1843) 10 Cl and F 200.

A more recent case which deals with the issue of insanity is *Brennan v HM Advocate*.[14] The accused had murdered his father as a result of extreme intoxication, and sought to raise the special defence of insanity on the basis of that intoxication. It was held that voluntary intoxication was not sufficient to raise the special defence of insanity and, moreover, that insanity required proof of a total alienation of reason due to mental disease or illness, or a defect or unsoundness of mind. As a result, his appeal against conviction for murder was refused. In *HM Advocate v Blake*,[15] the court again held that what was required for the defence of insanity was an alienation of reason in relation to the criminal act committed by the accused. This was to be proved by the accused on the balance of probabilities and on the basis of a common-sense interpretation of all relevant facts. The court also held that it was for the jury to decide whether the accused was insane at the time of acting, and this was not a decision to be made by the medical experts, again emphasising that the test for insanity is a legal rather than a medical one. The accused had been charged with attempted murder following an attack on his victim with an axe. He had struck her head and arms, causing her to suffer severe injury, including damage to her hearing. In response to the charge, he raised a special defence that he had been insane at the time. His assertion of insanity was rejected by the jury, who convicted him of assault to severe injury rather than attempted murder on the ground of diminished responsibility. The jury did not feel that his state of mind was sufficiently abnormal to be classified as insanity.

It can be seen that Scots law is not prepared to uphold the defence of insanity unless the accused can prove that he suffered from some mental disease or illness to such an extent that he was a stranger to reason. Even if successful, the defence of insanity is something of a double-edged sword, in that, although a variety of options are open to the court, there is still the possibility that the accused will be detained in hospital under a restriction order. The effect of this may be that the accused spends a longer period detained in hospital than he might have done in prison had he not raised the defence of insanity.

Insanity in bar of trial

This form of insanity operates to provide a defence for the accused who is insane at the time his case comes to trial, whether or not he was also insane at the time of commission. The argument put forward on his behalf will be that he suffers from some form of mental abnormality such that he cannot understand the court proceedings or adequately instruct his legal representatives.[16] This cannot be equated with the level of mental illness and alienation of reason required for the defence of insanity itself. The law is governed by the Criminal Procedure (Scotland)

---

[14] 1977 JC 38. This case will be discussed in more detail below with reference to the possibility of a defence of intoxication.
[15] 1986 SLT 661.
[16] He would thus, if tried, not benefit from the fair trial which is a fundamental right of the accused.

Act 1995, s 54(1), which states that the accused can be found unfit to stand trial if two doctors submit written or oral evidence to that effect. If this is complied with, the trial will be deserted. An examination of the facts will then follow, in order to establish whether the insane person had in fact committed the offence in question and whether there are grounds for acquittal. If the court concludes that the accused did not commit the offence or should be acquitted, he will be released. However, if he committed the offence without grounds for acquittal, or was also insane at the time of the offence, then the appropriate disposal under the 1995 Act will apply, whether that amounts to detention in a secure hospital or some less restrictive disposal.[17]

Mental abnormality can be found in some form of mental disturbance, or in a disability of some sort.[18] The effect of the plea in bar of trial is that the accused will be detained in a psychiatric hospital, although the Crown reserves the right to prosecute at a later date should the accused recover his cognitive abilities. A recent case can be cited to illustrate the view taken by the Scottish courts. In *Stewart* v *HM Advocate*,[19] the accused had been charged with a number of rapes and other sexual offences committed in respect of four complainers over a period of 10 years. He raised a plea in bar of trial based on psychiatric evidence that he suffered from a mental handicap and a very low IQ which placed him in the bottom 1 per cent of the population. It was clear that he understood the charges against him, but he was suggestible, particularly in relation to answering questions in court, and could not properly follow proceedings or instruct a defence. His plea in bar of trial was rejected and, on appeal, that decision was upheld on the basis that it was for the trial judge to determine this type of insanity on the facts of the case and he had been entitled to reach the conclusion that Stewart was not unfit to stand trial.

Self-defence

This defence is available where the accused has acted in contravention of the criminal law in order to defend himself, another person or property. Thus, the term "self-defence" is narrower than its legal meaning and is not, as it suggests on its face, limited to defence of one's own person. It is, however, less likely that the accused will succeed with a plea of self-defence in defence of his property, particularly if his defensive actions have gone so far as to kill. Even if the accused voluntarily intervened to defend someone else rather than himself, the defence will still be available to him. The defence justifies the use of some physical force in response to an attack of some sort, but only within certain parameters. The defence has been used to counter charges of murder, assault and breach of the peace, but it is most commonly used when the accused has killed someone while defending himself and will thus be used as a defence to a charge of murder or culpable

---

[17] On this, see C Connelly, "Insanity and Unfitness to Plead" 1996 JR 206 at pp 207–208.

[18] See *McLachlan* v *Brown* 1997 SLT 1059.

[19] 1997 SLT 1047.

homicide. However, there are limits imposed on its use to prevent the defence from becoming circular and unworkable. For example, the victim may defend himself against his attacker. Any injuries or death caused thus will be covered by a plea of self-defence. However, it is not open to the attacker to argue that he was defending himself against the counter-attack unleashed by his victim. The attacker's initial criminal act (the original attack) precludes him from raising self-defence when he then has to respond to the victim's attempts to fend him off. There are a number of requirements which must be met before the defence is established, not least that, as a special defence, notice must be given before trial.

The first requirement is that of an imminent danger to life or, for women, an imminent threat of rape.[20] The threat must be an imminent one (in the sense of having already begun, or being about to begin), rather than a threat for the future or a contingent one. Thus, if the accused has been threatened that he will be killed at a later date, he cannot strike first, kill the person threatening him, and claim self-defence. The accused must have reason to believe that his life is in danger,[21] but use of a weapon by the victim in his attack will often justify the accused's assumption that his life was in danger. However, if the accused mistakenly believes that his life is in danger, for example if he wrongly believes that the victim has a weapon, then, unless he had reasonable grounds for that mistaken belief, he will not be able to lead the defence.[22] The assessment is made on subjective grounds. The court will assess whether the accused himself reasonably believed that his life was in danger.[23] He must also show that he feared for his life, not that he simply feared an attack of some sort. This is shown in *Elliot* v *HM Advocate*,[24] where the accused had defended himself through fear of a homosexual advance. This was insufficient to establish self-defence. The accused must then show that the danger he faced was inescapable. There is a duty to retreat if possible. This has been established by cases such as *HM Advocate* v *Doherty*.[25] The accused was charged with culpable homicide following an attack during which his opponent used a hammer. Doherty had responded by using a bayonet, and had stabbed his attacker fatally. The accused was standing in front of an open door leading to a flight of stairs, which, it was held, he could easily have used as a means of retreat. As he failed to avail himself of this option, a plea of self-defence was rejected. The defence was likewise unavailable in *Fitzpatrick* v *HM Advocate*.[26] The accused had been involved in a fight in a bar. It was held that he had the option of leaving the bar and avoiding the danger which he faced, and therefore the defence was not open to him. However, it is equally clear that the law will not expect the accused to retreat or escape from

---

[20] *McCluskey* v *HM Advocate* 1959 JC 39.
[21] *Jones* v *HM Advocate* 1990 SLT 517.
[22] *Owens* v *HM Advocate* 1946 JC 119 and, more recently, *Lieser* v *HM Advocate* 2008 SLT 866.
[23] *Jones* v *HM Advocate* 1990 SLT 517, following *Owens*.
[24] 1987 SCCR 278.
[25] 1954 JC 1.
[26] 1992 SLT 796.

the danger in some way which is unreasonable or puts his life in danger, and thus he is not required to retreat using an escape route which is in itself inherently dangerous.[27] It is one thing to have the option of retreating through a door and out onto a passageway, or even down a flight of well-lit, well-maintained stairs, but quite another to be expected to run backwards, while defending oneself, down a flight of worn, uneven and poorly lit stairs.[28]

Having established that a plea of self-defence is available, the accused must then satisfy the requirement of proportionality. The rule is that the accused may use only such force as is reasonably necessary to fend off the attack in order to save his life. He cannot use excessive force. Thus, in *Pollock* v *HM Advocate*,[29] the accused had defended his girlfriend from assault with intent to rape. The victim had struggled with her and hit her, at which point the accused intervened and proceeded to stamp repeatedly on the victim's head, causing him 70 blunt force injuries. This response by the accused was held to be well outside the scope of a proportionate response.

Likewise, the defence is not available if the force used by the victim is in some way lawful. Thus, if the accused defends himself against force used by police officers in order to carry out his arrest, he will not be able to plead the defence. If the case involves defence of property, the courts will apply broadly the same tests, in that so long as the accused defends himself proportionately against, for example, a pickpocket who takes his wallet, he will be able to plead self-defence to any charge of assault. However, in *McCluskey* v *HM Advocate*[30] it was held that self-defence could be used as a defence to a charge of murder only if the deceased had threatened the accused's life. Thus, if the accused kills in defence of his property, he will not be able to raise the defence.

A further issue of note is the position of the accused who has instigated a fight. In *Burns* v *HM Advocate*,[31] the accused had started a fight following an argument. The fight had been carried out over a period of time in a number of locations. Immediately prior to the final and fatal assault by the accused, the victim had crossed the road towards him and the accused alleged that he had believed the victim was about to assault him. On the basis of this assertion, he argued that, when he inflicted fatal injuries on the victim, he had been acting in self-defence. At trial, the judge highlighted to the jury that one of the criteria for the defence of self-defence was that the accused had not instigated the fight. Following conviction, the accused appealed on the ground that this part of the direction to the jury was incorrect. It was held that the accused could raise the defence even though he had started the argument, so long as the victim's response to the accused's initial acts was disproportionate and justified the accused in feeling he was in imminent

---

[27] For example, leaping out of an upper storey of a building or running across a busy motorway.
[28] Gordon, *Criminal Law* (3rd edn, W Green/SULI, Edinburgh, 2001), vol 2, p 323.
[29] 1998 SLT 880.
[30] 1959 JC 39.
[31] 1995 SLT 1090.

danger. If the accused then responded in a proportionate way to defend himself, this would entitle him to raise the defence.

Incrimination

Incrimination can be used by the accused who wishes to establish, in his defence, that the crime was not committed by him but by some other person. This special defence has been raised in a wide variety of cases ranging from murder to theft and the possession of drugs. One of the issues raised in this area relates to the onus of proof in establishing the existence of such a defence, and whether that onus is placed on the Crown or the defence. In *Lambie* v *HM Advocate*,[32] the accused had been charged with the theft of money and had raised a special defence of incrimination, alleging that other people had committed the offence. His defence was rejected by the jury and he was convicted. He raised an appeal, contending, among other points, that the judge had been incorrect to direct the jury that the onus of proving a special defence lay on the accused. It was held on appeal that the requirements surrounding special defences existed simply to give the Crown fair warning that the accused would be raising one of them. Once given such warning, it was then for the Crown, as in other cases, to prove the accused guilty beyond reasonable doubt. It followed that the accused was required to do no more than raise a reasonable doubt in the jury's mind that someone else was guilty instead of him. He was not required to prove the existence of the defence of incrimination in his case, and therefore his conviction was quashed.

Alibi

The essence of the special defence of alibi is an assertion that, not only did the accused not commit the offence in question, but that he was elsewhere during the time in question. It is necessary to state where the accused was during the relevant time period in order to establish that he was not responsible and, in common with all special defences, notice must be given to the Crown before trial.

OTHER DEFENCES

Intoxication: involuntary and self-induced

Intoxication can operate as a defence to a charge only in certain circumstances. The approach taken by the courts varies depending on whether the intoxication has been caused by a voluntary act of the accused or by a substance he has unknowingly ingested. Intoxication can be caused by alcohol or drugs. Voluntary intoxication covers situations where the accused is to blame for having become intoxicated. It is also referred to as self-induced intoxication. Generally speaking, this type of

---

[32] 1973 SLT 219.

intoxication is not a defence, as the accused has voluntarily chosen to become intoxicated, knowing that he could cause harm, and must therefore be liable for any criminal act he commits. The accused can be liable on the basis that he knew the substance was intoxicating and took it regardless (or because) of its intoxicating nature. However, the law will also hold him liable on the basis that, even though he did not personally know the substance was intoxicating, he should have so known. A number of cases can be used to illustrate the approach taken by the courts to voluntary intoxication. In *Kennedy v HM Advocate*,[33] the accused argued that the charge should be reduced from murder to culpable homicide on the basis of his intoxication at the time of the offence. The court was required to consider the effect of intoxication on criminal responsibility and held that the accused should remain liable for murder unless it could be shown that he was intoxicated to such a level that he was incapable of forming the specific *mens rea* for murder. There was evidence before the court to show that the accused had been drinking but it was not sufficient for him to show that he was intoxicated, as this would not afford him a defence. Had he been so intoxicated that he did not know the nature or quality of his act, then he would be suffering from an alienation of reason which might lead the court to a different conclusion.[34]

Perhaps the most important case in this area is *Brennan v HM Advocate*.[35] Brennan stood charged with murder. During an argument, he had stabbed his father to death with a knife after having voluntarily consumed between 20 and 25 pints of beer during the day and taken LSD shortly before the attack. He raised a plea of insanity but also contended that the effect of his intoxication was such as to reduce the charge against him to culpable homicide. The jury were instructed that they were not entitled to convict of culpable homicide on the basis of his intoxication and he was convicted of murder. His appeal was heard by a Full Bench of seven judges. He argued that the instructions to the jury amounted to a misdirection and that his conviction should therefore be quashed. On appeal it was held that if the accused voluntarily and deliberately consumed substances he knew to be intoxicants for their intoxicating effect, then it was open to the court to convict him. This would apply regardless of the quantity taken, or whether their intoxicating effect was fully foreseeable.[36] It was clear that Brennan had voluntarily consumed both the alcohol and the drugs in the full knowledge of, and because of their intoxicating effects, and that he also knew that he might lose control over his subsequent actions. It was also held that his self-induced intoxication, when added to his other actions, constituted the type of criminal recklessness which the law aimed to prevent. The Lord Justice-General stated that "(t)here is nothing unethical or unfair or contrary

---

[33] 1944 JC 171.

[34] If total alienation of reason can be proved, the court would be entitled to treat the case as a straightforward instance of insanity brought on by the long-term effects of alcohol abuse, rather than an instance of drunkenness.

[35] 1977 JC 38.

[36] *Ibid* at 46.

to the general principle of our law that self-induced intoxication is not by itself a defence to any criminal charge ...".[37] The judgment in *Brennan* refers to intoxication caused by substances known by the accused to be intoxicating, but the courts will assume such knowledge in the majority of cases.[38]

Brennan has been applied consistently in this type of situation, as shown in the recent case of *Donaldson* v *Normand*.[39] The accused had been charged with culpably and recklessly endangering another person. Following his arrest on another matter, he had been asked whether he had any knives, sharp instruments or needles on his person. He had emptied his pockets of several needles but, when searched, another unguarded needle was found in his sock. He was charged with culpably and recklessly exposing the person who had discovered this needle to infection and injury. In the sheriff court, it was found that, because of his ingestion of heroin and temazepam, he had forgotten about the existence of the needle. His forgetfulness had been caused by the level of his intoxication, but this was treated as irrelevant and he was convicted. He appealed unsuccessfully, contending that, because of intoxication, he did not have the relevant *mens rea* for the offence. Thus, the court in *Donaldson* was able to state that, in any crime that could be committed recklessly, it was not sufficient for the accused to state that intoxication deprived him of the required *mens rea*. Becoming intoxicated was itself an act of recklessness which existed up to and during the commission of the offence, thereby supplying the *mens rea* in offences which could be committed recklessly. Thus, once the accused had been found to have satisfied the *actus reus* of the offence, he would be guilty as charged because the recklessness inherent in becoming intoxicated supplied the necessary *mens rea*.

Although voluntary intoxication is the most likely to lead to crime, it is also possible for the accused to have committed a crime while involuntarily intoxicated. This will apply in situations where the accused has unknowingly ingested the intoxicant, for example where his drink is "spiked" with either drugs or alcohol. It had been accepted that, if the accused was suffering from involuntary intoxication, he lacked *mens rea* for the offence.[40] The approach taken by the courts is to view involuntary intoxication as capable of establishing the relevant criteria for a finding of the defence of automatism.[41] Perhaps the most notable decision in this area came in *Ross* v *HM Advocate*.[42] The accused lost control and seriously assaulted several people. He was charged with a number of offences, including attempted murder and assault. He had left a can of lager unattended and, unknown to him, five or six temazepam tablets and some LSD were added to it. He then drank the remainder of the contents and shortly thereafter started screaming and lunging at

---

[37] 1977 JC 38 at 51.
[38] Gordon, vol 1, p 488.
[39] 1997 SLT 1303.
[40] See *HM Advocate* v *Raiker* 1989 SCCR 149.
[41] For further detail on automatism, see Chapter 2.
[42] 1991 SLT 564

those present, with a knife. In his defence, it was argued that he was intoxicated to the extent that he could not form the appropriate *mens rea* for the charges laid against him and that the jury should therefore consider whether he could be acquitted. The trial judge refused to uphold this argument and Ross was convicted accordingly. However, his appeal was successful and the court allowed involuntary intoxication to operate as a defence where, because it was not self-induced and not foreseeable, it amounted to non-insane automatism. In *Ross*, the Lord Justice-General said that

> "... if a person cannot form any intention at all because, for example, he is asleep or unconscious at the time, it would seem impossible to hold that he had *mens rea* and was guilty in the criminal sense of anything he did when he was in that state".[43]

Accordingly, Ross's convictions were quashed as there had been a miscarriage of justice.

A similar case, which followed the line laid down in *Ross*, is *Sorley* v *HM Advocate*.[44] The accused had been charged with assault and breach of the peace following an incident during which he had been almost helplessly drunk. He gave evidence that he had drunk a small quantity of alcohol 30 minutes earlier and had no recollection of anything else until the following morning. Unknown to him, his drink had been laced with LSD and sleeping tablets which had caused his intoxicated state. He was convicted at trial but appealed on the basis that *Ross* allowed involuntary intoxication to found a plea of automatism so long as the intoxication was not self-induced or foreseeable and resulted in a total loss of self-control. His appeal was unsuccessful, on the ground that the defence had not proved on the basis of expert evidence that he had suffered a total loss of self-control. Such evidence would be required, *inter alia*, to prove a causal link between the involuntary intoxication and the loss of control.

A similar case is that of *Ebsworth* v *HM Advocate*,[45] which again related to the availability of the plea of automatism to an intoxicated accused. The situation was slightly different to that in *Ross*, in that Ebsworth had voluntarily taken an excessive quantity of paracetamol and diamorphine. He had been prescribed both drugs in order to manage the pain from a fractured bone, but had taken an amount in excess of the prescribed dose without medical advice to that effect. As a result of his intoxicated state, he lost control and seriously assaulted his victim. He was convicted of assault to severe injury and permanent disfigurement and appealed on the ground that, because of his intoxication, he could not have formed the necessary *mens rea* for the offence. The sheriff had proceeded on the basis that, as stated in *Ross*, he should withdraw the defence from the jury if the accused had voluntarily and deliberately consumed the intoxicants. Since he felt this was clearly

---

[43] *Ross* at 566
[44] 1992 SLT 867.
[45] 1992 SLT 1161.

the case, he had withdrawn the defence. It was held on appeal that there would be circumstances where deliberate consumption of intoxicants would be justified, as there would be a legitimate medical purpose, and that, although deliberate, the intoxication would be viewed as if it had been involuntary. However, in this case, the court viewed that the fact that Ebsworth had taken an excessive quantity, well above that which had been prescribed, as sufficient to classify his conduct as reckless. He was bound to have foreseen the potential effects of taking such a quantity of the drugs without proper advice. It therefore amounted to self-induced intoxication which prevented him from raising the defence.

Necessity/coercion

The law in this area can prove confusing. The root of the problem lies in the reluctance of Scots law to recognise a defence of necessity. The essence of such a defence is that the accused acted in contravention of the criminal law in a situation where he had no other option, where his fortitude was overcome by threats he believed would be carried out.[46] The defence of coercion operates where the accused commits a criminal act (other than murder) because he has been threatened that he will be killed or very seriously injured if he does not comply. In *Cochrane* v *HM Advocate*,[47] the accused had lodged a special defence of coercion by his co-accused. Cochrane was 17 years old and in the bottom 4 per cent of the population in terms of intelligence. His co-accused had been the driving force behind the crime they committed, and had told Cochrane that he would blow up his house and physically assault him if he did not join in with the criminal activity. Cochrane believed the threats but was convicted. On appeal, it was argued that the sheriff should have instructed the jury to assess the effect of the threats on someone of Cochrane's level of intelligence and susceptibility to suggestion. It was held by the High Court that the proper test was objective and required the accused to have exercised reasonable firmness. It was further noted that the reason for insisting on objectivity was to prevent people, who should bear responsibility for their actions, escaping from liability because of a weakness in character which they should be able to overcome.

There is limited recognition by the Scottish courts of a defence of necessity. The major case in this area is *Moss* v *Howdle*.[48] It was felt that there was no reason why the accused should not benefit from a defence simply because the danger faced was one that arose from some cause other than the threat made by another party. Thus the court in *Moss* acknowledge the use of the defence if the accused had driven dangerously to avoid the imminent threat of death caused either by a heart attack or by a natural occurrence such as a flood, and also an immediate threat of death at the hands of a third party. The test specified for the defence of

---

[46] *Thomson* v *HM Advocate* 1983 JC 69.
[47] 2001 SCCR 655.
[48] 1997 SCCR 215.

necessity in that case was that the accused must have had no option but to do
what he did, and it will apply only in cases where he was faced with an immediate
threat of death or serious bodily harm to himself or others. The defence will not
apply if the crime committed is one committed against property in order to protect
that property. In *Moss*, the accused had been driving on the motorway when his
passenger shouted in pain. Assuming (incorrectly) that his passenger was seriously
ill, the accused drove to the nearest service station at over 100 miles per hour. He
was prosecuted for speeding, which is a crime of strict liability. There was no need
for the prosecutor to establish that the accused acted with *mens rea*, as the act of
speeding was sufficient to constitute the offence. The accused raised the defence of
necessity and this was rejected by the sheriff on the basis that, although it existed,
it did not apply to cases of medical emergency. On appeal, the court considered
first the issue of necessity and recognised that it had already been established as an
available defence in Scots law. It noted that the defence required that the accused
had been faced with immediate danger of death or serious bodily harm resulting
from threatened violence if he did not commit the crime in question. It concluded
that coercion and necessity were not distinguishable in any relevant sense and
that "necessity" was simply the Scottish term to be applied to situations where the
circumstances gave the accused no option but to contravene the criminal law. The
only difference between coercion and necessity lay in the source of the imminent
danger facing the accused. In cases of necessity, it could arise from illness or natural
disaster[49] and would apply where the accused committed a crime to escape from
that danger himself, or to allow another to escape.[50] However, in this case the court
concluded that the accused had been presented with a real choice (he could have
stopped on the hard shoulder). He had not therefore been forced to commit the
crime, and so the court upheld his conviction.[51]

Moss v *Howdle* has been applied in subsequent cases. In *Dawson* v *Dickson*[52] the
accused was charged with driving under the influence of alcohol. He was a fireman
who accompanied a colleague to the scene of an accident. He had been drinking
but drove one of the fire engines to the scene and also stepped in to move a fire
engine which was preventing an ambulance from leaving the scene, crashing into
a police car in the process. He asserted that it had never crossed his mind that
he might be unfit to drive. The defence of necessity was raised before the sheriff
but rejected on the ground that it was clear he would have driven whether or
not the patient's life had been in danger. It was held on appeal that the defence
of necessity was appropriate only where the accused had faced a real conscious
dilemma between contravening the criminal law and saving a life. The accused
had not consciously deliberated on this issue and had therefore not met the criteria
required for the defence.

---

[49] 1997 SCCR 215 at 222.
[50] *Idem*.
[51] *Ibid* at 224.
[52] 1999 SLT 1328.

Moss has also been applied in a factually more unusual case. In *Lord Advocate's Reference No 1 of 2000*,[53] the three accused had been charged with malicious damage to a ship which had a role in the Trident missile programme. Their argument rested on the alleged criminality of the Government's actions under customary international law regarding the deployment of nuclear missiles. They argued that their actions in causing damage to the ship were justified under the doctrine of necessity. The court reiterated that, for the defence to succeed, the danger which the accused faced must be immediate and there must have been no alternative course of action available to them. Moreover, they had to show that they had good reason to fear that death or serious injury would follow if they did not act, although it was not necessary to show that such consequences would be visited on those already known to the accused, or solely on persons in the vicinity of the *locus* of the crime. They would also need to show that they had reason to think that their acts would have some chance of avoiding the inherent danger, that their acts were roughly proportional to the risk involved, and that a sober, reasonable person would have acted similarly. In the light of this, the court concluded that the accused could not rely on the defence of necessity.

Error

The concept of error can be divided into two parts: errors of law and errors of fact. An error of law arises where the accused has made a mistake in his assessment of the relevant criminal law. Errors of law can be further subdivided into errors as to the general criminal law and errors as to civil (non-criminal) law. The latter may be relevant as a defence to a charge of dishonesty. However, errors as to the general criminal law are not relevant and the accused will be convicted regardless of his ignorance. This is based on the principle *ignorantia iuris neminem excusat*, or "ignorance of the law excuses no one". If the accused is somehow unaware that it is a criminal offence to bring illegal drugs through Customs, he will be convicted even though he was unaware that he was committing a crime.

Errors of fact are more frequently used to found a defence. However, not all such errors are relevant. An error relating to the object or victim of the crime is not relevant, unless an error is made as to the identity of the victim of the crime, and their identity is crucial to the definition of the offence. For example, if an assault is carried out on a policeman but the accused is not aware that his victim is a policeman, then such an error would operate as a defence to a charge of assaulting a police officer. If the accused intends to commit a crime by a particular method and instead accomplishes it by some other means, this is irrelevant. Beyond factual errors as to the object or method of the crime, other factual errors are relevant to the question of conviction. The stance taken is that the accused's guilt should be assessed on the basis of his subjective understanding of the facts. In other words,

---

[53] 2001 SLT 507.

the courts will take account of the facts as the accused believed them to exist. If he is labouring under an error of fact, then that mistaken assumption will be relevant to the case. However, the accused's error must be both genuine and reasonable in the circumstances.[54]

SUMMARY OF MAIN POINTS

Defences
- no liability

Mitigating pleas
- reduce the charge against the accused

Special defences
- notice requirement
- insanity, self-defence, incrimination, alibi (and coercion and automatism)

Insanity at the time of the offence
- acquittal, but leads to hospital order etc
- absolute alienation of reason
- result of mental defect

Insanity in bar of trial
- incapable of instructing solicitor
- disposal by way of hospital order etc

Self-defence
- commit offence in defence of self/another/property
- imminent danger to life/of rape
- danger inescapable, no means of retreat
- force used to defend self must be proportionate
- cannot defend self against lawful force
- self-defence not available if kill in defence of property

Incrimination
- allege crime committed by someone else

Alibi
- allege elsewhere at time offence committed

Other defences
- no notice requirement

---

[54] See the discussion on this in respect of self-defence cases.

Intoxication
- self-induced intoxication is no defence
- involuntary intoxication removes *mens rea*
- can be used to found a plea of automatism

Necessity/coercion
- commit crime in face of threat to life/serious bodily injury
- or where circumstances leave the accused with no other option

Error
- of law – irrelevant: *ignorantia iuris neminem excusat*
- of fact – if genuine and reasonable, relevant

INSANITY

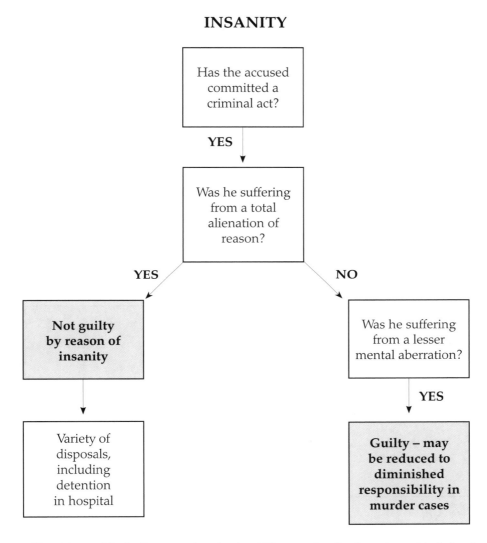

Note: Use of the word "guilty" is a convenient shorthand. There may be other issues to consider before the accused is convicted.

SELF-DEFENCE

Was there an imminent danger or reasonable belief of threat to life/of rape?

YES — Was the danger inescapable?

NO — **Guilty**

YES — Was the force used by accused excessive?

NO — **Guilty**

NO — Was the force used by victim lawful?

YES — **Guilty**

NO — **Justificatory defence – complete acquittal**

YES — **Guilty**

Note: Use of the word "guilty" is a convenient shorthand. There may be other issues to consider before the accused is convicted.

INTOXICATION

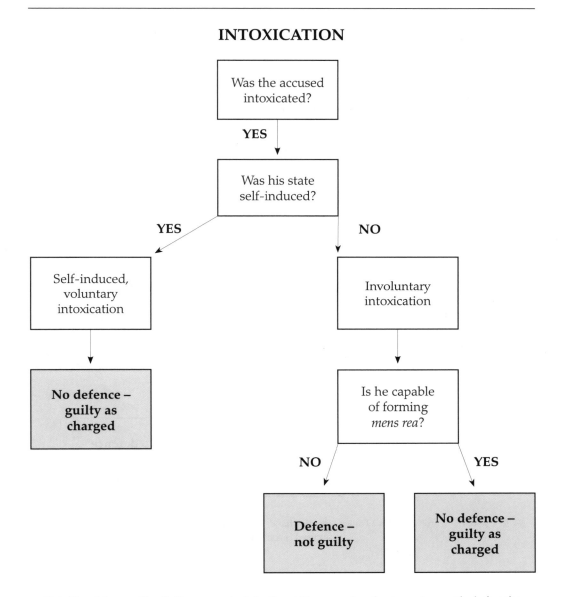

Note: Use of the word "guilty" is a convenient shorthand. There may be other issues to consider before the accused is convicted.

NECESSITY/COERCION

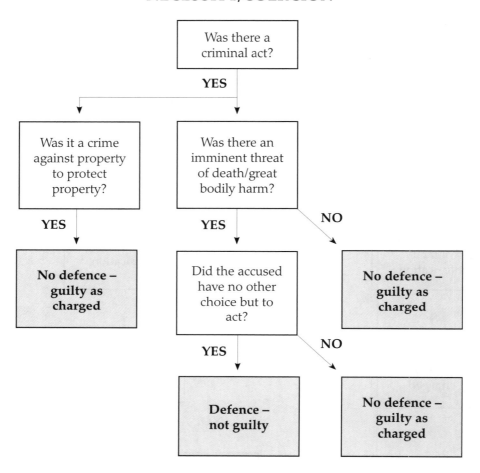

Note: Use of the word "guilty" is a convenient shorthand. There may be other issues to consider before the accused is convicted.

SELF-ASSESSMENT QUESTIONS (see Appendix for answers)

1   The accused has been charged with murder and wishes to plead self-defence. He had been drinking in a bar when a quarrel broke out between himself and the deceased. The deceased became violent, drew a knife and stated that he was going to kill the accused. There was an open door behind the accused, but he decided to defend himself against the deceased and, in doing so, struck him a fatal blow. Will his plea of self-defence succeed?

2   The accused has been prescribed strong pain-killers by his doctor. The advice on the label makes it very clear that the patient should under no circumstances take more than the prescribed dose. He takes double the prescribed dose in a desperate attempt to reduce the pain he is suffering, and becomes extremely violent. He attacks his wife and kills her, but maintains that he has no memory of the incident whatsoever. Can he raise a successful plea in response to the charge of murder?

3   Imagine that the Government has recently passed a statute making it illegal to transport sheep for more than 100 miles without stopping to ensure that they have adequate water supplies. The offence is punishable by a fine. A farmer who lives and works on a remote hillside farm with little contact with the outside world continues to transport his sheep 150 miles to market without any break at all. When charged, he argues that he was completely unaware of the new legislation. Is this a valid defence?

Further questions

1   What is the relationship between the defences of intoxication and automatism? Why did the court in *Ross* v *HM Advocate* feel it was necessary to change the existing law relating to criminal liability in cases of involuntary intoxication?

2   Why can the defence of insanity be described as a "double-edged sword"?

3   Can the instigator of a fight raise a plea of self-defence if he kills his assailant in the course of an attack which he started?

Further reading

Jones and Christie, *Criminal Law* (4th edn), pp 166–207.

McCall Smith and Sheldon, *Scots Criminal Law* (2nd edn), pp 117–153.

P Ferguson, *Crimes Against the Person*, pp 101–117 and 153–173.

C Connelly, "Insanity and Unfitness to Plead" 1996 JR 206.

M Christie, "The Mother of Invention? *Moss v. Howdle*" 1997 Edin LR 479.

P Ferguson, "Necessity and Coercion in Criminal Law" 1997 SLT (News) 127.

8 HOMICIDE

"Homicide" is the term used to describe the killing of a human being and, so far as the criminal law is concerned, it is restricted to situations where that killing is unlawful. Depending on the precise type of situation involved, the degree of criminality of the conduct and the range of sanctions available to the court will differ. "Homicide" is used as a blanket term which covers distinct and identifiable types of behaviour; murder and culpable homicide are respectively the most serious of the homicide crimes, followed by some aspects of suicide and abortion. However, "homicide" is also the term used to describe killings which are classified as non-criminal homicide, with which the law is not concerned.

MURDER

The traditional definition of murder covers any wilful act causing death which is done either with a wicked intent to kill (re-defined from the traditional requirement of an intention to kill[1]), or with such wicked recklessness that it can be inferred from what is done that the accused had no regard for whether his victim lived or died.[2] It requires that a self-existent human life has been brought to an end and thus the charge will apply only once a child has been born alive.[3] This is traditionally viewed as starting from the point where the child takes its first independent breath. If a child dies before birth and the mother miscarries as the result of her injuries, the death of her child cannot be classified as murder, as no self-existent human life has been destroyed. However, if the child is born alive and dies as a result of injuries inflicted before birth, the situation is more complex. If the law looks for evidence of independent existence and is satisfied by the child taking its first breath, then the accused should be liable for causing death by inflicting fatal injuries before birth, so long as causation can be established. In *McCluskey* v *HM Advocate*,[4] the accused was responsible for a car accident through his reckless driving. As a result, he caused injuries to a pregnant woman and also to her unborn and almost full-term child, causing it to be born prematurely. Although the child was born alive, it died as a result of

---

[1] See discussion of *mens rea* below.
[2] J Macdonald, *A Practical Treatise on the Criminal Law of Scotland* (1867; 5th edn, 1948), p 89.
[3] Hume, *Commentaries*, i, 186.
[4] 1989 SLT 175.

the injuries it had suffered before birth. The accused was charged with causing death by reckless driving under the applicable legislation at the time – the Road Traffic Act 1972, s 1, which simply required that the accused's reckless driving caused the death of another person. He argued at trial that the statute required him to have caused the death of another person who was alive at the time of the incident. The argument was rejected and he was convicted accordingly.[5] Similarly, it is no defence to show that, had the accused not intervened fatally, the victim would have died anyway. If, for example, the accused had poisoned the victim just before they boarded a plane which subsequently ditched into the sea, killing all the passengers, then the accused would still be liable for murder because his acts were still wickedly intentional acts aimed at bringing about the death of another person. If the victim had a terminal illness which would have killed him within the week, it would still be murder to deprive him of his life even for that short period.

Actus reus of murder – an act causing death

What is required is conduct capable of raising an inference that either variant of *mens rea* is present. It is clear that a vast array of types of conduct are covered by this, including assaulting either by punching or using a weapon, poisoning, shooting, drowning, suffocating and covering both acts leading to death and, in certain cases, failures to act, such as criminal neglect.[6]

Mens rea of murder – wicked intent or wicked recklessness

There are two alternative forms of *mens rea*, both of which can establish a charge of murder. The definition quoted above talks in terms of either a "wicked intent to kill" or "wicked recklessness",[7] but there is no requirement that the killing is premeditated. Intentional killing will arise where the accused has acted deliberately, intending to murder his victim, and has done so in a way which he knows or believes will bring about that result. The case of *Drury* v *HM Advocate*[8] is important in this area, although it deals primarily with the issue of provocation and, as such, is discussed later in this chapter. However, in *Drury*, the Lord Justice-General stated that the *mens rea* of murder required a wicked intent to kill, or wicked recklessness. His reason for modifying the traditional *mens rea*, which simply required an intent to kill, was that the accused may have intended to kill, and yet still not meet the standard required to convict them of murder, if provocation could be established. Under the traditional formulation (an intent to

---

[5] 1989 SLT 175 at 177.
[6] On liability for omissions, see Chapter 2.
[7] For general discussion of intention and recklessness, see Chapter 3.
[8] 2001 SLT 1013.

kill) the provoked accused would, in the heat of the moment, have been shown to have intended to kill (murder) but, because of the provocation, the charge would have been reduced to culpable homicide. It was held in *Drury* that, if the *mens rea* for murder instead specified *wicked* intent, it would remove the anomaly whereby the provoked accused technically met the requirements for murder but was convicted of culpable homicide. Following *Drury*, Lord Rodger's approach now requires the jury to treat provocation as an element to weigh in deciding whether the accused's intent was wicked (murder) or not (culpable homicide). Thus, an intent to kill driven by provocation fails to show the "wickedness" necessary for murder, and therefore cannot be prosecuted as such.[9]

If the accused does not show any intention to kill, he may still be guilty of murder under the alternative form of *mens rea*. Wicked recklessness requires that the accused has decided to commit an act which could lead to the death of the victim, and was wholly and callously unconcerned about the consequences of that act. He must act with a wicked disregard for the consequences of his actions. In other words, he must act in a way which could cause death, and show that he does not care whether his victim lives or dies. This is a more extreme form of recklessness than would usually be found as a form of *mens rea*, reflecting the greater degree of recklessness required before it can be the basis of a conviction and sentence for murder. Wicked recklessness will be inferred from the facts, and may be shown, for example, through the severity of the assault on the victim. It will be clear that the accused who carries out a savage assault did not care whether the victim survived, and this type of conduct is viewed as sufficiently reprehensible to warrant conviction for murder.

However, given the particular circumstances of the case, a much less serious assault may also justify the conclusion that the accused was wickedly reckless. For example, if the victim is disabled in some way, or clearly frail, then a relatively minor assault may be held sufficient to justify the conclusion that the accused did not care whether they lived or died as a result. It is also clear that the use of a weapon in an attack will at least point to the existence of wicked recklessness, given the increased likelihood that the victim will die in the course of this more serious assault, although this will not be conclusive. Thus, it is much more likely that an accused who set about his victim with a metal bar rather than his fists would be convicted of murder, even if he did not intend to kill. He would find it very difficult to argue that he was not being wickedly reckless as to whether the victim survived. Such recklessness is assessed objectively under Scots law, and so the question for the court is whether the reasonable person would have realised that such conduct could lead to the death of the victim. Whether or not the accused himself realised this is irrelevant.[10]

---

[9] On this, see Gordon, vol 2, pp 291–293.
[10] See Goff, "The mental element in the crime of murder" (1989) 104 LQR 30 at p 55.

One further point worth noting is that a killing which occurs during the course of a robbery amounts to murder even if there is no wicked intent to kill and no wicked recklessness. Robbery is classified as a crime of violence and, thus, if there is a fatal assault on the victim during the course of a robbery, it can result in a conviction for murder. So long as the accused has met the relevant criteria for a conviction for robbery, he will be liable for murder if a death results from his actions, even though he did not have the *mens rea* for murder. This will apply so long as some degree of force is used, and so long as the death is not the result of an accident. The modern authority for this is *Miller and Denovan*.[11] The accused had carried out a series of assaults and robberies, during which one of their victims was fatally injured. The jury was charged as follows: if the assault showed such wicked recklessness "as to imply a disposition depraved enough to be regardless of the consequences", the accused were guilty of murder.[12] The trial judge continued by stating that "[i]f in perpetrating this crime of robbery a person used serious and reckless violence which may cause death without considering what the result may be, he is guilty of murder if the violence results in death (even though) he had no intention to kill".[13] This direction was upheld on appeal.

Causation

There must be a causal link between the act or omission committed and the death that results. However, the causation requirement can equally be satisfied by a failure to act which results in a death. For example, the wilful neglect and failure to care for a dependent person such as a child or elderly relative will lead to a conviction for murder if that dependent person dies as a result of the failure to provide appropriate care. Thus, liability for murder is said to arise from either an act or an omission. For liability to attach to a failure to act, it must, however, be shown that the failure occurred against the background of a duty to act. Scots criminal law, unlike some other systems, will not impose a general duty to act but will instead restrict liability for omissions to cases where the accused was under a duty to act. Such cases are limited to instances where there is a close personal or contractual tie between the victim and the accused, to police officers who have a duty to prevent crime, and to situations where the accused's own previous behaviour has created a situation of danger which he then fails to avert. Thus, a parent who, with wicked intent, fails to provide adequate food for their child and watches that child starve to death would be liable for murder because they will have met the *actus reus*, *mens rea* and causation requirements of the offence. Similarly, someone who starts a fire in a building and leaves it

---

[11] Unreported, 1960, High Court on appeal: in Gordon, vol 2, pp 303–305.
[12] *Ibid* 304.
[13] Gordon, vol 2, pp 303–305.

to burn would be liable for any deaths which occurred as a result because his own prior dangerous actions (leaving the fire to burn out of control, rather than trying to put it out) created a dangerous situation which he then did nothing to avert. If anyone died in the fire, the accused would be liable for murder because he caused their deaths by his failure to avert the danger he had created. There is also no requirement that the victim die within a set period of time after the accused's act. However, the longer he survives, the more likely it is that there will be some other cause of his eventual death, thereby depriving the prosecution of proof of causation and, with it, the possibility of conviction. Once *actus reus* and *mens rea* have been proved, the accused can still escape liability for the death if he can show that the causal requirement has not been met. In order to achieve this, he must show that there was an independent and subsequent act which he did not cause and which resulted in the death. This subsequent, independent act is called the *novus actus interveniens*.[14]

However, the accused must show not only that there was a subsequent independent act which caused the death, but also that the subsequent act was a separate cause of the death. Thus, if the accused's attack on his victim leaves him in hospital on a life-support machine, the doctor's decision that continued life support was medically inappropriate and his subsequent act of switching off that support will not amount to a separate cause of death which breaks the chain of causation. Although it is an independent act of a third party which, in a very physical sense, causes death, that death is still a direct consequence of the attack and therefore liability remains with the accused.[15] A further point to note relates to inappropriate medical treatment which renders the patient's condition worse. This is known as malregimen. If a patient has suffered a wound which, in the normal course of events, would not be fatal, but is treated incompetently and dies, the wound is not viewed as the cause of the death. Instead, the medical treatment may be viewed as the legally significant cause of the death. However, if the wound is irretrievably fatal and the treatment received is sub-standard, that treatment will not be viewed as the cause of the death, as it would be clear that death would have resulted no matter whether the quality of treatment received was good, bad or indifferent.

CULPABLE HOMICIDE

A definition of culpable homicide is not easy to find, although, as a working definition, it would be fair to use the description given in *Drury* and define it as any unlawful killing in a situation which does not, in legal terms, amount to murder.[16] Problems have arisen in cases where the judge has instructed the

---

[14] On which, see Chapter 2.
[15] *Finlayson* v *HM Advocate* 1978 SLT (Notes) 60.
[16] *Drury* v *HM Advocate* 2001 SLT 1013 at 1017.

jury on the distinction between murder and culpable homicide. For example, in *Charles* v *HM Advocate*,[17] the jury was instructed to determine whether, during the assault, the accused had shown wicked recklessness (murder) or simply negligence (culpable homicide). It was argued that this amounted to a misdirection, as culpable homicide can never be established by straightforward negligence. Insofar as it can be established by negligence at all, it requires gross negligence. As a proposition, the above is correct, but the appeal failed because, when the disputed section of the direction was taken in context, the judge had properly directed the jury.

Actus reus of culpable homicide

The *actus reus* of culpable homicide is satisfied by any type of act which causes death. The reason for it not being treated as murder stems from the accused's lack of appropriate *mens rea* or the availability of a partial defence. An example of the breadth of conduct which will satisfy this requirement is provided by *Lourie* v *HM Advocate*,[18] where the accused had entered an elderly woman's house and stolen her handbag. It was alleged that the victim had watched from another room where she was hiding while the theft took place and was put in a state of fear as a result. She had heart disease and, as a result of the shock, suffered a heart attack and died. At trial, the judge told the members of the jury that, if they found that the accused had unlawfully stolen the bag, put the victim in a state of alarm and that she had died as a result, they were entitled to convict of culpable homicide. The accused argued that what was required for the *actus reus* of culpable homicide was a physical act against the victim, whereas they had neither been violent towards her nor threatened her in any way. While it is clear that any unlawful act will satisfy the *actus reus* requirement, the appeal court also upheld the trial judge's comments that if the result of them putting her in a state of fear was her death, then they were liable for culpable homicide. What was necessary was an illegal act which was likely to, and did, result in some physical harm to the deceased, and this was clearly present. However, the appeals were allowed and the convictions quashed on the basis that there was not enough evidence to show that the victim had watched them commit the crime and therefore that it was not possible to say that she had been placed in a situation of alarm *as a consequence* of witnessing their unlawful acts. Likewise, in *Bird* v *HM Advocate*[19] it was held that physical injuries are not necessarily required and if the victim can be proved to have died of shock, this will be sufficient for conviction. In this particular case, the accused followed the deceased, believing, incorrectly, that she had stolen money from him. This put her in such a state of alarm that she collapsed and died, and as a result the accused was convicted. It was held

---

[17] Available at http:/www.scotcourts.gov.uk/opinions/c90_01.html
[18] 1988 SCCR 634.
[19] 1952 JC 23.

that it was perfectly competent to view the cause of her death as the level of fear to which she had been subjected, and that the fact that she also suffered from a weak heart was irrelevant.

The "thin skull" rule applies to cases of culpable homicide. Thus if, viewed on the basis of external facts alone, the assault should not have caused the death, a particular peculiarity of the victim which makes him more vulnerable than one might expect or foresee, and which therefore leads to an unexpected death, is irrelevant. Thus, for example, a heart condition unknown to the accused would not relieve him of liability for culpable homicide if the victim died from a relatively minor assault. However, the unforeseeable nature of the death would probably be reflected in the sentence imposed.

Mens rea of culpable homicide

Although the *actus reus* for culpable homicide is substantially the same as for murder, the *mens rea* differs in that it varies depending on the type of crime involved. Traditionally, four separate categories of culpable homicide are identified, of which the first three are classified as involuntary culpable homicide, while the final category is classed as voluntary culpable homicide.

The first is an assault which leads to an unintended death, hence lacking the necessary *mens rea* to be classified as murder (wicked intent or wicked recklessness). However, if the assault is a very serious one, it may be possible for the court to infer the necessary *mens rea* to convict of murder on the basis of wicked recklessness, rather than culpable homicide. All that is required here is that the accused assaulted the victim in a way which conforms to the general definition of assault,[20] and thus the range of conduct covered is extremely wide. In *Mowles v HM Advocate*,[21] a firearm was pointed at the victim. It was defective and could not be fired in the normal way, but could fire if it was knocked. Pointing a weapon at someone is an action amounting to threatening conduct that would lead the victim to fear for his life, and so amounts to an assault. In this case, in the course of a struggle, the firearm was knocked, causing it to fire and resulting in the unintended death of the victim. The accused was convicted of culpable homicide. Even a simple push which causes the victim to stumble, fall over and hit his head would suffice if death resulted. Any individual peculiarities of the victim are viewed as irrelevant through the application of the "thin skull" rule, and thus the fact that the victim has an unusual physical characteristic will not relieve the accused of liability for involuntary culpable homicide. This is described as "taking one's victim as one finds him": in other words, it provides that any unusual weakness from which the victim suffers, but which is not common to everyone else, is not taken into account. Thus, if the victim has an

---

[20] On this, see Chapter 9.
[21] 1986 SCCR 117.

unusually weak heart such that a relatively minor assault would produce a fatal result, then the accused will be liable for involuntary culpable homicide because his assault has caused an unintended death, albeit unexpectedly. The unusual and invisible weakness of his victim will not provide a defence. An example of this is provided by *HM Advocate* v *Robertson and Donoghue*,[22] where the accused were charged with assault, robbery and murder. They had assaulted an elderly man, causing him minor injuries. He subsequently died of a heart attack and was found to have had a very weak heart. It was held that culpable homicide required that the death had been caused by the accused and it did not matter whether that accused knew of the particular condition of his victim. He took his victim as he found him. Thus the convictions were upheld.

The second category encompasses an unlawful act (other than assault) which leads to injury and was carried out recklessly, but which was not intended to cause harm. An illustration of such a situation is provided by *Sutherland* v *HM Advocate*,[23] where the accused had set fire to his property in order to claim the insurance money. It was held that this amounted to an unlawful act carried out in a reckless manner and that therefore the deaths which resulted from his conduct were properly instances of culpable homicide. This case is particularly interesting in that the deceased was also involved in the fire-raising but his willing participation in the criminal activity which killed him did not provide the accused with a defence.

Thirdly, a lawful act carried out recklessly may lead to conviction for culpable homicide, the classic example here being cases where death arises from reckless driving, since driving itself is not a crime.[24]

Finally, those situations which would lead to a conviction for murder but which are subject to a mitigating plea are also classified as instances of voluntary culpable homicide and are discussed below as partial defences.

Relevance of surrounding conduct

In some areas, a charge of culpable homicide can also require examination of the accused's conduct both before and after the time of the offence. In *McDowell* v *HM Advocate*,[25] the accused had been charged with culpable homicide by reckless driving. He had tried to overtake a car but had to pull back into his lane because of oncoming traffic. There was insufficient room to allow for his manoeuvre and he collided with the car he was overtaking, causing it to crash into the oncoming traffic and killing some of the passengers. Surrounding evidence showed that

---

[22] Unreported, Gane and Stoddart, *A Casebook on Scottish Criminal Law* (3rd edn, W Green, Edinburgh, 2001), pp 114–115.

[23] 1994 SLT 634.

[24] See *McDowell* v *HM Advocate* 1999 SLT 243.

[25] *Idem.*

he had been driving in a reckless manner before the accident, including driving at speed on the wrong side of the road, and that immediately afterwards he had fled the scene. The judge directed the jury that they could take into account the evidence of his conduct prior to and after the accident in deciding whether he was guilty of culpable homicide. The issue of causation was not disputed, it being clear that McDowell's accident had caused the deaths, and he was convicted. He appealed on the basis that his conduct before and after the event were not relevant issues to put to the jury. Refusing his appeal, it was held that his conduct was relevant to determining whether he was acting with utter disregard for his victims' safety and that it helped to show his state of mind at the time of the accident.

Causation

One of the areas where a charge of culpable homicide can arise is in the unlawful and reckless act of supplying dangerous drugs to another who dies as a result. Clearly, this raises questions relating to the causation requirement and whether the death can be attributed to the ingestion of the drugs. Scots law took a particularly robust stance in such cases, until recent developments gave rise to a change in direction. The earlier position is exemplified by *Lord Advocate's Reference (No 1 of 1994)*,[26] where the accused had supplied potentially lethal amounts of amphetamines to several people, one of whom subsequently died. As a result, he was charged with, among other offences, culpable homicide. He argued that, although he was clearly guilty of supplying an illegal narcotic, he was not guilty of culpable homicide because he had not caused the death. The deceased had voluntarily asked for the drug, selected her own dose, ingested it, and had not been encouraged in the slightest by the accused. At trial, the judge concluded that this was sufficient to break the chain of causation and remove liability for her death from the accused. The case was referred to the appeal court on the ground that this was an incorrect decision, following the authority of *Khaliq v HM Advocate*[27] and *HM Advocate v Ulhaq*.[28] Both these cases involve convictions for culpably, wilfully and recklessly supplying solvents. In both cases, the accused had supplied glue-sniffing kits, knowing that the buyers would abuse that substance, but had not actively encouraged the abuse. The victims had voluntarily used the glue but that voluntary action was not sufficient to break the chain of causation. Likewise, on appeal in *Lord Advocate's Reference (No 1 of 1994)*, the voluntary act of the accused was not found to be sufficient to break the chain of causation leading from the accused's criminal act of supplying the drugs to the death of the victim. Since the accused had supplied the drugs, knowing the use to which they would be put, he had caused the death. However, it is now

---

[26] 1995 SLT 248.
[27] 1984 SLT 137.
[28] 1991 SLT 614.

necessary to revise this view, given the opinions delivered in *MacAngus* v *HM Advocate*,[29] following the English lead in *R* v *Kennedy (No 2)*[30] and stating that an adult's voluntary decision to take drugs offered to them may break the chain of causation and frustrate any prosecution.[31]

The issue of causation in cases of culpable homicide has arisen in other areas beyond the supply of drugs. In *Hendry* v *HM Advocate*,[32] the accused had punched and kicked an elderly man, causing relatively minor injuries. However, after climbing the stairs back up to his flat, the victim had collapsed and suffered a fatal heart attack. The post mortem revealed that he had been suffering from heart disease, and angina and had alcohol in his bloodstream at the time of death. Following conviction, the accused appealed on the basis that there was not enough evidence to show a causal link between his assault and the victim's death because of the number of other contributory causes. Three medical experts were called, all of whom gave evidence to the effect that a stressful situation would have caused the death and that, although the assault was clearly an extremely stressful event, so too were climbing stairs and drinking alcohol in the victim's condition. The judges referred to an earlier case, *HM Advocate* v *McGinlay*,[33] where the expert witnesses would only go so far as to say that there was a possible or, on balance, probable causal link between the assault and the heart attack. However, the court was not satisfied that *McGinlay* had been decided correctly. In *Hendry* the court held that it was for the jury, not the expert witness, to decide whether the death had, beyond reasonable doubt, been caused by the assault. It was held further that there was sufficient evidence to allow the jury to ignore the other possible causes of the heart attack and convict on the basis that the assault was the factor which caused the death.[34]

PARTIAL DEFENCES

If the accused is found to have both the *actus reus* and *mens rea* for murder, he will be guilty as charged and subject to an appropriate sentence. However, there are two specific concepts which require further consideration. Whether or not there are any general defences available to the accused, there may be scope for him to raise a plea of either diminished responsibility or provocation. The effect of diminished responsibility is not to acquit the accused, but rather to mitigate the severity of the sanction imposed on him by reducing the charge from murder to the lesser crime of culpable homicide. If provocation is proved, the accused will

---

[29] [2009] GWD 4–61.
[30] [2008] 1 AC 269.
[31] On both of these cases, see discussion in Chapter 2 on causation.
[32] 1987 JC 63.
[33] 1983 SLT 562.
[34] For criticism of this, see "Causation and expert evidence" 1987 JLSS 468.

have failed to meet the definition of murder (*wicked* intent) and will therefore be charged with culpable homicide.

Voluntary culpable homicide – diminished responsibility

Diminished responsibility operates as a mitigating plea to reduce a charge of murder to culpable homicide. The basic requirement for a successful plea of diminished responsibility is that the accused suffers some form of mental weakness. This covers a variety of situations but is used within fairly stringent parameters, such that, for example, mental "states" such as insanity or voluntary intoxication are not sufficient. The definition of what amounts to diminished responsibility for Scots law was set out originally in *HM Advocate v Savage*.[35] The accused had been convicted of murdering the deceased by slitting her throat. At trial he pleaded not guilty by reason of insanity and evidence was led to show that he had in the past suffered a head injury which had left him prone to erratic behaviour. He was also a chronic alcoholic who often became violent when under the influence and was shown to have been drunk on the night in question. The prosecution argued that he was otherwise sane, but prone to the type of behaviour commonly exhibited by someone who was an alcoholic. In his direction, the trial judge told the jury that, as well as considering whether Savage was insane, they also had to consider whether, if he failed to satisfy the criteria for insanity, his situation was of such a type as to reduce the charge against him from murder to culpable homicide on the ground of diminished responsibility. He instructed them that, to do so, they must find Savage's state of mind to have been something short of insanity. The accused must fit into a class of people who, while not responsible for their actions, were also not wholly irresponsible.[36] The judge was at pains to state that mere drunkenness was not sufficient to excuse the accused, as he would still be responsible for his condition. He went on to list four descriptions of the type of mental state that would reduce something normally classed as murder to culpable homicide. These have been referred to subsequently as the "*Savage* criteria". The accused was required to show an unsound mind; a state of mind bordering on (although not amounting to) insanity; an aberration or weakness of mind; or a state of mind so affected that responsibility is diminished from full to partial responsibility. As a result of his partial responsibility, he would benefit from a partial defence. However, the jury was not satisfied that Savage was insane or even that he was only partially responsible, and so convicted him of murder.

There are a number of more modern cases that illustrate the types of situation in which diminished responsibility will be accepted. In *LT v HM Advocate*,[37] the accused had been convicted of culpable homicide on the

---

[35] 1923 JC 49 at 51.
[36] *Ibid* at 50.
[37] 1990 SCCR 540.

ground of diminished responsibility and sentenced to 10 years' imprisonment. She had murdered her sons by setting fire to the house while they were inside but had the charge against her reduced on the grounds that she was suffering from pre-menstrual tension and had been intoxicated at the time, and that she had previously been sufficiently depressed to take an overdose. The trial judge noted that, although he was not convinced that pre-menstrual tension amounted to a mental disease as required by *Savage*, he had felt that there was some evidence of diminished responsibility which justified the issue being put to the jury. The High Court admitted surprise that the trial judge had allowed the issue of diminished responsibility to proceed but decided that it had to accept the jury's decision. In *Strathern* v *HM Advocate*,[38] the accused had been suffering from post-traumatic stress disorder following an incident where his son was sexually assaulted by the deceased. The jury accepted this as sufficient to amount to diminished responsibility. In *Lindsay* v *HM Advocate*,[39] the accused had strangled a young girl to death with a metal dog leash. He was convicted of murder, sentenced to 15 years' imprisonment, and appealed against conviction on the basis that he should have been found guilty of culpable homicide, rather than murder, on the ground of diminished responsibility. At trial it had been argued that it was for the accused to prove the necessary elements for the mitigating plea on the balance of probabilities. The accused appealed on the ground that the law in this area was unfair and a larger court should consider whether or not it should be changed. On appeal, the court upheld the conviction on the basis that the trial judge had instructed the jury in accordance with the current law and any reform of that position was properly the province of Parliament. The court also stated that it is wrong to describe diminished responsibility as a defence to a charge of murder, since it is properly a mitigating factor rather than a full defence.

The law on diminished responsibility must now be read in the light of the High Court of Justiciary's opinion in *Galbraith* v *HM Advocate (No 2)*.[40] The case concerned long-term domestic violence, as a result of which the accused had been charged with murdering her abusive husband. It was argued in her defence that she had been suffering from a form of post-traumatic stress disorder. At trial, the jury was instructed to consider whether the four elements from *Savage* had been met and, further, whether the accused was suffering from some form of mental disorder. The accused appealed on the ground that the directions given were based on a flawed interpretation of *Savage* which came from *Connelly* v *HM Advocate*.[41] The alleged flaw is found in the interpretation of the four criteria. In *Savage* itself, the criteria are given in the alternative, clearly intended as examples of the type of state of mind required for diminished responsibility to apply. However, in *Connelly*,

---

[38] 1996 SLT 1171.
[39] 1997 JC 19.
[40] 2001 SLT 953.
[41] 1991 SLT 397.

they were interpreted as joint pre-requisites, such that, to succeed, the accused must show that he exhibited a state of mind which covered all four of the criteria. This interpretation makes the *Savage* definition of diminished responsibility much harder to satisfy. In *Galbraith*, the accused's appeal rested on two main points: the contention that *Connelly* was wrongly decided and that this misinterpretation had restricted the application of the defence to her detriment; and the contention that *Savage* was wrong to require evidence of mental disorder, it being sufficient to show evidence of abuse and psychological expert evidence as to its effect. The High Court held that *Connelly* had misinterpreted *Savage* and that the former case should be overruled. The trial judge's direction in *Galbraith* was therefore unsound, as the law had been interpreted too restrictively in the intervening years. It was held further that it was not necessary to establish that the accused's state of mind bordered on insanity, unless the real issue was whether the accused was sane at the time. All that was required for diminished responsibility was an abnormality of mind which had a substantial effect on the accused's actions. This abnormality could be found in a number of different forms, whether congenital, organic or psychological. Specifically, it could encompass severe psychological trauma induced by abuse. Galbraith's appeal was thus allowed, although the Crown was given leave to bring a fresh prosecution against her.

Voluntary culpable homicide – provocation

Requirements of the doctrine

The doctrine of provocation applies to cases of assault, but is of more practical importance in cases where the accused has killed without manifesting the wicked intent necessary for murder. It will apply in cases where the accused has lost his self-control and killed the deceased in the heat of the moment in circumstances which would likewise have caused the ordinary person to lose control. The classic definition comes from Macdonald:

> "Being agitated and excited, and alarmed by violence, I lost control over myself and took a life, when my presence of mind had left me, and without thought of what I was doing."[42]

However, this definition dates from the 19th century and is no longer as comprehensive as once it was. Provocation is traditionally viewed as a concession to human frailty, so long as the circumstances are such that the ordinary man would also be unable to withstand them.[43] As traditionally defined, it used to reduce the charge to culpable homicide and recognised that the accused was not as guilty as someone who had killed in cold blood. Following *Drury*,[44]

---

[42] Macdonald, p 94.
[43] Hume, i, 249.
[44] 2001 SLT 1013.

however, if the criteria which follow are met, the accused will be charged with culpable homicide in its own right, rather than as a reduction from a charge of murder, because establishing the criteria for provocation will show that the accused has not acted with the wicked intent needed for murder. The courts will not allow the plea where the accused has responded in a state of anger or bad temper, since what is required is the level of uncontrollable rage that deprives the ordinary man or woman of their self-control and reason.[45] The difficult question in this area is how to determine the standard of conduct required. The Scottish courts have not provided any real guidance on this issue but it is clear that, while Scotland has maintained a very objective approach to such issues, other jurisdictions have moved away from this stance. Previously, the standard used in most jurisdictions was highly objective. The test used was that of the "reasonable man" and he was assumed to be free of the vast majority of human characteristics and weaknesses. However, the more recent trend in other jurisdictions has been to move to a subjective assessment whereby the court examines whether the reasonable man endowed with some of the characteristics of the accused would have reacted as the accused did. This then begs the question of which characteristics should be taken into account and raises complex issues as to whether those characteristics should be widened, thus making the test even more subjective. While, for example, English law has taken this route, it seems clear from *Gillon* v *HM Advocate*[46] that Scots law steers clear of imputing any specific characteristics of the accused to the concept of the ordinary man or woman.

Recognised types of provocation

Certain types of conduct are recognised as capable of being provocative. Generally speaking, provocation requires an assault. Words, no matter how abusive or taunting, will not be sufficient under Scots law. The most obvious and traditional example of provocation is violent conduct in the form of a serious provocative assault, such that the accused loses control in the face of the violent attack and inflicts fatal injuries on his attacker in response. However, as an exception to this general rule, it has long been established that if a husband finds his wife (or vice versa) in the act of committing adultery, that will amount to sufficient provocation if he kills either or both of them, providing that the situation is such that the adultery would cause the ordinary person to lose control.[47] This concept was then extended to cover cases where, although the husband never witnessed the adultery, he heard his wife confess to it, since this is viewed as tantamount to finding her in the act.[48] It is worth noting that the courts refuse to draw the

---

[45] 2001 SLT 1013.
[46] 2006 SLT 799.
[47] *HM Advocate* v *Gillon* 1938 JC 1.
[48] *HM Advocate* v *Hill* 1941 JC 59.

definition of provocation too restrictively. In *Thomson* v *HM Advocate*,[49] it was held that it would not be useful or necessary to define precisely what would amount to provocative conduct. Confessions of infidelity operate as an exception to the rule that words are insufficient provocation but, in more modern times, this exception has been extended further to reflect modern relationships. In *HM Advocate* v *Callander*,[50] it was applied in a case of assault arising from a wife's infidelity with her lesbian lover and, in *HM Advocate* v *McKean*,[51] provocation was allowed in a case where a woman heard a man confess to his infidelity with her lesbian lover. A case which brings out several of these modern extensions to the doctrine of provocation is *Rutherford* v *HM Advocate*.[52] The accused was charged with murdering a woman with whom he had lived for some time but from whom had separated shortly before her death. Two days prior to her murder, she had told him that she had been unfaithful to him twice. On the day in question, they met again and she repeated her confession of unfaithfulness to him, but in somewhat different terms. She stated that, instead of having been unfaithful twice, she had been having an affair for months and told the accused that he was "spineless" and a "waste of space". In response, he stabbed her to death and threw her body off a bridge. At trial, the issue of provocation was withheld from the jury because the accused already knew that the victim had been unfaithful before the day of the incident. There was therefore no new confession which could cause him to lose control and respond violently. On appeal, it was held that the trial judge had been wrong to deal with the case as he did. Given the substantively different account the victim had presented to the accused at their second meeting, the fact that she had been consistently unfaithful over a period of time was sufficient to amount to a fresh confession which had caused him to lose control and kill her. The appeal court also held that, although the couple were not married and had not been living together immediately prior to her death, their relationship had been the equivalent of marriage and that therefore this aspect of the doctrine of provocation could properly be applied. It also held that, had the victim simply repeated exactly what she had confessed to the accused previously, he would not have been able to plead provocation because there would have been no new and provocative revelation on which to base the plea.

Proportionality

A further requirement for provocation is that the accused's response is proportionate to the provocative conduct. If the accused has attacked and killed the person who provoked him, it would require a great deal of provocation from the deceased to justify a fatal attack in response. This can cause problems

---

[49] 1985 SCCR 448.
[50] 1958 SLT 24.
[51] 1996 SCCR 402.
[52] 1998 SLT 740.

in situations where people react in a particularly violent way to a non-violent approach from the deceased. In *Robertson* v *HM Advocate*,[53] the deceased was a homosexual who had approached the accused, placed his hand on his thigh, asked for a kiss and then produced a knife, striking the accused. Robertson had responded by killing him and was convicted of murder on the basis that there was no proportionate relationship between the provocation and his response. He appealed, arguing that provocation should be rejected only in circumstances where the response of the accused was *grossly* disproportionate. He argued that his response was not so extreme. On appeal, the High Court maintained that there must be reasonable proportion between the deceased's provocative act and the accused's response. Since there was no proportion in this case, the accused's plea of provocation was not accepted.

The High Court has recently given lengthy consideration to the issue of proportionality, and the whole doctrine of provocation, in *Drury* v *HM Advocate*.[54] Drury had murdered his ex-lover after discovering that she had begun a relationship with another man. He had confronted her, repeatedly assaulted her and hit her over the head with a hammer, causing such extensive and serious injuries that she died the next day. He was unanimously convicted of her murder, but appealed on the basis that the jury had been misdirected on the applicability of provocation. The appellant contended that he had seen another man leaving the deceased's house and, when he had questioned her, she had replied in terms which led him to believe that she had been unfaithful to him. In response, he lost control and remembered nothing else until he saw her lying on the ground, covered in blood. He had then left the scene. There was some uncertainty as to the nature and extent of any continuing relationship between the appellant and the deceased at the time of her death. It appeared that their relationship had ceased at least for a time, but it was possible to construe the evidence in a way which was consistent with a continuing relationship of some sort. The trial judge left the issue of provocation to the jury since there was some evidence, if the jury accepted it, to suggest that Drury could expect fidelity from the deceased. He directed the jury that, for provocation to succeed, it was necessary that the accused's actions were not grossly disproportionate to the provocative conduct of the deceased. Counsel for the appellant criticised these directions and invited the court to substitute a verdict of culpable homicide, or allow the Crown to bring a fresh prosecution.

After some consideration of general issues relating to murder, culpable homicide and provocation, the Lord Justice-General returned to the case in hand. He noted that the jury had been left to determine the state of mind of the appellant at the time of the homicide, particularly whether he had acted with wicked intent or wicked recklessness, or whether conviction for culpable homicide was more

---

[53] 1994 JC 245.
[54] 2001 SLT 1013.

appropriate. Counsel for the appellant argued that, if his client had been subjected to provocation, then he had lost control. If the appellant had indeed lost control, there was little point in looking into his state of mind or determining whether he had acted proportionately, since someone who has lost control cannot exercise any restraint, let alone enough restraint to keep his response proportionate. Thus, the trial judge's direction requiring the jury to consider whether his conduct was disproportionate in the circumstances was a misdirection.[55] This novel argument was rejected by the court as being inconsistent with established notions of provocation. The Lord Justice-General noted that counsel's argument effectively branded someone responding to provocation as having so little control as to be suffering from a form of temporary insanity. He stated that, were this true, the law would respond appropriately by acquitting on such grounds. But this has never been the approach of the Scottish courts. Under Scots law, provocation is relevant in only limited circumstances, where the accused has himself been assaulted[56] and subjected to substantial provocation. There is an assumption that the accused will exercise restraint and therefore the plea is not open in cases of verbal or other insults. The only exception to this limiting approach is in the context of discoveries of infidelity where fidelity might reasonably be expected.[57] However, the precise question to be determined in *Drury* was whether the trial judge was wrong to direct the jury to consider whether the accused's violence was grossly disproportionate. The court concluded that the judge was indeed wrong to give such a direction. The difficulty arises because the direction as given required the jury to measure the accused's conduct against the provocative nature of the deceased's supposed infidelity. These two issues are not commensurable, and previous cases on sexual infidelity had not established that such measuring was necessary. Thus, the Crown's argument, based on the correctness of the trial judge's direction, was rejected. The court was prepared to accept the approach outlined by counsel for the appellant, under which, instead of insisting on the concept of proportionality, the court looked at whether the ordinary person in the same situation would have behaved in the same way.[58] Lord Rodger describes this as "workable (and) ... consistent with our law as a whole".[59] He concluded that, if the situation was one where fidelity might be expected, the jury should be instructed to consider whether the accused had lost self-control at the time of the killing as a result of provocation, and then whether the ordinary man would have reacted this way in the same situation. In determining these issues, the nature and degree of violence used by the accused will be relevant. However, in giving his direction to the jury, the trial judge was wrong to use the "proportionality" test which would have been required had the provocation

---

[55] 2001 SLT 1013 at 1020.
[56] This is more restrictive than in England.
[57] *Drury* at 1020–1021.
[58] *Ibid* at 1022.
[59] *Idem.*

taken the form of an assault. This misdirection had resulted in a miscarriage of justice and the conviction was quashed unanimously.

Cumulative provocation and domestic violence

One of the more intractable problems in this area is the requirement that the accused respond instantly to the provocation in the heat of the moment. Cumulative provocation refers instead to situations where the provocative conduct has occurred over a period of time and the overall effect is to cause the accused to lose control, rather than the specific instance in question. One of the more prevalent areas where pleas of provocation are raised is in cases of domestic violence. The approach taken by the courts in some jurisdictions has become markedly more lenient over recent years. The traditional requirement for provocation is that the accused snaps in the heat of the moment when faced with sufficient provocation, and kills the deceased. However, it is well documented that women who suffer domestic abuse tend not to respond in this fashion. They are much more likely to endure suffering in silence for considerable periods of time, and eventually react violently to the overall situation, rather than reacting immediately in response to one particular instance of violence from the accused. The Scottish courts have a long history of rejecting the relevance of cumulative provocation, and convicting in those cases where the provoking incident occurred prior to the fatal attack. However, in cases such as *Walker* v *HM Advocate*,[60] there is a clear indication that, in practice, prosecutors can adopt a more lenient attitude. In *Walker*, the accused had suffered 2½ years of verbal and physical abuse from her cohabitee. The prosecution accepted a plea of culpable homicide, on the ground that the previous history of violence had caused the accused to lose her self-control as a result of cumulative provocation, and the accused was sentenced to 6 years' imprisonment.

However, not all such cases are successful, often because it is clear that the accused has had time to plot revenge, and the final incident of provocation is not a flashpoint, but rather a convenient instance which the accused can use to exact that revenge. In *Parr* v *HM Advocate*,[61] constant nagging over a long period of time and a history of being physically assaulted were not sufficient to allow the plea of provocation. In the face of her prolonged nagging, the accused had argued with his mother, lost his temper when she threw an object at him, and had struck her violently and repeatedly over the head with a hammer. Both parties were alcoholics and had a poor relationship at the time of the incident, which was characterised by the court as a tendency to mutual criticism. At trial, the judge refused to allow the jury to consider provocation and thus it found the accused guilty of murder. He appealed on the basis that this had been a misdirection and that the cumulative nature of the arguments between the

---

[60] 1996 SCCR 818.
[61] 1991 SCCR 180.

parties in the past was such as should have reduced the charge against him. It was held that the provocation must lead immediately to the fatal assault and since it was clear that there was an interval between the two, the conviction for murder was upheld. Although this presents a gloomy picture for battered women who kill their abusers, it is of course possible to plead diminished responsibility, following *Galbraith*.

OTHER HOMICIDE CRIMES

Suicide

Since suicide is not a crime under Scots law, it follows that the person who attempts suicide and survives also does not commit an offence, although it is possible that, if the attempt is carried out in a way which would cause alarm to the public, it could be prosecuted as a breach of the peace. However, several other issues related to suicide merit some discussion. These relate to questions of euthanasia and assisted suicide. "Euthanasia" is defined as the intentional, premature termination of life by a doctor in situations where the individual is suffering incurable pain, but the fact remains that the individual has been killed. The question is whether this killing can be justified. A distinction must be drawn here between voluntary euthanasia (where a patient in acute pain or suffering from a recognised terminal illness has requested that their life should come to an end); non-voluntary euthanasia (where the patient cannot express their desires and the request is made by a relative or an attendant instead); and involuntary euthanasia (where their life is terminated in their best interests without them or their family requesting such action). A further distinction to be drawn here is in the manner in which euthanasia of whichever sort is carried out. This can be by active or passive means: either the doctor can actively take some step which terminates the patient's life or, less controversially, he can withdraw or withhold certain types of treatment or fail to take invasive or heroic measures to maintain the patient's life. As regards active euthanasia, it is clear that the doctor intends to kill and carries out an act to achieve that end. As a result, he is liable for murder and, in the absence of any provision relating to mercy killings, he has no defence. As was stated in *Airedale NHS Trust* v *Bland*,[62] mercy killings, no matter how laudable the doctor's intentions, amount to murder. The doctor's motive is irrelevant; he has committed the relevant act and had an intention to kill, thereby establishing the criteria for the offence of murder, and his reasons for taking that course of action do not give him any legal defence, although they may affect the moral response to his act. The issue of passive euthanasia involves a failure to act on the part of

---

[62] [1993] 1 All ER 821 at 890. However, this issue must be considered in the light of the changes made to the definition of murder in *Drury*. To be liable for murder, the doctor would have had to act with *wicked* intent or wicked recklessness.

the doctor. He will either withdraw treatment, such as life support, or fail to treat a condition. The withdrawal of treatment will be of particular relevance in cases concerning patients in a persistent vegetative state, where such extensive brain damage has occurred that they are incapable of supporting life themselves and are kept alive purely by artificial means and are wholly dependent on nursing care. Following *Bland*, a recent Scottish case, *Law Hospital NHS Trust* v *Lord Advocate*,[63] held that, if it was no longer in the patient's best interests to be kept alive in this way, it would be competent to withdraw life support.

However, there is a clear intuitive difference between a doctor who actively causes the death of his patient and one who helps in some less active way. An example of this is provided by the doctor who leaves tablets within reach of the patient, but does not actually administer them. This is often referred to as "physician-assisted suicide" and, although it is the subject of legislation abroad, has yet to receive much attention in the UK.[64] The recent and high-profile case brought by Diane Pretty raised the issue of the right to assistance in committing suicide. Although her case was heard through the English courts, the final hearing came before the European Court of Human Rights and dealt with the interpretation of various rights under the European Convention on Human Rights.[65] Thus, the decision at this final stage will be relevant to a Scottish court in the future. Mrs Pretty had contended throughout that, since she was incapable through illness of taking her own life, her husband should be allowed to help her to commit suicide when her condition[66] became intolerable. She had consistently failed before the English courts because the Suicide Act 1961, s 2(1), criminalises anyone who provides assistance to another in committing suicide. She had failed to secure any assurance from the Director of Public Prosecutions that her husband would not be prosecuted under this statute. The applicant had raised a number of human rights arguments before the European Court of Human Rights, but all were rejected. Among the provisions raised by the applicant, Art 2 enshrines a right to life, but the court refused to interpret this to accommodate a right to die at a time and in a manner of one's own choosing. So far as Art 3 was concerned, the prohibition on cruel and inhumane treatment was interpreted so as to grant individuals such protection until the natural end of their lives, and not to give them the right to seek help in procuring an earlier death.[67]

Abortion

The crime of abortion covers any intentional and unlawful killing of a foetus in the womb. However, there are instances where abortion is medically justified

---

[63] 1996 SLT 848.
[64] See, eg, the Oregon Death with Dignity Act and the position in the Netherlands and Switzerland.
[65] *Pretty* v *United Kingdom* (2002) 35 EHRR 1.
[66] Motor neurone disease.
[67] The courts also considered Arts 8, 9 and 14, but the arguments based on these Articles also failed.

and will not amount to an offence. This is now regulated under the Abortion Act 1967 which provides for a termination of a pregnancy if carried out up to the 24th week of pregnancy by a qualified doctor in response to opinions from two other doctors that continuation with the pregnancy would cause greater risk of physical or mental injury to the mother or her existing family.[68] It is also legitimate to perform an abortion at any stage if there is a risk to the mother's life or of causing her grave permanent injury by continuing with the pregnancy,[69] or if there is a substantial likelihood that the child will be born seriously handicapped.[70] It is further possible for a medical practitioner to perform an abortion without two other opinions if it is immediately necessary to save the life, or prevent grave permanent injury to the physical or mental health, of the mother.[71] Any unlawful termination of a pregnancy other than by natural causes amounts to a criminal offence. There is a right to refuse to participate in any procedures authorised by the Act if that person raises a conscientious objection to the abortion. The right subsists unless the abortion is necessary to save the mother's life or prevent grave injury to her.[72]

NON-CRIMINAL HOMICIDE

Homicide arises where a human being has been deprived of life and, as shown, applies in a variety of different situations. It may be possible to argue, in unusual cases, that the victim consented to, or even encouraged, their own death at the hands of the accused. However, this will not be taken into consideration by the court, as it is not possible to consent to be killed.[73] There remains one further category of homicide (non-criminal homicide) which deserves brief mention for the sake of completeness. Non-criminal homicide is not the concern of the criminal law, for one of two possible reasons. The killing will be entirely accidental, in situations where the death is wholly unintentional. Alternatively, it may be, in some way, justifiable, for example in the course of carrying out a duty during war time or, most importantly, killing in self-defence.[74]

---

[68] Abortion Act 1967, s 1(1)(a), as amended by the Human Fertilisation and Embryology Act 1990, s 37.
[69] Section 1(1)(b) and (c).
[70] Section 1(1)(d).
[71] Section 1(4).
[72] Section 4(1).
[73] See *HM Advocate* v *Rutherford* 1947 SLT 3.
[74] See Chapter 7.

SUMMARY OF MAIN POINTS

Murder

- *actus reus* – any act causing death which raises the inference that the accused had the *mens rea* for murder
- *mens rea* – a wicked intent to kill, or wicked recklessness as to whether the victim lives or dies

Culpable homicide

- involuntary culpable homicide, where
    - an assault leads to an unintended death
    - an unlawful act is carried out recklessly and results in an unintended death
    - a lawful act is carried out recklessly and leads to death
- voluntary culpable homicide, where either diminished responsibility or provocation applies

Diminished responsibility

- mental weakness falling short of insanity, rendering the accused only partially responsible for his actions
- *Savage* criteria
- *Galbraith (No 2)* – requires an abnormality of the mind which has a substantial effect on actions

Provocation

- a sudden loss of self-control in response to an attack or confession of infidelity, leading to death
- several requirements apply: death must occur in circumstances where the ordinary person would also have lost control, and the response must be proportionate
- the response to provocation must be immediate, meaning cumulative provocation is difficult to establish

Suicide

- attempted suicide is not an offence in itself, although it may amount to breach of the peace
- active euthanasia amounts to a criminal offence. Passive euthanasia can be exonerated if in the patient's best interests – *Bland* and *Law Hospital Trust*
- assisted suicide illegal in UK

Abortion

- unless carried out in accordance with the Abortion Act 1967, amounts to a criminal offence

HOMICIDE

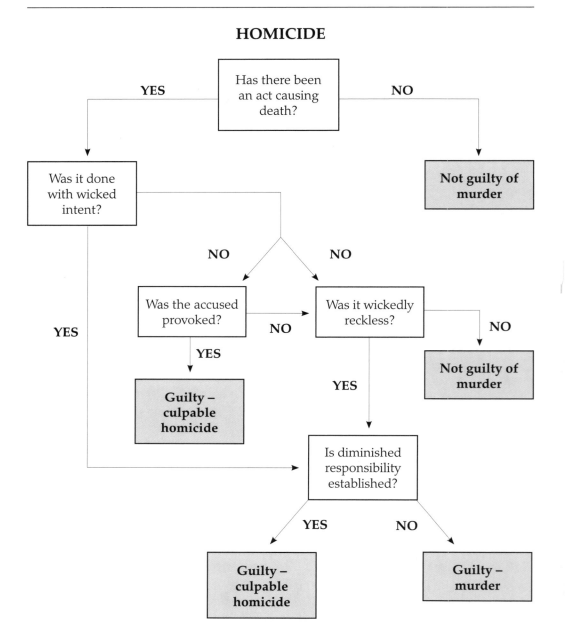

Note: Use of the word "guilty" is a convenient shorthand. There may be other issues to consider before the accused is convicted.

SELF-ASSESSMENT QUESTIONS (see Appendix for answers)

1   X is annoyed by something Y has said to him and decides to teach him a lesson. He confronts Y and lands a moderate punch on him. Y has an unusual medical condition which leaves his arteries particularly vulnerable to rupture even if only moderate force is applied to them. As a result of X's actions, one of Y's major arteries is ruptured and he suffers major internal bleeding and dies. X wishes to argue in his defence that he had no idea Y was so vulnerable and that he never intended to kill him. Will X be guilty and, if so, of what?

2   What differences did *Galbraith (No 2)* introduce into the law on diminished responsibility?

3   What are the requirements for the plea of provocation?

Further questions

1   Should attempted suicide amount to a crime when suicide itself is not longer criminal?

2   How is the requirement of proportionality treated in sexual infidelity cases?

Further reading

Jones and Christie, *Criminal Law* (4th edn), pp 240–265.
McCall Smith and Sheldon, *Scots Criminal Law* (2nd edn), pp 170–190.
Gordon, *Criminal Law* (3rd edn), vol 2, pp 285–312.
"Causation and expert evidence" 1987 JLSS 468.
P Ferguson, *Crimes Against the Person* (2nd edn), pp 21–43 and 117–142.

9 OFFENCES AGAINST THE PERSON

ASSAULT

Actus reus of assault

The crime of assault is constituted by any attack made by the accused on another person. There is, however, no requirement that such an attack causes physical injury and thus putting someone in fear of being injured, menacing them with threatening gestures, or pointing a gun at someone will also amount to assault.[1] The use of threatening words without threatening actions or gestures will not amount to assault, as words are not viewed as sufficient to constitute a criminal threat. There is no requirement that the attack should be sufficient to cause any injury to the victim and, thus, a relatively trivial attack still amounts to assault; and it is also not necessary to show that the victim put up any resistance in the face of the attack. However, the act must be a voluntary one and therefore any "assault" committed as a result of a reflex or any other automatic action will not be sufficient to lead to conviction.

It is also possible to commit an assault indirectly. If the accused deliberately sets in motion a series of incidents which are intended to cause or threaten harm without any further direct involvement on the part of the accused, he can be liable for assault if the victim suffers injury as a result of those incidents. Classic cases involve setting dogs on the victim, frightening the horse he is riding so that it throws him, or any other behaviour which amounts to an attack on the victim without directly involving the accused.

Mens rea of assault

Historically, the *mens rea* for assault has always been intention, specifically evil intention, and this requirement has been restated consistently through to modern times.[2] Modern, detailed discussion of the requirement of evil intent is to be found in *Lord Advocate's Reference (No 2 of 1992)*.[3] In this case, the accused maintained that he had not exhibited the evil intent necessary for conviction because, after

---

[1] *Atkinson v HM Advocate* 1987 SCCR 534.
[2] See, eg, *HM Advocate v Harris* 1993 SLT 963.
[3] 1993 SLT 460.

bursting into a shop and waving what appeared to be a gun at some shop assistants and demanding the contents of the till, he had started to laugh. He argued that it had all been a joke and that he never had an evil intent to assault anyone. However, such arguments, aimed at negating intent by claiming that the actions were carried out in jest, are viewed rather dimly by the courts. It was held on appeal that the requirement of evil intent was designed to ensure that assault as a crime would always be one of intention rather than recklessness or negligence. Thus, it would seem that the requirement of evil intent is synonymous with a requirement of intention and does not need any further evidence of evil on the part of the accused beyond an intention to commit an assault. Conceptually, assault must be a crime of intention, in that it is hard to envisage an accused who could voluntarily attack his victim in a reckless or negligent fashion. However, there appears to be some doubt on this point, and at least two modern cases would tend to suggest that there may be some room for recklessness in the *mens rea* of assault. In *Roberts* v *Hamilton*,[4] the court was concerned with the likelihood of injury and stated that the accused would be liable if injury to any other person was likely to occur. This moves the *mens rea* requirement for assault beyond pure intention and into what is known as "transferred intention". This applies where the accused intends to assault his victim, but foresees that someone else might be hurt as well as, or instead of, that victim, because the blow might fall astray. The doctrine of transferred intent makes the accused liable for assaulting that other person because, although he intended to assault only his victim, he could foresee that he might also injure the other party. However, in *HM Advocate* v *Harris*[5] the court specifically said that foreseeing injury as likely was not sufficient for assault, thereby establishing the *mens rea* of assault firmly within the realms of intention.

A final point to note in relation to the *mens rea* of assault is that the mitigating plea of provocation applies as it does to charges of homicide. However, given the less serious nature of the offence, the plea is construed rather less strictly. It has been established since Institutional times that in assault, in contrast with cases of murder, provocation can be found in simple words. Thus, the accused who commits an assault in response to provocative language by the victim can plead provocation successfully, whereas the accused who goes further and kills the victim cannot raise the plea.[6] However, as in murder cases, the provocation must lead immediately to an assault carried out in the heat of the moment.

AGGRAVATED ASSAULT

Assaults can be described and treated as aggravated assaults in a number of different circumstances. Perhaps the most common means by which a charge

---

[4] 1989 SLT 399. See also *Connor* v *Jessop* 1988 SCCR 624.
[5] 1993 SLT 963.
[6] Gordon, vol 2, p 418.

is raised from plain assault to aggravated assault is where the accused has used a weapon, especially a firearm, in the course of his attack. However, almost anything that can be wielded as a weapon will aggravate the assault.[7] The law also views assault by stabbing and by throwing acid or similar substances as serious aggravations. An assault can also be viewed as aggravated if the consequences for the victim fall within certain parameters. Assault to severe injury or permanent disfigurement is an aggravated assault, as can be seen in *HM Advocate* v *Harris*,[8] where the victim was seized and pushed down a flight of stairs such that she landed in the roadway, and was hit by a car. It is also possible to charge the accused with assault to permanent impairment, or to the danger of the victim's life. An attack against certain types of victim will also make an assault an aggravated offence, such as the elderly, infirm, children or on-duty policemen. An assault on the Sovereign, a judge, sheriff or justice of the peace[9] will likewise be an aggravated assault, if it can be proved that the accused knew of the status of the victim at the time of the attack. Where the aggravating quality of the assault is found in the character of the victim, it is for the prosecution to establish that the accused was aware of the characteristic. An assault will also be aggravated if it is carried out with an intention to commit a further crime such as rape or robbery.

DEFENCES TO ASSAULT

Lawful force

There are circumstances where physical force of some kind can be used without rendering the individual liable on a charge of assault. A clear example of such a situation arises in the context of lawful force. These situations all involve the use of justifiable force by the accused in order to defend himself or others, prevent crime or carry out lawful chastisement. It is also possible to exert necessary force against someone in order to secure compliance. For example, staff in a secure hospital would be entitled to exercise reasonable force in order to ensure that a patient complied with treatment or to prevent them from injuring themselves or others.

Self-defence
The defence of self-defence has already been discussed in some detail.[10] In brief, it requires that the accused responded proportionately to an attack made upon himself or another which was life threatening. The circumstances must be

---

[7] This will include broken bottles, garden tools etc.
[8] 1993 SLT 963.
[9] Or any other "officer of the law".
[10] See Chapter 7.

such that there is no opportunity to retreat and the act of self-defence must be necessary in the circumstances.

Crime prevention

The police are entitled to use force in order to prevent the commission or continuation of crime. Inevitably, this will involve them in inflicting intentional injury, but such a use of force is justified in the circumstances so long as it is reasonable and not excessive.[11] A private citizen is also entitled to use reasonable force to prevent a serious crime which he witnesses. It is necessary for the citizen making the arrest to bring himself within the precise scope of what is permissible as a citizen's arrest, and these parameters have been construed rigidly by the courts. It used to be imperative that the person making the citizen's arrest had actually observed the offence taking place. In *Codona* v *Cardle*,[12] an employee had told the accused who was responsible for breaking a window on his premises, but the accused had not actually seen the crime being committed. The accused then grabbed the supposed vandal by the arm and twisted it up his back. Since the accused had not seen the crime being committed, it was held that he was not entitled to make a citizen's arrest and was himself convicted of assault. Similarly, in *Bryans* v *Guild*,[13] the accused was convicted of assault because he had not seen the supposed criminal in the act or received information which could be construed as the equivalent of personal observation. However, in *Wightman* v *Lees*,[14] it was held, in the context of theft, that this rule (that the citizen must witness the crime themselves) could not be applied rigidly. It was held that where the citizen had "a moral certainty that a crime had been committed"[15] and that a particular person had committed it, he would then be justified in making a citizen's arrest. It would be necessary to show that the circumstances were strongly indicative of the criminal activity in question, and thus a citizen's arrest could not be made on the basis of a mere suspicion.

Chastisement

The issue of the lawful chastisement of children has been a rather controversial one. It applies to those who have children in their charge, not simply to parents. The requirement for a conviction of assault in these circumstances remains the same; there must be evidence of evil intent, which can be shown by the use of excessive force beyond that which is reasonable for disciplinary purposes.[16] The Criminal Justice (Scotland) Act 2003, s 51, requires the court to look at a number of factors when the accused argues that their physical punishment of a child

---

[11] *Marchbank* v *Annan* 1987 SCCR 718.
[12] 1989 JC 99.
[13] 1990 JC 51.
[14] 2000 SLT 111.
[15] *Ibid* at 113.
[16] Smith, "Spare the rod and spoil the child" 1999 SLT 139.

was justified as the exercise of a parental or quasi-parental right. These factors are the nature and reason for the punishment; the circumstances, duration and frequency of the use of force; the effects on the child; and its age, sex and health status. Blows to the head, shaking the child, and the use of an implement are all classified as unjustifiable.

Consent

It is clear that the accused cannot avoid liability for assaulting his victim by stating that the victim consented. For example, in *HM Advocate* v *Rutherford*,[17] the accused had strangled a woman to death, apparently at her request, but was denied the defence of consent because it was not possible for her to have consented to her own death. In *Smart* v *HM Advocate*,[18] the accused was charged with assaulting his victim by kicking, punching and biting him in the course of a fight. Since the victim had accepted Smart's challenge to a fight, he argued that he could not be guilty of assault because, as the victim had consented to the fight, he had therefore also consented to the possibility of injury. On appeal, the court held that the victim's state of mind was irrelevant and that, since Smart had clearly objectively committed an assault, he had rightly been convicted. However, *Smart* recognises an exception to this rule, in that any "assault" occasioned in the normal and accepted course of consensual sporting activities will not amount to an offence. Although the court accepted that there was an exception, this exception did not apply to Smart himself, as the fight had not taken place in the context of a consensual sporting activity. There are a number of sports which involve the infliction of injury as a normal and expectable part of playing the game and where it is clear that such injury is not inflicted with the requisite evil intent. Activities such as rugby and boxing provide clear examples. So long as the violence in question is within the normal parameters of the particular sport, then there is no evil intention. However, if a player were to inflict injury well beyond what would be expected within the normal course of the game, this would amount to assault. A further area where consent removes liability for assault occurs in cases involving medical professionals. Doctors, nurses and other such professionals often cause injury intentionally, in order to carry out their duties. Health professionals need to secure the patient's or their representative's voluntary and informed consent[19] before treatment, otherwise a wide range of medical procedures, particularly in surgery, would clearly amount to assaults. However, if the patient requires treatment in an emergency, and delaying in order to secure consent would threaten their life, then a doctor could proceed in the absence of consent without being liable for assault.

---

[17] 1947 SLT 3.
[18] 1975 SLT 65.
[19] Informed consent is a thorny area in medical law, particularly in relation to considerations of how much information the patient should be given.

OTHER OFFENCES

Culpable and reckless conduct

Culpable and reckless conduct can arise in a wide variety of situations. In *Robson* v *Spiers*,[20] the accused was charged with chasing bullocks across a field and cornering them by the fence, with the result that they jumped the fence and made their way onto a railway line and a road, all to the danger of the public. The accused appealed against his conviction, alleging that there was no evidence from his actions of the level of recklessness which would be required for conviction. He had admitted that it was a stupid thing to have done, but maintained that the eventual result of his conduct was not obvious from the outset. The Crown contended that it had been entirely foreseeable that serious injury could have been caused by the animals. The High Court agreed with the Crown and also stated that the appellant's conduct in chasing the animals until they were cornered showed, in itself, sufficient evidence of utter recklessness as to the consequences of his action.

Culpably or recklessly causing injury or the risk of injury to others is also an offence. The accused must be shown to have acted with utter disregard of the consequences of his actions, in a highly reckless manner. There is no requirement that the victim suffers any actual injury, as the offence can be made out simply by creating a risk of injury. In assessing whether the accused's conduct was reckless, there is no need to investigate the accused's state of mind. The question is simply whether, objectively, his conduct was reckless. In *Allan* v *Patterson*,[21] the accused was charged with driving his motorbike across a school crossing at some speed, while ignoring the sign requiring him to stop. It was held that the issue was whether the driver had fallen below the expected standard of care and, if so, whether the extent to which he had fallen below that standard was such as the jury would objectively describe as being reckless. On this basis, he was convicted. In *HM Advocate* v *Harris*,[22] the accused had pushed the victim down the stairs to a nightclub which had resulted in her landing in the road and being hit by a passing car. He had been charged with assault to severe injury and permanent disfigurement and, in the alternative, with culpable, wilful and reckless conduct to the same end. An objection was raised to the relevancy of the alternative charge, arguing that no such crime existed in Scots law, and that the charge amounted to a duplication of the main charge of assault. This objection was upheld by the sheriff and the alternative charge was dismissed. The Crown appealed and, in allowing the appeal, it was held that reckless conduct which caused injury was a crime, as was such conduct which endangered the lieges. It was held further that it was appropriate to bring the charge as an alternative to assault, as a jury could

---

[20] 1999 SLT 1141.
[21] 1979 JC 57.
[22] 1993 SLT 963.

competently find that the accused lacked the *mens rea* of intention necessary for the assault charge, but that he had displayed the recklessness necessary for the alternative charge. In holding as it did, it was necessary for the court to consider the case of *Quinn* v *Cunningham*.[23] The accused was charged with riding his bicycle in a reckless manner and colliding with two pedestrians, causing them injury. It was held that, since the charge had not been framed so as to include "to the danger of the lieges", it was not competent. It was held necessary to charge the accused with a level of recklessness which could be classified as criminal, that is "recklessness so high as to involve an indifference to the consequences for the public generally"[24] – hence the need to specify a danger to the lieges. In *Harris*, the court overruled *Quinn*, holding that recklessly causing injury is a crime under Scots law, regardless of whether there is evidence of indifference of the public at large.[25]

Reckless endangerment

Some reckless behaviour is viewed as being capable of causing danger to others even if, in a particular instance, it has not. Society is protected against such potentially harmful behaviour by the offence of recklessly endangering the lieges. "Lieges" simply means other people and the essence of the offence is that other people might be harmed by the reckless conduct in question. The offence has been charged in cases of setting fire to a field in such a manner that the smoke caused hazardous driving conditions on a nearby road. Visibility for road users was so badly affected that two cars collided. However, the accused did nothing to avert the danger and carried on with other work on that field. It was held that he had exhibited such reckless indifference to the safety of the public at large, and particularly those involved in the collision, that he was found guilty of reckless endangerment.[26] The charge has further been used where the accused had dropped a glass bottle from the 15th floor of a block of flats, with utter disregard for the consequences of his act.[27] It was also held in *Normand* v *Morrison*[28] that a charge of culpably and recklessly endangering the lieges could be brought where the accused, who had been taken to a police station and was to be searched, denied that she had any sharp objects on her person. During the search, an uncovered syringe was found, to the obvious danger of the officer who had searched her and who could have been injured by the needle. The court described her actions as showing complete indifference to the safety of the public, here represented by the police officer involved in the

---

[23] 1956 SLT 55.
[24] *Ibid* at 57.
[25] *HM Advocate* v *Harris* 1993 SLT 963 at 965–966.
[26] *MacPhail* v *Clark* 1983 SCCR 395.
[27] *RHW* v *HM Advocate* 1982 SCCR 152.
[28] 1993 SCCR 207.

search. Although this type of conduct had never been the subject of such a charge before, the court was adamant that the beauty of the common law was its ability to adapt to new circumstances and deal with them accordingly. Consequently, the accused's argument that the charge against her was irrelevant was repelled. A similar situation gave rise to an appeal in *Donaldson* v *Normand*,[29] where the accused allowed himself to be searched, having incorrectly denied that there were any sharp objects on his person. He had been asked if he had any sharp objects, and had removed several guarded needles from his pocket. He was then asked the same question again. Because of his consumption of both heroin and temazepam, he had forgotten that he had placed an unprotected needle in his sock. Since his forgetfulness was attributable to self-induced intoxication,[30] it did not afford him any protection and his conviction for recklessly exposing another to injury and infection was upheld. More recently, the High Court on appeal heard the case of *Mallin* v *Clark*[31] following the accused's conviction for culpably and recklessly concealing a used syringe on his person which he did not mention when being searched. The officer carrying out the search felt the needle graze the back of his hand, but did not realise what had happened until the appellant removed his jacket and took out a syringe. At this point, the officer was taken to hospital and given treatment for possible infections. Counsel for the appellant acknowledged that, following previous cases, there could be liability for falsely denying the existence of a concealed needle, but maintained that the accused had to either deny its existence or engage in some comparable conduct. He contended that, in this case, there was no such conduct. His response to the police had been, at best, equivocal and he had not, at any point, actually denied having a needle on his person. Further, it was submitted that, since the police had proceeded with the search in ways which minimised their actual physical contact with the accused, it could be presumed that they had at least taken account of the fact that he might have had concealed sharp objects on his person. For the Crown, it was noted that the accused knew prior to the search that he had concealed a needle in his shirt pocket, that the needle had been used, and that he was a drug user. In this context, the Crown argued that he had been culpably reckless in failing to alert the police to its existence prior to the search. In the particular circumstances of this case, the court held that the Crown had failed to show any positive duty on the accused to volunteer this information to the police, but it did acknowledge that there may still be circumstances where such a failure might be classified as culpable and reckless conduct.

Culpable and reckless conduct is not, however, confined to this type of case. In *Normand* v *Robinson*,[32] the accused had organised a rave in a building which was

---

[29] 1997 SLT 1303.
[30] The court applied the *dicta* from *Brennan* v *HM Advocate* 1977 JC 38.
[31] 2002 GWD 26-862.
[32] 1994 SLT 558.

awaiting demolition because it was unsafe. This was held to amount to recklessly endangering the lieges (in other words, those who attended) if it could be proved that the accused had reached a sufficient level of recklessness to amount to criminal culpability. A variant of reckless endangerment is found in the crime of recklessly discharging a firearm. In *Gizzi* v *Tudhope*,[33] the appellants had set up a clay pigeon shoot close to a line of trees which obscured the ground behind from view. The line of trees was well within range, so that, when the appellants fired their shots, the bullets went beyond the line of trees. They were unaware that there were men working behind the trees, one of whom was injured by their shots. The court held that members of the public might have been expected to be behind the trees and that, as a result, the appellants had acted recklessly by firing without knowing who might be there.

Noxious substances

It is an offence to administer or supply noxious substances to another. If this is done deliberately, it amounts to culpable and reckless endangerment or, if a greater disregard of consequences can be shown, it may amount to reckless injury. The offence will apply where the accused has either forced the victim to take the noxious substance or has administered it to someone who does not know its nature. The most interesting development in this area is the charge of supplying potentially noxious substances, which charge was upheld in *Khaliq* v *HM Advocate*[34] and *Ulhaq* v *HM Advocate*,[35] where both the accused were convicted of supplying solvents as part of a kit with other equipment which would make it possible to inhale the fumes.

Recklessly causing infection

It would seem that there would be scope for using the criminal law to penalise conduct which is aimed at passing on infection or disease. Thus, if someone who had AIDS or was HIV positive was to deliberately have unprotected sexual intercourse with the victim without telling them of the risks, it might be possible to argue that charges should be brought under some heading. Reckless endangerment is a potential candidate but is not without its own problems.[36]

---

[33] 1983 SLT 214.
[34] 1984 SLT 137.
[35] 1991 SLT 614.
[36] See Tadros, "Recklessness, consent and the transmission of HIV" 2001 Edin LR 371, commenting on *HM Advocate* v *Kelly* (unreported). For the position in England, see *R* v *Konzani* [2005] 2 Cr App R 14 and *R* v *Brady* [2007] Crim LR 564, where the possibility of conviction for reckless transmission is clear, so long as an appropriate direction is given on the meaning of "recklessness".

Stalking

There has been much discussion in recent years of the legal response to stalking. It will usually amount to some form of distressing conduct during which the stalker follows his victim or somehow intimidates them, either physically or psychologically. It has always been competent to charge the stalker with causing a breach of the peace in cases where his conduct has caused alarm. However, victims of stalking can now benefit from sanctions imposed on the stalker under the Protection from Harassment Act 1997. Section 8(1) makes it an offence to carry out conduct intended to harass another, or where, if not intended by the accused, the conduct would be viewed as harassment by the reasonable man. Section 8(3) of the 1997 Act defines "harassment" as conduct (including speech) which causes distress or alarm to the victim on a minimum of two occasions. The 1997 Act inserts s 234A into the Criminal Procedure (Scotland) Act 1995 which allows for a non-harassment order to be made in such circumstances, preventing the accused from engaging in specific types of conduct for specified periods of time. However, it is necessary to establish a course of conduct which amounts to harassment and, for these purposes, such a course of conduct is established by evidence of two separate incidents.[37] This requirement has caused some difficulties, as shown in *McGlennan* v *McKinnon*.[38] The accused had been convicted of a breach of the peace for shouting at a former partner, causing her distress. The prosecution sought a non-harassment order and, to satisfy the requirements of s 8(3), it brought evidence of four previous convictions. However, the sheriff refused to make the order, on the ground that the case before him involved only one incident of harassment and did not, therefore, amount to a course of conduct as specified in the legislation. The High Court, on appeal, upheld the sheriff's position and refused the Crown's appeal. It is thus necessary to establish a course of two or more incidents of harassing behaviour arising from the context of the case in hand, and not arising from prior convictions. This clearly limits the usefulness of the orders by removing from their scope those offenders who commit a string of single incidents, no matter how distressing each individual incident is to the victim.

THREATS

Making a threat against another person is a criminal offence, whether that threat is to do him physical injury or to damage his property. It is equally criminal whether spoken or written. Some threats have been recognised as criminal in themselves.[39] Further instances of threatening conduct are covered by other classes of crime, for example extortion or breach of the peace.[40]

---

[37] Section 8(3).

[38] 1998 SLT 494.

[39] *James Millar* (1862) 4 Irv 238. These include threats of death, serious bodily injury and burning down one's house, as well as doing serious damage to the victim's reputation.

[40] Gordon, vol 2, pp 430–434.

SUMMARY OF MAIN POINTS

Assault
- requires an attack on another, whether or not it causes any injury
- attack can be direct or indirect
- there must be evidence of evil intention
- can be aggravated by the use of a weapon, consequences for victim, age or status of the victim, or if there is an intention to commit a further crime

Defences
- *lawful force* – where justified in using necessary force in self-defence, to prevent crime, or chastise
- *consent* is no defence except in the context of sport or medicine

Culpable or reckless injury
- where show utter disregard for the consequences to the victim
- sufficient if accused creates risk of causing injury

Reckless endangerment
- behaviour capable of causing danger to the lieges

Supply of noxious substances
- covers administration or supply
- can amount to either culpable and reckless endangerment or reckless injury, depending on level of disregard shown

Stalking
- course of conduct causing alarm or distress
- some kind of physical intimidation
- Protection from Harassment Act 1997, s 8

ASSAULT

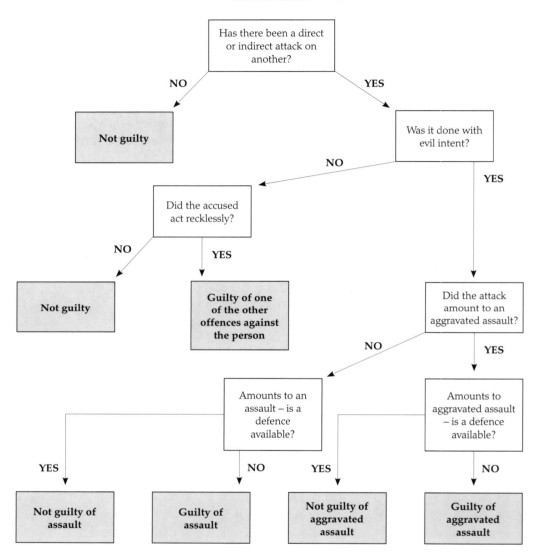

Note: Use of the world "guilty" is a convenient shorthand. There may be other issues to consider before the accused is convicted.

SELF-ASSESSMENT QUESTIONS (see Appendix for answers)

1 When can a member of the public make a citizen's arrest?

2 Can consent ever be a valid defence to a charge of assault?

3 If the accused has hit someone but not caused them any injury, can he use this as a defence?

Further questions

1 Should there be criminal liability for recklessly causing infection?

2 Why should an accused who uses a weapon in a threatening way as part of a joke be convicted of assault?

3 If someone is alarmed by being followed, what charges can be brought? Are these sufficient?

Further reading

Jones and Christie, *Criminal Law* (4th edn), pp 208–236.

McCall Smith and Sheldon, *Scots Criminal Law* (2nd edn), pp 154–169.

Gordon, *Criminal Law* (3rd edn), vol 2, pp 397–434.

Ferguson, *Crimes against the person* (2nd edn), pp 1–20.

Laurie, "AIDS and criminal liability under Scots law" 1991 JLSS 312.

10 SEXUAL OFFENCES

SEXUAL OFFENCES (SCOTLAND) ACT 2009[1]

The Sexual Offences (Scotland) Act 2009 was passed by the Scottish Parliament on 10 June 2009 and received Royal Assent on 14 July 2009. At the time of writing (July 2009), this widescale reform of the law on sexual offences has not yet come into force. The Bill was introduced into the Scottish Parliament in June 2008, following a Report[2] from the Scottish Law Commission and a subsequent consultation on that Report by the Scottish Government.[3] The impetus behind this ongoing law reform was the need to modernise the law on sexual offences and answer the growing criticisms levelled at the common law, particularly in relation to the restrictive approach taken in admitting of rape only where there was a male accused and a female victim. In abolishing a number of common law sexual offences (rape; sodomy; clandestine injury to women; and lewd, indecent or libidinous practices), the Act instead provides for a statutory offence of rape alongside a range of other sexual offences, including sexual coercion, sexual assault, and sexual exposure.

Rape

Section 1 addresses much of the gender-related criticism of the common law of rape, which was defined so as to require penile penetration of the victim's vagina, and thus excluded cases of anal or other forms of penetration. The Act defines "rape" as occurring when a person, intentionally or recklessly, penetrates their victim's vagina, anus or mouth with their penis. Section 1(4) allows for conviction where the accused's penis or victim's vagina were created as part of a sex change operation. The accused will be guilty of rape if the penetration takes place without the victim's consent, and without any reasonable belief on the part of the accused that the victim consented. The prosecution will therefore

---

[1] My thanks are due to Gery McLaughlin and Patrick Down of the Sex Offences Law Team at the Criminal Justice Directorate for their most helpful comments on this section of the text. Responsibility for any errors remains, however, mine.

[2] Scottish Law Commission, Report 209 on Rape and Other Sexual Offences: http://www.scotlawcom.gov.uk/downloads/rep209.pdf, para 1.25.

[3] Scottish Government Consultation on the Scottish Law Commission Report on Rape and Other Sexual Offences: http://www.scotland.gov.uk/Topics/Justice/crimes/8980/Scottishgovtconsultation.

have to show either that the accused knew that the victim was not consenting, or that, while the accused alleged they believed that the victim consented, that belief was unreasonable. This focus on consent is another departure from the traditional common law definition, which originally looked for a situation where the accused had forcibly overcome the victim's will in order to have sex with them. This was then modified by *Lord Advocate's Reference (No 1 of 2001)*[4] where it was held that the common law crime of rape was defined as a man having sexual intercourse with a woman without her consent. It is common, when discussing rape, to refer to a lack of consent, and the focus in the legislation has now shifted to looking for consent, defined as free agreement. Section 1(3) allows for a conviction for rape when, although consent was initially given, the victim withdrew that consent during the course of penetration. The section defines "penetration" as an on-going act, from insertion to withdrawal and thus it will amount to rape from the point at which consent is withdrawn. This offence is prosecutable only on indictment, with a maximum penalty of life imprisonment and a fine.

Sexual assault

Sexual assault is dealt with in two separate sections: s 2 deals with sexual assault by penetration, while s 3 deals with sexual assault. Section 2 requires that the accused has sexually penetrated the victim's vagina or anus to any extent with any part of their body or any other item.[5] The *mens rea* requirement is one of intention or recklessness. The penetration must take place without the victim's consent, and without any reasonable belief on the part of the accused that the victim consented.[6] If consent is given but then withdrawn, the offence is committed from the point at which consent is withdrawn, by virtue of s 2(3). The offence is prosecutable only on indictment, with a maximum penalty of life imprisonment and a fine.

The new offence of sexual assault under s 3 is capable of being committed by five distinct types of conduct. These are:[7]

- sexual penetration of the victim's vagina, anus or mouth, by any means and carried out either intentionally or recklessly;[8]
- sexually touching the victim, either intentionally or recklessly;

---

[4] 2002 SLT 466.

[5] Section 2(1). Section 2(4) overlaps with s 1 in stating that the penetration here can also be achieved by the accused's penis. This is intended to cover situations where the victim cannot say for certain whether they were penetrated by the accused's penis or something else.

[6] Section 2(1)(a) and (b).

[7] Section 3(2)(a)–(e).

[8] "Penetration" here is also construed to include penile penetration (s 3(5)), again overlapping with s 1 and providing for those situations where the victim cannot say whether the penetration was penile or otherwise.

- any other sexual activity involving intentional or reckless physical contact with the victim, whether bodily contact or through the use of an implement, and whether clothed or not;
- intentional or reckless ejaculation onto the victim; and
- intentional or reckless emission or urine or saliva onto the victim if done sexually.

As before, the offence will be committed where the victim does not consent, and the accused has no reasonable belief that the victim consents.[9] Section 60 defines "sexual" in this context as meaning conduct which the reasonable person would, in all the circumstances of the case, consider to be sexual. Section 3(3) again construes penetration as a continuing act and so allows for sexual assault to be proved if consent is initially given but then withdrawn. The maximum penalties are imprisonment for a year, a fine or both (summary) or life imprisonment, a fine or both (indictment).

Sexual coercion and related offences

Section 4 sets out a new offence of sexual coercion to deal with situations where the accused intentionally forces another to participate in sexual activity where they do not consent, and the accused does not have a reasonable belief that they are consenting to such participation. "Sexual" is again to be construed by reference to the reasonable person's assessment of the activity in the circumstances.[10] The maximum penalties are imprisonment for a year, a fine or both (summary) or life imprisonment, a fine or both (indictment). However, beyond coercing someone to take part in sexual activity, two further offences are created. Under s 5, it is an offence to coerce a victim into being present while the accused or a third party intentionally engages in sexual activity for the purpose of either obtaining sexual gratification, or humiliating, distressing or alarming the victim.[11] In this, and all sections using this phrasing, the above purposes are established if they can be reasonably inferred from the accused's conduct, and it is not necessary for the Crown to prove that the victim was actually affected in the ways specified.[12] The offence will only be committed if the victim does not consent, and the accused does not have a reasonable belief that the victim is consenting and, again, "sexual" is defined by reference to the reasonable person.[13] The maximum penalties are imprisonment for a year, a fine or both (summary) or imprisonment for 10 years, a fine or both (indictment). Section 6 criminalises the act of coercing someone into looking at an image of sexual activity. The image can be of any type (either moving or still, and including images sent by text or e-mail) and

---

[9] Section 3(1).
[10] Section 60.
[11] Sections 5(1) and (2).
[12] Section 49.
[13] Section 60.

involve either the accused, a third party or an imaginary person engaging in such activity, which will presumably therefore also cover the use of images involving cartoon figures and CGI creations.[14] It also covers images of either the accused's or a third party or imaginary person's genitals.[15] The accused must have intentionally caused the victim to look at such an image without their consent, and without any reasonable belief that the victim was consenting.[16] Section 6(2) states that the purpose behind the accused's conduct must be one of obtaining sexual gratification or humiliating, distressing or alarming the victim. "Sexual" is again defined by the reasonable person's assessment of what is sexual in the circumstances.[17] The maximum penalties are imprisonment for a year, a fine or both (summary) or imprisonment for 10 years, a fine or both (indictment).

Section 7 deals with indecent communications between the accused and their victim. The maximum penalties are imprisonment for a year, a fine or both (summary) or imprisonment for 10 years, a fine or both (indictment). It requires that the accused has intentionally, and for the purpose of obtaining sexual gratification or humiliating, distressing or alarming their victim, either sent a written sexual communication to, or directed a verbal sexual communication at, their victim. This must be done without the victim's consent to receive a communication of that nature, and without any reasonable belief that the victim consents. Section 7(2) extends this prohibition to situations where the accused intentionally causes their victim to see or hear such a communication, other than by directing or sending it to the victim themselves. "Written" includes the accused's own words, as well as copying sections from other authors, and "verbal" includes speech, sound recordings and sign language. "Sexual" is defined by reference to the reasonable person as above.

Other sexual offences

Sexual exposure is dealt with in s 8 and will apply where the accused has, without either consent or a reasonable belief in consent, intentionally exposed their genitalia in a sexual manner to their victim, intending the victim to see them. Under s 8(2), the exposure must be done for the purposes of obtaining sexual gratification, or humiliating, distressing or alarming the victim. The maximum penalties are imprisonment for a year, a fine or both (summary) or imprisonment for 5 years, a fine or both (indictment). Section 9 introduces a new offence of voyeurism for conduct which would previously have been (and may alternatively still be) covered by breach of the peace. It will apply in a number of situations:

---

[14] Section 6(3)(a).
[15] Section 6(3)(b).
[16] Section 6(1)(a) and (b).
[17] Section 60.

- if the accused, for the purposes of obtaining sexual gratification or humiliating, distressing or alarming the victim, observes the victim carrying out a private act, without their consent or a reasonable belief in their consent;[18]
- if the accused, for the same purposes and similarly without consent, operates equipment (eg a webcam) with the intention of allowing themselves or another to observe the victim carrying out a private act;[19]
- if the accused, again without consent, records the victim carrying out a private act with the intention that they or another party look at the image for the purposes of obtaining sexual gratification or humiliating, distressing or alarming the victim;[20]
- or if the accused installs equipment or constructs or adapts any structure (eg by drilling a peephole or making a hide) for the purpose of allowing themselves or another to do any of the above.[21]

Section 10 provides that a person is doing a private act if that person is in a place which, in the circumstances, would reasonably be expected to provide privacy, and either (a) the person's genitals, buttocks or breasts are exposed;[22] (b) the person is using a lavatory; or (c) the person is engaging in a sexual act not normally done in public. The maximum penalties are imprisonment for a year, a fine or both (summary) or imprisonment for 5 years, a fine or both (indictment). Section 11 provides that it is an offence for a person intentionally to administer a substance to another person without their knowledge, and without any reasonable belief that they know. This applies where administration is carried out for the purpose of stupefying or overpowering that person so as to enable the accused or a third person to engage in sexual activity involving that person. "Sexual" is defined in the same way as in earlier sections. Although this offence is not committed if the other person knows that they are taking the substance, if the victim is deceived, by act or omission, into believing that the substance is of a substantially lesser strength or quantity, then the victim's knowledge is to be disregarded, and the accused can be convicted under s 11. The maximum penalties are imprisonment for a year, a fine or both (summary) or imprisonment for 5 years, a fine or both (indictment).

Consent and reasonable belief

The foregoing offences have made frequent reference to these two specific concepts, without providing further clarification in their respective sections. Part 2 sets out, in ss 12–16, how these concepts are to be understood. This is a

---

[18] Section 9(2).
[19] Section 9(3).
[20] Section 9(4).
[21] Section 9(5).
[22] Either naked or covered only by underwear.

particularly important part of the new regime, as these two issues have stood at the heart of much of the criticism of the common law. As regards the use of the term "consent", it is defined in s 12 to mean "free agreement". The notion of free agreement here is very clearly tied to the Scottish Law Commission's emphasis on promoting sexual autonomy, which is evident in its report.[23] While "free agreement" is not defined further, s 13 lists a number of situations where free agreement is absent. This list is not exhaustive, so there can be other situations where there is no free agreement even though they do not appear in the list. Section 13 provides that free agreement will not be present where:

- the sexual activity takes place when the victim is incapable of consenting as a result of the effects of alcohol or any other intoxicating substance;
- the victim agreed or submitted to conduct because they or a third party were subjected to violence or threats of violence;
- the victim agreed or submitted to conduct because they were unlawfully detained by the accused;
- the victim agreed or submitted to conduct because they were deceived by the accused as to the nature or purpose of the conduct (eg the accused deceived the victim into believing that the activity was a medical procedure);
- the victim agreed or submitted to conduct because their agreement to the conduct in question was induced by the accused impersonating someone known to the victim; or
- where the only expression or indication of consent is made by someone other than the victim themselves.

This provides a fairly extensive list of situations in which any expression or indication of consent given by the victim will be ignored because it will fail to meet the threshold for free agreement (because of coercion, deception or incapacity). The previously controversial issue of the sleeping or unconscious victim is dealt with under s 14 and simply provides that any victim who is asleep or unconscious is incapable of consenting. Section 15 goes on to deal with a few other points in relation to consent: that consent to any conduct cannot be said of itself to imply consent to any other conduct, and that consent, once given, can yet be withdrawn at any time prior to commencement of the conduct in question, or indeed, if the conduct is of a continuing type, such as sexual intercourse, during the course of the conduct. When consent is withdrawn, if conduct continues to take place, it takes place without consent.

---

[23] "Autonomy" in the sense of being able to determine one's own choices and actions, applied here in the context of freedom to make one's own sexual choices: Scottish Law Commission, Report 209 on Rape and Other Sexual Offences (Scot Law Com Report 209) (http://www.scotlawcom.gov.uk/downloads/rep209.pdf).

Section 16 provides that, in determining whether an accused's belief that the victim consented is reasonable, regard is to be had as to whether the accused took any steps to establish whether the victim was consenting (or in the case of s 11, whether the victim had the required knowledge), and if so, the nature of those steps. It will depend on the facts and circumstances of each case, and be up to the judge or jury to assess whether the belief was reasonable.

Vulnerable groups

The Act then deals with specific measures designed to offer protection to particular vulnerable groups; mentally disordered persons, children and those situations involving an abuse of trust where such a relationship exists between the accused and the victim.

Mentally disordered persons (s 17)

In relation to the offences set out in ss 1–9 (rape through to voyeurism), any apparent consent given by a mentally disordered person is to be disregarded where their mental disorder means that they cannot understand the sexual conduct in question, form a decision about whether to take part in it or agree to its taking place, or communicate any decision they have taken. "Mental disorder" is construed in the same way as in s 328 of the Mental Health (Care and Treatment) (Scotland) Act 2003 which defines it as any mental illness, personality disorder or learning disability. Someone is, however, not mentally disordered as a result of only one of: sexual orientation; sexual deviancy; transsexualism; transvestism; dependence on or use of alcohol or drugs; behaviour that causes or is likely to cause harassment, alarm or distress to another; or behaviour that no prudent person would exhibit.

Young children

Part 4 deals exclusively with offences against, or involving, children. Sections 18–26 provide for offences against children under the age of 13 years ("younger children"). The Act provides that a person under the age of 13 years is incapable of consenting to sexual activity, and the prosecution is thus not required to prove the absence of consent. Section 18 deals with rape of a young child which is defined as the intentional or reckless penile penetration of the child's vagina, anus or mouth by the accused, where that child is under 13 years of age. Prosecution is on indictment only and the maximum penalty is set at life imprisonment and a fine.

Section 19 introduces an offence of sexual assault on a young child by penetration, in terms paralleling s 2 except that the victim must be a child under the age of 13, and there is no reference to consent by that child, as it is irrelevant. The maximum penalty on indictment is set at life imprisonment and a fine.

Section 20 deals with sexual assaults on children under 13 and is specified in exactly the same terms as s 3, except that there is no mention of the effect of any consent or belief in consent as it is irrelevant. The maximum penalties are imprisonment for a year, a fine or both (summary) or life imprisonment, or a fine or both (indictment).

Section 21 creates the offence of causing a child under 13 to participate in a sexual activity. It requires the accused to have intentionally caused their child victim to participate in a sexual activity[24] and the maximum penalties are imprisonment for a year, a fine or both (summary) or life imprisonment, a fine or both (indictment).

Section 22 (causing a young child to be present during a sexual activity) provides a parallel version of s 5, the only differences being that the victim must be under 13 years of age, and all references to the victim's consent are deleted. The maximum penalties are imprisonment for a year, a fine or both (summary) or imprisonment for 10 years, a fine or both (indictment).

Section 23 (causing a young child to look at an image of a sexual activity) similarly provides a parallel version of s 6, the only differences again being that the victim must be under 13 years of age, and all references to the victim's consent are deleted. Again the maximum penalties are imprisonment for a year, a fine or both (summary) or imprisonment for 10 years, a fine or both (indictment).

Section 24 covers indecent communications made to a young child and is also a parallel of s 7, the only differences again being that the victim must be under 13 years of age, and all references to the victim's consent are deleted. The maximum penalties are imprisonment for a year, a fine or both (summary) or imprisonment for 10 years, a fine or both (indictment).

Section 25 sets out the offence of sexual exposure to a young child which is phrased in the same terms as s 8 except that the victim must be under 13 and there are no references to the victim's consent.

Section 26 introduces an offence of voyeurism towards a young child, which is also a mirror provision of that found in s 9 except that it requires a victim under the age of 13 and makes no reference to the issue of their consent. The maximum penalties for ss 25 and 26 are imprisonment for a year, a fine or both (summary) or imprisonment for 10 years, a fine or both (indictment).

Section 27 provides that it is not a defence to the charges under ss 18–26, that the accused believed the child to be over 13.

Older children

Sections 28–39 deal with offences against "older" children. These are defined as children who have reached 13 years of age, but are not yet 16. The Act provides that it will be an offence for a person over the age of 16 to engage in sexual activity with an older child, irrespective of whether the child consents to sexual

---

[24] That is, one which a reasonable person would view, in the circumstances, as sexual (s 60).

activity, though, where a lack of consent can be proven, it would be possible to prosecute under the comparable offences under Pt 1 of the Act, which have higher maximum penalties.

Section 28 creates an offence of having intercourse with an older child and applies where the accused (who must be 16 or over) intentionally or reckless penetrates the victim's vagina, anus or mouth with their penis. The maximum penalties are imprisonment for a year, a fine or both (summary) or imprisonment for 10 years, a fine or both (indictment).

Section 29 introduces the offence of engaging in penetrative sexual activity with an older child. It applies where an accused who is over 16 intentionally or recklessly penetrates[25] the victim's vagina or anus with any part of their body or any other item. The victim must be over the age of 13 but not yet 16. The maximum penalties are imprisonment for a year, a fine or both (summary) or imprisonment for 10 years, a fine or both (indictment).

Section 30 then widens the scope of criminal conduct here by creating the offence of engaging in sexual activity with an older child. It applies where the accused who is over 16 either intentionally or recklessly carries out one of the activities in s 30(2) in respect of an older child. These activities are:

(a)   penetrating[26] the victim's vagina, anus or mouth;

(b)   sexually touching the victim;

(c)   engaging in any other form of sexual activity involving physical contact with the victim, clothed or not;

(d)   ejaculating semen onto the victim; or

(e)   emitting urine or saliva onto the victim sexually.

Section 60 defines "sexual" for these purposes, by reference to what the reasonable person would, in the circumstances, believe to be sexual, and the maximum penalties are the same as for s 28. Causing an older child to participate in a sexual activity is set out in s 31, with the same maximum penalties, and requires the accused to have intentionally caused an older child to participate in something which a reasonable person would regard as sexual activity.

Section 32 provides that it is an offence to cause an older child to be present during a sexual activity. This requires the accused intentionally to engage in a sexual activity themselves in the presence of their victim, or intentionally cause the victim to be present while a third party engages in such an activity, all for the purpose of obtaining sexual gratification or humiliating, distressing or alarming the victim. The penalties are again the same except that the maximum period

---

[25] "Penetration" here is also construed to include penile penetration (s 29(2)), again overlapping with s 28 and providing for those situations where the victim cannot say whether the penetration was penile or otherwise.

[26] Again defined to include penile penetration, as in earlier sections.

of imprisonment on indictment is 5 years. Again, there are provisions dealing with causing an older child to look at an image of sexual activity (s 33) and communicating indecently with an older child (s 34). Both these provisions are equivalent to ss 23 and 24 in respect of young children, the only difference here relating to the relative ages of the accused (over 16) and victim (at least 13 but not yet 16).

Sections 35 and 36 introduce provisions dealing respectively with sexual exposure to an older child, and voyeurism towards an older child. Again, these are in parallel with the provisions set out in ss 8 and 9, except that the accused must be over 16; the victim between 13 and 16; and there is no reference to the victim's consent. The maximum penalties are imprisonment for a year, a fine or both (summary) or imprisonment for 10 years, a fine or both (indictment).

Section 37 deals with older children engaging in sexual conduct with each other. In these cases, both children must be in the "older child" age bracket. If one older child engages in penile sexual penetration of another older child's vagina, anus or mouth, either intentionally or recklessly, or intentionally or recklessly touches the victim's vagina, anus or penis in a sexual way with their mouth, then they commit the offence of engaging, while an older child themselves, in sexual conduct with another older child. Where the other older child has consented to the sexual penetration or touching, they too commit an offence under section 37(4) (of engaging, while an older child themselves, in consensual sexual conduct with another older child).

Section 38 provides a definition of "consent" for the purpose of s 37 which mirrors the definition in ss 12–15, and s 60 defines "sexual" by reference to the reasonable person. The maximum penalties are imprisonment for a year, a fine or both (summary) or imprisonment for 10 years, a fine or both (indictment).

Section 39 sets out defences available in respect of offences against older children. The accused can raise a defence that they reasonably believed the victim to be 16 or over, so long as they have not been charged previously with a relevant offence[27] and are not subject to a risk of sexual harm order.[28]

In cases brought under s 37(4), it would be a defence for the older child who consents to the penetration or touching to assert that they reasonably believed the other child to be 16 or over, under the same proviso as above. There is a further defence for the accused if the difference between the accused's and victim's ages is not more than two years, but the defence is not available in respect of s 37, or the conduct covered by that section (as set out in s 39(4)).

Abuse of trust

Further sanctions were provided by the Sexual Offences (Amendment) Act 2000, which protected young persons against the potential for abuse by those

---

[27] "Relevant sexual offences" are defined as sexual offences involving children and are listed in Sch 1.
[28] Under the Protection of Children and Prevention of Sexual Offences (Scotland) Act 2005.

entrusted to care for them, and by s 3 of the Criminal Law (Consolidation) (Scotland) Act 1995, which provides for offences relating to familial sexual abuse of trust. The relevant parts of these Acts are repealed and replaced with the offence provisions at ss 42–45. The Act creates an offence of sexual abuse of trust under s 42. This applies to an accused over the age of 18 who intentionally engages in sexual activity in respect of a person under 18, in relation to whom they are in a position of trust. Section 43 defines "position of trust" by reference to five specified conditions, any one of which is sufficient to establish such a position. If the person under 18 is detained in an institution by a court order and the accused looks after persons under 18 in that institution, then the accused is in a position of trust. Such a position is also established if the person under 18 lives in a children's home or other form of accommodation provided by the local authority for that purpose and the accused looks after persons under 18 there. If the person under 18 is accommodated and cared for in a hospital or facility run by an independent health care service or care home provider, a residential facility or accommodation provided by a school care accommodation service or secure accommodation provider, and the accused looks after persons under 18 in that place, then they are in a position of trust. If the person under 18 receives education at a school and the accused looks after persons under 18 in that school, or receives education at a further or higher educational establishment (including a university[29]), and the accused looks after them there, a position of trust is established. Finally, if the accused carries out parental responsibilities or exercises parental rights (or used to do so but no longer does), or does so by arrangement with the person who holds those same rights or responsibilities, or treats the person under 18 as a child of their family, and the person under 18 lives in their household, then they are in a position of trust over that person.

Section 45 provides defences to charges of sexual abuse of trust, where the accused reasonably believed either that the victim was 18 years of age, or that there was no position of trust capable of being abused. It is also a defence to show that the victim was, at the relevant time, either the accused's spouse or civil partner or that a sexual relationship was already in place between the accused and victim, prior to the position of trust coming into existence.[30] The maximum penalties are imprisonment for a year, a fine or both (summary) or imprisonment for 5 years, a fine or both (indictment).

In the case of sexual abuse of trust in cases involving mentally disordered persons, s 46 requires that the accused intentionally engages in a sexual activity in respect of a mentally disordered person. The offence repeals and replaces the offence in s 313 of the Mental Health (Care and Treatment) (Scotland) Act 2003. The accused must either provide care services to the victim, or be employed in, contracted to, or manage a hospital, independent health care service or state

---

[29] Section 44.
[30] This applies only if the position of trust is not based on parental rights or responsibilities.

hospital at which the victim is being treated. If the accused can prove that they reasonably believed that the victim was not mentally disordered or that they did not meet the definition of a person providing care services as outlined above, then they can raise a defence under s 47. It is also a defence if it can be shown that the mentally disordered person was the accused's spouse or civil partner, or if there was a pre-existing sexual relationship between the two prior to the accused providing care services to the victim, or prior to the victim's admission into the hospital or similar facility.

In respect of all the sections dealing with children and mentally disordered victims, s 51 provides that an individual is not guilty of inciting or being art and part in any of those offences if they acted in order to either; protect that child or mentally disordered person from an STD, protect their physical safety, prevent them from becoming pregnant, or protect their emotional wellbeing by providing advice. This will preclude them from being charged with any of the offences so long as they did not act to obtain sexual gratification for themselves, humiliate, distress or alarm the child or mentally disordered individual, or to cause or encourage the sexual activity to take place.

CONTINUITY OF COMMON LAW CRIMES

Section 52 of the Act abolishes the common law crimes of rape; clandestine injury to women; sodomy; and lewd, indecent or libidinous practices from the point at which each of the relevant new offences come into force. However, s 53 provides for the continuity of these common law crimes in certain circumstances. It may be the case that the accused could be charged with, for example, an offence of rape under s 1, and the common law crime of rape, where it is unclear whether the incident took place just before or after the coming into force of s 1, or before or after the abolition of common law rape. So long as it was clear that the accused had satisfied all the other aspects of the offences with which they were charged, then s 53(3) allows the accused to be found guilty of the "old" crime if the maximum penalty is less than for the new statutory offence, or the new offence if the maximum penalty set for it is lower than the old common law crime. What follows, then, is a brief overview of the common law in relation to these four areas, which will continue to be relevant in some cases.

The common law of rape requires that the male accused has vaginal sexual intercourse with a female victim, without her consent, intending to do so, or reckless as to her consent.[31] The need to prove a lack of consent on the part of the victim comes from the decision in *Lord Advocate's Reference (No 1 of 2001)*,[32]

---

[31] Controversy was caused here by the acquittal of those accused who held a mistaken belief in the victim's consent. See *Meek* v *HM Advocate* 1982 SCCR 613; *DPP* v *Morgan* [1976] AC 182; and *Jamieson* v *HM Advocate* 1994 SCCR 181.

[32] 2002 SLT 466.

which itself represented a significant change in the law. Prior to 2001, the law had required that the male accused had sexual intercourse with his female victim forcibly and against her will. This was a source of controversy under the pre-2001 law because, since the definition required that the victim's will was overcome, cases where the woman had been asleep or unconscious could not be prosecuted as rape, but rather as either clandestine injury to a woman (which is also abolished by the new Act) or indecent assault. Clandestine injury had, as a separate charge in its own right, already become questionable following the re-definition of rape in *Lord Advocate's Reference (No 1 of 2001)*. The common law on rape also precludes conviction in a number of situations which would be covered by the statutory definition of rape, most notably, perhaps, those cases where the accused was female, or the victim male, and those cases where penetration was either oral, anal or by means of some implement.[33] It had also previously been the case that a man could not be guilty of raping his wife, although this had been overruled by *Stallard* v *HM Advocate*.[34]

Sodomy – that is, non-consensual anal penetration where both accused and victim are male – is a common law crime, as is consensual penetration in these circumstances unless both parties are over the age of 16 and the acts take place in private.

At common law, it is an offence to indulge in lewd, indecent or libidinous practices towards children under the age of puberty. There is no prospect of the child being able to consent to the practices in question, as they are deemed incapable of consent on account of their age. The crime can be used to prosecute indecent exposure or the performance of sexual acts in front of children, indecently touching children, showing them pornographic material or inducing them to commit indecent acts themselves.

OTHER SEXUAL OFFENCES

Indecent assault

Indecent assault covers any assault in indecent circumstances. Thus, it is a species of assault and has the same basic requirements, including physical contact of some sort, and the necessary evil intent. It can be committed by someone of either sex, on a victim of either sex. The assault must involve either a sexual part of the body or a contiguous part, although it is possible that it also covers touching a non-sexual part of the body if there is also suggestive behaviour. However, the behaviour must be outwardly, objectively indecent. There is a defence of consent, so that, if the "victim" had consented to the physical and indecent contact, there

---

[33] Under the common law, these situations would have been covered by the crime of indecent assault, which lacks the severe penalties imposed for common law rape.

[34] 1989 SLT 469.

can be no prosecution. The position is less clear if the accused only believed that the victim consented. However, in *Marr* v *HM Advocate*,[35] the court acknowledged that juries would not believe an accused in circumstances which showed his belief in consent to be unreasonable. At trial, the jury in *Marr* was directed to consider the genuineness of his belief, but was not directed to consider whether his belief in consent was reasonable. On appeal, the High Court declined to make the reasonableness of the mistaken belief a requirement of the direction to the jury in indecent assault charges.

Public indecency

The concept of public indecency is a fairly new development in the law in this area. Previously, the crime was classified as one exhibiting shameless indecency, which was wide and flexible, covering a variety of activities which the courts saw as unacceptable.

The historical position

In *McLaughlan* v *Boyd*[36] the court adopted an earlier statement which classified *all* shamelessly indecent conduct as criminal, but did not offer any detailed definition of the term. In general, it required conduct which was aimed at a person and intended to corrupt or deprave them.[37] It was charged against those who arranged, for example, a sexually stimulating performance, so long as that performance involved some form of corruption and did more than stimulate ordinary sexual desires.[38] It was for the judge or jury to decide whether the conduct in question fell into this category. Thus, the precise scope of the definition was for the courts to interpret without the aid of expert evidence.

Two classic cases in this area illustrated the breadth of the definition. On the one hand, the accused in *Lockhart* v *Stephen*[39] was not convicted of shameless indecency, despite his actions. He had organised erotic dancers in his bar who went as far as to simulate sexual intercourse on stage. However, this was only likely to stimulate normal, heterosexual desires and therefore did not warrant conviction. This can be set against *Watt* v *Annan*,[40] where showing a pornographic film, including scenes of perversion, to consenting adults warranted conviction. This was held despite the fact that the owner operated a private club in which to show such films to members only. However, it was noted by the court that it was very easy to obtain membership at the door and no real control was exercised over who might become a member. Thus, even though the film was,

---

[35] 1996 SLT 1035.
[36] 1934 JC 19.
[37] *Dean* v *John Menzies Holdings* 1981 SLT 50.
[38] *Gellatly* v *Laird* 1953 JC 16.
[39] 1987 SCCR 642.
[40] 1978 JC 84.

strictly speaking, shown in private, this still amounted to shameless indecency as the film included material felt likely to corrupt morals and give rise to depravity and lust. It was made clear by Lord Cameron that a conviction of shameless indecency required the court to consider the level of shamelessness involved. It was stated in *Lockhart* that the conduct in that case was not shamelessly indecent in the social climate of 1987. It may well be that the difference in verdict between the two cases related more to changes in what was viewed as acceptable over the course of a decade than it did to substantive changes in the crime of shameless indecency. The *mens rea* of shameless indecency was considered in *Usai* v *Russell*.[41] The accused had stood naked at his window, exposing himself and staring at two women who were passing by. However, it became clear from the evidence that the accused was not wearing his contact lenses at the time and so could not have been intentionally staring at anyone, nor, indeed, could he have been aware that there were witnesses to his actions. On appeal, he argued that the Crown must show intention or reckless indifference on his part regarding the likely effects of his conduct. It was held that there was no need to show that the accused actually knew his conduct had been witnessed by other persons in order to classify it as shamelessly indecent. It was sufficient to show that it was likely that there would be witnesses who would be affected by his conduct, and that he had been recklessly indifferent as to the presence of witnesses. It had also been determined that shameless indecency would be used to cover such conduct as fell short of any other nominate sexual offence, but which was felt to deserve punishment.

The change to public indecency

However, the law on shameless indecency took a fairly dramatic turn in 2003 with the case of *Webster* v *Dominick*,[42] which reverted to the much earlier definition found in *McKenzie* v *Whyte*[43] and insisted that the conduct must have taken place in public in order to amount to a crime against morality and public order. Hence, the case overrules *Watt* and brings into Scots criminal law a crime of public indecency. It was held that the definition laid down in *McLaughlan* had rested on a misinterpretation of older texts, and that the truer interpretation of the foundation of the law in this area could be found in *McKenzie*. Public indecency, then, requires that the accused engages in indecent conduct to which the public is exposed in some way. This would exclude situations where private members' clubs screen films behind locked doors. Examples given of public indecency include indecent exposure,[44] sexual intercourse in public and perhaps sexual gestures or acts in the course of a stage show, unless the audience were entirely

---

[41] 2000 JC 144.

[42] 2003 JC 65.

[43] (1864) 4 Irv 570.

[44] It is possible that this conduct would also meet the definition set out in s 8 of the Sexual Offences (Scotland) Act 2009 for the offence of sexual exposure.

knowledgeable as to the context, and were willing spectators. The distinction between "public" and "private" is clear in this context. If conduct takes place in private but is capable of being viewed by members of the public, then it takes place in a public place for these purposes. The necessary level of indecency is to be judged by contemporary standards, allowing for changes in social and sexual mores over time.

INCEST

The Criminal Law (Consolidation) (Scotland) Act 1995 regulates the law on incest, although it was traditionally based on an Act of 1567 with heavy reliance on Leviticus 18:6–18. The existence of such laws was justified on moral, religious and genetic grounds, many of which are still relevant. The one major change since the Act of 1567 is the removal of the prohibition on grounds of affinity. This used to mean that someone could not have sexual intercourse with anyone related to them in the prohibited degrees by virtue of marriage, as well as by blood. This has been abolished. It remains forbidden for anyone to have sexual intercourse with someone related to them by blood within certain degrees of relationship. These degrees are based either on blood ties or on adoptive or former adoptive relationships,[45] and apply whether the relationship is one of half-blood or full-blood, and legitimate or illegitimate.[46] Sexual intercourse is required and has traditionally been taken to cover only vaginal intercourse between these relations, so that oral or anal penetration does not amount to the crime of incest.[47] Consent is irrelevant, and thus cannot be raised as a defence by the perpetrating party.[48] Figure 10.1 illustrates the prohibited relationships, in the shaded boxes. It is based on X, a man, although clearly it would also apply to a woman by substituting male relatives for female. The list of prohibited relationships also extends as far as great-grandparents and great-grandchildren, although the prospect of them even being alive, let alone feasible sexual partners, is remote.

The accused can argue that he did not know, and had no reason to believe in the existence, of a prohibited relationship between himself and his sexual partner, but the onus is on him to prove such lack of knowledge. Likewise, those accused would have a defence if they were subjected to rape by their relative or could show that they were validly married under the law of some other country which allowed marriage between close relations.[49] Step-parents or former step-parents cannot have sexual intercourse with a step-child or former step-child where they

---

[45] Criminal Law (Consolidation) (Scotland) Act 1995, s 2.

[46] *Ibid*, s 1(2)(a) and (b).

[47] Such acts would still be prosecutable under other headings: public indecency would be a candidate if the conduct met the requirements of that crime, as would one of the sexual offences set out in the 2009 Act.

[48] Section 1(1)(b); and see also *McDade* v *HM Advocate* 1998 SLT 68.

[49] Criminal Law (Consolidation) (Scotland) Act 1995, s 1(1)(a)–(c).

Figure 10.1

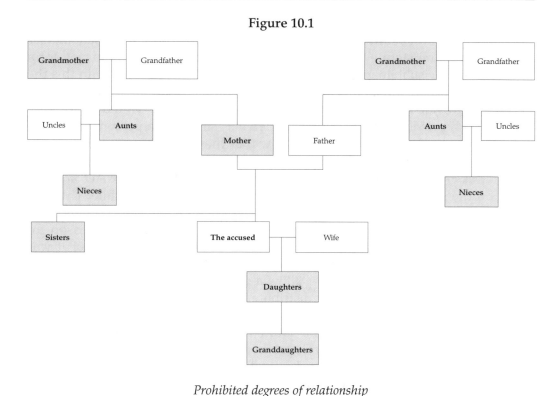

Prohibited degrees of relationship

are under the age of 21, or had lived with them as a child of the family at any time before they reached the age of 18.[50] Defences are provided to cover situations where the accused did not know or have reason to suspect the other party was their step-child or former step-child; reasonably believed the other party to be 21 or over; did not consent; or was validly married to them at the time.

Obscene material

Under the Civic Government (Scotland) Act 1982, it is an offence to display obscene material in either a public place, or in a place in which the public might have sight of it.[51] It is also an offence to publish, sell or distribute obscene material, or to make, keep or print such material with a view to selling it at a later date.[52] The nature of obscene "material" has been subject to broader definition as

---

[50] Criminal Law (Consolidation) (Scotland) Act 1995, s 2.
[51] Civic Government (Scotland) Act 1982, s 51(1).
[52] *Ibid*, s 51(2).

time has passed and thus, in *Ross* v *HM Advocate*,[53] the accused was convicted of operating a bulletin board on the Internet which included obscene visual images and text files. The statute defines "material" to cover, among others, any form of recording of visual images. The court was prepared to include within this the text files concerned and, in any event, noted that the relevant provision[54] did not purport to provide an exhaustive list of those "materials" that would be covered. Section 51(4) provides a "due diligence" defence, such that a person will not be guilty under this heading if they can show that they did everything possible to prevent commission of the offence.

So far as child pornography is concerned, s 52A(1) of the same Act imposes a ban on the simple possession of an indecent photograph of a child. This also covers "pseudo-photographs" which include photograph-type images generated by a computer. There is a defence if the accused had a legitimate reason for possessing the picture, had not taken it and did not know or suspect it was indecent, or had received it unsolicited and disposed of it promptly. Section 52(1) extends to cover those who take or allow a photograph or pseudo-photograph of a child under 18 to be taken, or distribute or advertise it. There is, however, a defence if there was a legitimate reason for having possession of the picture, or if the possessor was unaware of the nature of the photograph, or if it was sent to him unsolicited and he returned it promptly.[55] In *Ogilvie* v *HM Advocate*[56] the accused had downloaded and stored a total of 22,000 obscene photographs of children and had been sentenced to 2 years' imprisonment. In his appeal against sentence, the High Court took account of the scale of his offending and the fact that he had immediately replaced his previous computer which had been confiscated so that he could continue offending. However, they also noted that he was a first-time offender with no previous convictions for sexual offences, who had pled guilty and so substituted a more lenient sentence. The court also observed that there were instances where the statutory maximum sentence should be imposed: where the case is contested or where there is evidence of commercial exploitation coupled with a large quantity of material. Conversely, non-custodial options were only appropriate where there was a small amount of material for personal use by a first-time offender who pled guilty.[57] Ogilvie fell somewhere in the middle of this spectrum and therefore the court had to consider other factors, including the quality, nature and quantity of the material, the level of exploitation, distribution or commercial gain, the accused's character, and his level of co-operation.[58]

---

[53] 1998 SLT 1313.
[54] Civic Government (Scotland) Act 1982, s 51(8).
[55] *Ibid,* s 52(5)(a) and (b).
[56] 2001 SLT 1391.
[57] Following the English case of *R* v *Toomer* [2001] 2 Crim App R (S) 8.
[58] *Ogilvie* v *HM Advocate* 2001 SLT 1391 at 1394.

Prostitution

Prostitution is in a somewhat anomalous position insofar as the criminal law is concerned. Although many would view it as immoral, in itself the practice of prostitution is perfectly legal. However, this is considerably diluted by several statues regulating associated activities. The Civic Government (Scotland) Act 1982, s 46 prohibits loitering in public and soliciting of clients in public places, and applies to both male and female prostitutes. The Criminal Law (Consolidation) (Scotland) Act 1995, s 11(1)(b) makes it an offence for a man to persistently solicit for immoral purposes in public. If he were to make only one sexual suggestion to someone in public, this would not be sufficient for a section which requires persistent conduct on the part of the accused, but it could render him liable to prosecution for breach of the peace. This is confined to soliciting for heterosexual activity, either by the man himself, or by a woman on whose behalf he is acting. Soliciting in a homosexual context is prohibited by s 13(9) of the same Act. Further ancillary activities are also criminalised. It is an offence to procure women for prostitution, to run a brothel, or to allow premises to be used as such.[59] It is also an offence for a man to live wholly or partly off the proceeds of prostitution,[60] and for a woman to act as a brothel madam.[61]

The Prostitution (Public Places) (Scotland) Act 2007 turned the tables and introduced an offence aimed specifically at clients soliciting a prostitute's services. Most commonly, this would cover what is known as "kerb crawling". Section 1 sets out an offence of soliciting a prostitute in order to obtain their services and applies whether or not the accused solicits from a private motor vehicle or public transport. It also applies regardless of whether the person solicited happens not to be a prostitute. The offence also applies to those who loiter in a specific place in order to obtain the services of a prostitute.[62] The soliciting or loitering must take place in a public place, meaning any place to which to public have unrestricted access or to which they have permitted access, whether or not payment is required.[63]

---

[59] Criminal Law (Consolidation) (Scotland) Act 1995, s 11(5).
[60] *Ibid*, s 11(1).
[61] *Ibid*, s 11(4).
[62] Prostitution (Public Places) (Scotland) Act 2007, s 1(3).
[63] *Ibid*, s 1(6)(a) and (b).

SUMMARY OF MAIN POINTS

Rape

Sexual Offences (Scotland) Act 2009, s 1
- intentional or reckless penile penetration of victim's vagina, anus or mouth
- without the victim's consent and where accused does not reasonably believe there was consent

Sexual assault by penetration

2009 Act, s 2
- intentional or reckless penetration of victim's vagina or anus by any means
- without the victim's consent and where accused does not reasonably believe there was consent

Sexual assault

2009 Act, s 3
- intentional or reckless sexual penetration of vagina, anus or mouth by whatever means
- intentional or reckless sexual touching
- intentional or reckless physical contact
- intentional or reckless ejaculation onto the victim
- intentional or reckless emission of urine or saliva onto victim, if done sexually
- without the victim's consent and where accused does not reasonably believe there was consent
- "sexual" determined by reference to the reasonable person (s 60)

Sexual coercion and related offences

2009 Act, s 4 – intentionally forcing another to participate in sexual activity
- without the victim's consent and where accused does not reasonably believe there was consent
- "sexual" determined by reference to the reasonable person (s 60)

2009 Act, s 5 – coercing another to be present while the accused or a third party engages in sexual activity
- done intentionally and in order to obtain sexual gratification, or humiliate, distress or alarm the victim

- without the victim's consent or where accused does not reasonably believe there was consent
- "sexual" determined by reference to the reasonable person (s 60)

2009 Act, s 6 – intentionally coercing another into looking at an image of sexual activity

- without the victim's consent and where accused does not reasonably believe there was consent
- "sexual" determined by reference to the reasonable person (s 60)
- done intentionally and in order to obtain sexual gratification, or humiliate, distress or alarm the victim

2009 Act, s 7 – sending or directing an indecent communication

- written or verbal
- done intentionally and in order to obtain sexual gratification, or humiliate, distress or alarm victim
- without the victim's consent and where accused does not reasonably believe there was consent

Other sexual offences

- "sexual" determined by reference to the reasonable person

2009 Act, s 8 – sexual exposure

- intentional exposure of genitalia with intent that causes alarm or distress, or reckless as to whether causes alarm or distress
- done without consent or belief in consent
- done intentionally and in order to obtain sexual gratification, or humiliate, distress or alarm the victim

2009 Act, s 9 – voyeurism

- observes or records victim engaging in private act, without consent and without reasonable belief in consent
- done intentionally and in order to obtain sexual gratification, or humiliate, distress or alarm the victim

2009 Act, s 11 – administering substances

- done in order to overpower or drug the victim so can engage in sexual activity with them
- victim's knowledge that they are taking a substance (unless deceived by accused), and the accused's reasonable belief that they know, precludes conviction

Consent

2009 Act, ss 12–15

- free agreement
- consent is invalid if victim is: intoxicated, coerced by threats of violence, unlawfully detained by accused, deceived by accused about nature of sexual activity, deceived by accused impersonating someone they know, or if the consent is given by someone other than the victim
- victim does not consent if asleep or unconscious,
- consent can be withdrawn at any time
- consent to one thing does not imply consent to something else

Reasonable belief

2009 Act, s 16

- for judge/jury to determine if belief is reasonable by looking at whether accused took steps to establish consent, and if so, what steps

Mentally disordered victims

2009 Act, s 17

- any consent given is to be disregarded if their mental disorder means that they cannot
    - understand the sexual conduct in question
    - form a decision about taking part or agreeing to the conduct or
    - communicate that decision
- mental disorder is not established by one only of; sexual orientation, sexual deviancy, transsexualism, transvestism, dependence on intoxicants, behaviour likely to cause alarm, distress or harassment, or imprudent behaviour

Young children

2009 Act, s 18 – rape – intentional or reckless penile penetration of child's vagina, anus or mouth
- under 13, any consent is irrelevant

2009 Act, s 19 – sexual assault on young child by penetration – as specified for adults, except that child must be under 13 and any consent is irrelevant

2009 Act, s 20 – sexual assaults – as specified for adults, except that child must be under 13 and any consent is irrelevant

2009 Act, s 21 – intentionally causing a young child to participate in sexual activity

2009 Act, s 22 – causing a young child to be present during a sexual activity – as specified for adults, except that child must be under 13 and any consent is irrelevant

2009 Act, s 23 – causing a young child to look at an image of sexual activity – as specified for adults, except that child must be under 13 and any consent is irrelevant

2009 Act, s 24 – indecent communications made to a young child – as specified for adults, except that child must be under 13 and any consent is irrelevant

2009 Act, s 25 – sexual exposure to a young child – as specified for adults, except that child must be under 13 and any consent is irrelevant

2009 Act, s 26 – voyeurism – as specified for adults, except that child must be under 13 and any consent is irrelevant

2009 Act, s 27 – no defence that believed the child to be over 13

Older children
- "older" defined as over 13 years but not yet 16

2009 Act, s 28 – having intercourse with an older child – intentional or reckless penile penetration of vagina, anus or mouth

2009 Act, s 29 – sexual assault on older child by penetration – as specified for adults, except that child must be between 13 and 16, and any consent is irrelevant

2009 Act, s 30 – engaging in sexual activity with an older child
- intentional or reckless sexual penetration of vagina, anus or mouth by whatever means
- intentional or reckless sexual touching
- intentional or reckless physical contact
- intentional or reckless ejaculation onto the victim
- intentional or reckless emission of urine or saliva onto victim, if done sexually
- accused must be over 16

2009 Act, s 31 – intentionally causing an older child to participate in sexual activity

2009 Act, s 32 – causing an older child to be present while accused or a third party engages in sexual activity

- done for the purpose of obtaining sexual gratification, or distressing, humiliating or alarming the child

2009 Act, s 33 – causing an older child to look at an image of sexual activity

- as specified for adults, except that child must be over 13 but under 16 and the accused must be over 16

2009 Act, s 34 – indecent communications with an older child

- as specified for adults, except that child must be over 13 but under 16 and the accused must be over 16

2009 Act, s 35 – sexual exposure to an older child – as specified for adults, except that child must be between 13 and 16, and any consent is irrelevant

2009 Act, s 36 – voyeurism towards an older child – as specified for adults, except that child must be between 13 and 16, and any consent is irrelevant

2009 Act, s 37 – sexual conduct between older children

- requires intentional or reckless penile penetration of vagina, anus or mouth, or intentional or reckless sexual touching of victim's vagina, anus or penis with the accused's mouth
- done with consent
- both parties are guilty

2009 Act, s 39 – defences – reasonable belief that victim over 16, although only effective if accused has not previously been charged with a relevant offence or subject to a risk of sexual harm order

Abuse of trust

2009 Act, s 42 – sexual abuse of trust

- accused must be over 18 years, victim under 18
- accused must be in a position of trust in relation to victim

2009 Act, s 45 – defence if reasonably believed over 18 or reasonably believed no position of trust existed, or if victim and accused are married, or in a pre-existing sexual relationship

2009 Act, ss 46 and 47 – sexual abuse of trust of mentally disordered person, where accused provides care for them.

- defences available where accused reasonably believed the victim was not mentally disordered, they were not providing care for the victim, or they were married to the victim or in a pre-existing sexual relationship

Common law

- Sexual Offences (Scotland) Act 2009, when fully in force, will abolish common law rape; clandestine injury; lewd, indecent or libidinous practices; and sodomy

Indecent assault

- the basic requirements are the same as those for assault
- must touch a sexual or contiguous part of the body, or a non-sexual part of the body if the surrounding conduct is sufficiently suggestive
- defence of consent

Public indecency

- until 2003, categorised as shameless indecency
- very wide definition
- conduct which is aimed at a person/s which it is intended to corrupt
- *Webster* v *Dominick* sets out criteria for public indecency – need to expose the public in some way to the indecent conduct
- level of indecency required is to be assessed by current social standards

Incest

- Criminal Law (Consolidation) (Scotland) Act 1995, ss 1–2
- prohibits sexual intercourse between persons related by full-blood, half-blood or adoptive relationships, whether legitimate or not
- consent is irrelevant
- defence available if the accused can prove that he did not know of the prohibited relationship, did not consent or was married to the victim

Obscene material

- Civic Government (Scotland) Act 1982, ss 51–52A
- simple possession is not an offence, unless the subject-matter is an indecent image of a child
- offence to display, publish, sell or distribute
- due diligence defence

Prostitution

- soliciting clients and loitering outlawed, along with living off the earning of prostitution, allowing premises to be used for such, running premises, procuring women for the purposes of prostitution
- prostitution itself is not illegal
- Prostitution (Public Places) (Scotland) Act 2007 – offence of soliciting by clients looking to obtain the services of a prostitute.

RAPE (under the 2009 Act)

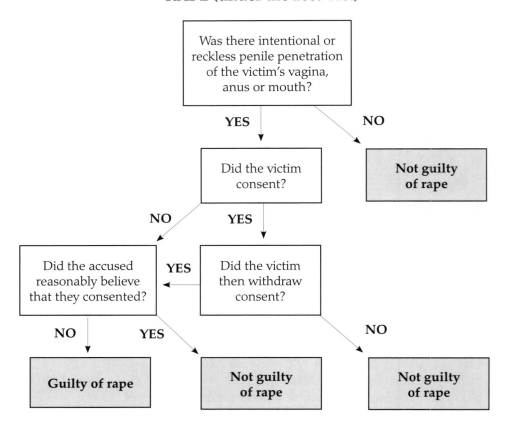

Note: Use of the word "guilty" is a convenient shorthand. There may be other issues to consider before the accused is convicted.

SEXUAL ASSAULT

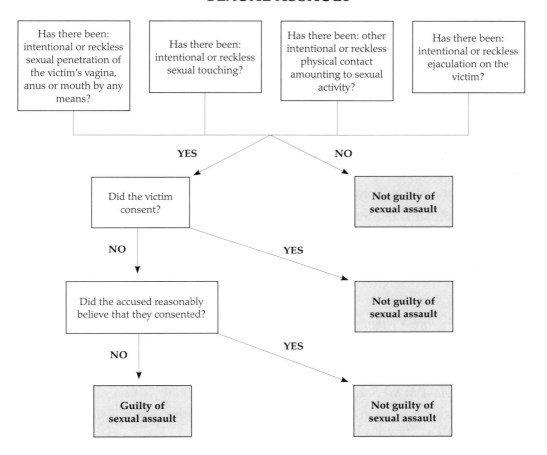

Note: Use of the world "guilty" is a convenient shorthand. There may be other issues to consider before the accused is convicted.

SELF-ASSESSMENT QUESTIONS (see Appendix for answers)

1 How has the law on public indecency developed from its predecessor?

2 Would the accused in *Watt* v *Annan* have been convicted today?

3 What developments in the law have been brought about by the Prostitution (Public Places) (Scotland) Act 2007?

Further questions

1 To what extent will the reforms to the law on sexual offences remedy some of the criticisms levelled at the common law in this area?

2 What is the reason behind the laws governing incestuous relationships?

3 How effective is the extra protection afforded to vulnerable victims in sexual offence cases?

Further reading

On the common law

Jones and Christie, *Criminal Law* (4th edn), pp 267–282 and 372–376.

McCall Smith and Sheldon, *Scots Criminal Law* (2nd edn), pp 191–209.

Gordon, *Criminal Law* (3rd edn), vol 2, pp 507–555.

On the provisions in the Sexual Offences (Scotland) Act 2009

Scottish Law Commission, *Report 209 on Rape and Other Sexual Offences,* http://www.scotlawcom.gov.uk/downloads/rep209.pdf

11 OFFENCES AGAINST SOCIETY

BREACH OF THE PEACE

So far as offences against society are concerned, breach of the peace is perhaps the most broadly defined and frequently used. It covers almost any kind of anti-social behaviour, so long as it is likely to create fear, alarm, annoyance or upset among the general public. Thus it can cover a whole multitude of sins, from the commonplace to the more exotic, including fighting in the streets; shouting abuse in public; staring persistently at someone; protesting against nuclear weapons; or attempting to commit suicide in public. As can be seen, this is but a flavour of the types of conduct which could be prosecuted as breach of the peace, and shows the breadth of interpretation which is possible when considering the definition. This in itself presents a significant problem. Generally speaking, it is not satisfactory for a legal rule to be drawn in terms which are so broad that the individual who plans an activity cannot be sure whether that conduct is criminal or not. Scots criminal law enshrines the notion that the accused should be informed of the nature of the charge against him. This is mirrored in the European Convention on Human Rights, Article 6(3)(a), which requires that the accused be informed, promptly, in detail and in language which he understands, of the precise nature of the charge against him. Arguably, breach of the peace could fall foul of this because of the breadth of the definition. However, the European Court of Human Rights has upheld the English version of breach of the peace, which is defined in a similar way, against attack under Art 6.[1]

A recent Scottish case on breach of the peace and Convention compliance is *Smith* v *Donnelly*,[2] which arose from an anti-nuclear protest during which the accused had lain in the road, disrupting traffic and causing a breach of the peace. The accused had argued that the Convention would not allow for a criminal charge which did not clearly define the limits of acceptable behaviour and that, since breach of the peace was such an all-encompassing charge, it was therefore too vague to be Convention-compliant under Art 7. This Article states that no one can be guilty of a criminal offence on account of an act or omission which

---

[1] See Oliver, "Prosecutorial Precision and the European Convention on Human Rights" 2000 *Scottish Law and Practice Quarterly* 111.
[2] 2001 SLT 1007.

was not criminal at the time of its commission. The implication from this is that individuals must be able to ascertain from the law in force at any given time, and its interpretation by the courts, what is and what is not criminal. The argument for the accused was therefore that the definition of breach of the peace in Scotland had been broadened over time to the extent that she could not know with any certainty whether her actions would amount to a crime or not. The importance of Art 7 is underlined by the fact that states cannot opt out of achieving compliance with its terms. However, the High Court was convinced that the extensive catalogue of previous cases dealing with breach of the peace in Scotland did provide a clear and understandable definition which would also be Convention-compliant. Lord Coulsfield noted that there are many ways of committing a breach of the peace and that "it is neither possible nor desirable to derive a comprehensive definition"[3] which would embrace all of these. However, he went on to state what he felt would be necessary to constitute the crime: the accused must be shown to have engaged in conduct serious enough to alarm ordinary people *and* threatened to cause serious disturbance to the community.[4] This is the central criterion of breach of the peace as established in early cases, and the court did not feel that subsequent cases had modified or redefined this. However, unless accompanied by other conduct, bad language *per se*,[5] failure to co-operate with the police and the use of words or actions of a disgusting character are not enough to amount to breach of the peace.[6] What is also clearly excluded is behaviour which is simply annoying or irritating without additionally causing alarm. The definition in *Smith* has been repeated by subsequent courts,[7] notably in *Peterson* v *HM Advocate*,[8] where the sheriff's direction to the jury that breach of the peace was constituted by causing serious alarm *or* disturbance to the community was held to be a misdirection, as it wrongly set out the definition given in *Smith*.

The range of Scottish cases over the last century and more gives an idea of the type of conduct which can be charged as breach of the peace. It includes swearing and cursing in public in the early hours of the morning;[9] peering in at lighted windows;[10] swearing and making obscene gestures to the opposing fans at a football match in circumstances likely to provoke a disturbance;[11] stopping

---

[3] 2001 SLT 1007 at 1011.

[4] *Idem*, reflecting the *dicta* in *Ferguson* v *Carnochan* (1889) 16R 93, which looked for a breach of public order to the alarm and annoyance of the public.

[5] On this see *Miller* v *Thomson* 2009 SLT 59 where twice shouting "I've done fuck all – you're not talking to me" was, following *Smith*, not enough for breach of the peace.

[6] *Smith* v *Donnelly* 2001 SLT 1007 at 1012.

[7] The approach taken to Art 7 in *Smith* was specifically approved in *Jones* v *Carnegie* 2004 JC 136.

[8] 2008 JC 327.

[9] *Ferguson* v *Carnochan* (1889) 16R 93.

[10] *Rafaelli* v *Heatly* 1949 SLT 284.

[11] *Wilson* v *Brown* 1982 SLT 361.

people in the street to ask for money and cigarettes;[12] following one's wife by car from bus stop to bus stop;[13] and repeatedly driving slowly past a group of teenaged girls while staring at them.[14] Even the wearing of reflective sunglasses, while the accused stared into a shop through the window, sat across the road and kept watch on the premises, and repeatedly joined and left the queue at the till, was sufficient to cause alarm and amount to breach of the peace.[15] The purpose behind breach of the peace is social protection – the desire to prevent harm to society by upholding certain standards of behaviour. It is considered unacceptable to indulge in behaviour which is likely to upset the public. On the one hand, this argument is unassailable. In order to maintain society and social cohesion, it is necessary to protect the public such that they can go about their own business without the prospect of being alarmed by another's conduct. Those who find fault with the breadth of conduct covered by breach of the peace, however, attack it on the grounds that it is over-protectionist and hopelessly vague. In effect, this difference of opinion is one which is perennial within criminal law and to which there is no straightforward solution. However, given the clear criteria set out in *Smith*, it is unlikely that cases where the victim was merely concerned would still amount to breach of the peace.

A charge of breach of the peace will state that the accused indulged in conduct which was "likely" to cause alarm to the public. It is important to remember here that the law does not require proof of *actual* alarm. All that is required is that the conduct was likely to cause such a reaction should a member of the public happen upon the accused committing a breach of the peace.

> It is well settled that a test which may be applied in charges of breach of the peace is whether the proved conduct may reasonably be expected to cause any person to be alarmed, upset or annoyed or to provoke a disturbance of the peace. Positive evidence of actual alarm, upset, annoyance or disturbance created by reprisal is not a prerequisite of conviction.[16]

This is illustrated by a number of cases. In *MacDougall* v *Dochree*[17] the accused had locked himself in a lavatory and peered through a small hole near the ground into a ladies' solarium, in order to spy on customers in a state of undress. He was arrested when staff became suspicious and had looked under the lavatory door, to see him on his hands and knees peering through the hole. They had called the police who had observed him from under the lavatory door, and had also

---

[12] *Wyness* v *Lockhart* 1992 SCCR 808, although it has subsequently been stated that begging itself is not a breach of the peace (*Donaldson* v *Vannet* 1998 SLT 957). It appears that it can be made so by virtue of the circumstances in each case.

[13] *Lees* v *Grier* 1996 SLT 1096.

[14] *Faroux* v *Brown* 1997 SLT 988.

[15] *McKenzie* v *Normand* 1992 SLT 130.

[16] *Wilson* v *Brown* 1982 SLT 361 at 362.

[17] 1992 JC 154.

gone through to the solarium and seen him peering through the hole. The sheriff dismissed the case on the ground that, although what he had done was a breach of the peace, no one would be alarmed by his conduct, unless they too were peering through the hole the other way, into the lavatory, which in itself would be a breach of the peace. On appeal, this decision was overturned. If someone had become suspicious of his conduct and investigated it, as the staff in fact had done, they would have found conduct which would be likely to alarm or upset the public. Thus the accused was convicted, despite that lack of actual alarm caused.

Similarly, in *Wyness* v *Lockhart*[18] the accused had approached two plain-clothes policemen and two other persons in the street, patted them on the shoulder and asked for money. In the district court it was held that, although none of the victims was alarmed in any way, an old lady might have been alarmed if she had been approached in this fashion. Thus the accused was convicted. On appeal, the decision was upheld as the conduct was of a type which might reasonably be expected to cause alarm or upset, despite the fact that it did not cause any such response on this occasion. In contrast, the accused in *Thompson* v *MacPhail*[19] locked himself in a restaurant toilet and injected himself with an illegal drug. He had been in the lavatory for so long that the manager became suspicious and called the police. When the door was forced, the accused was found removing a hypodermic needle from his arm and the walls of the cubicle were spattered with blood. It was accepted that this conduct could amount to breach of the peace, but his conviction was quashed on the ground that so much was left to conjecture. It was impossible to say whether the amount of time during which he had occupied the cubicle would inconvenience other members of the public and lead to investigations which would have brought to light the nature of his actions, and thereby caused a breach of the peace. It was held that, although the conduct could have amounted to breach of the peace, this would depend on the circumstances of the case.

It has also been argued that, if the only persons who witness the breach of the peace are police officers, then there were no witnesses who were capable of being affected by the conduct and therefore there should be no conviction. This argument has been rejected. In *Saltman* v *Allan*[20] the conduct in question amounted to shouting and swearing but the only people who heard the accused were the police. It was argued that the police were not liable to be affected by such conduct, but the court held that even if police officers were the sole witnesses of the conduct, it did not prevent conviction. This contrasts with the approach taken in *Logan* v *Jessop*[21] where the accused was acquitted on the

---

[18] 1992 SCCR 808.
[19] 1989 SLT 637.
[20] 1989 SLT 262.
[21] 1987 SCCR 604.

ground of insufficient evidence because their obscene language had only been heard by police officers. Although the same approach was taken in the later case of *Cavanagh* v *Wilson*,[22] the judges in *Saltman*[23] had previously stated that *Logan* was restricted to its own facts and found the accused in *Saltman* had presented much more provocative behaviour than was the case in *Logan*. This kind of situation would now have to be dealt with in light of *Smith* v *Donnelly* which precludes conviction for breach of the peace based purely on the use of bad language.

Questions have been raised about whether it is permissible to cause a breach of the peace in order to stop a separate breach of the peace. In *Palazzo* v *Copeland*[24] some drunk and disorderly youths were creating a disturbance. In order to prevent them from continuing with their breach of the peace, the accused fired a shotgun into the air. There was evidence that at least some of the youths were alarmed by this and ran for cover. The court held that to fire a gun into the air in a residential area in the early hours of the morning was an act calculated to cause alarm and fear to the public in general and therefore amounted to a breach of the peace in its own right. It was further held that the accused was not absolved from committing a crime himself simply because he was trying to stop another crime taking place. However, the court did not dismiss the appellant's arguments out of hand. The Lord Justice-General stated:

> [t]he proposition was that an act which is committed to stop a breach of the peace ought not to be regarded itself as a breach of the peace. While the proposition is attractive, however, we regret to say that we cannot give effect to it in law ... the fact that the appellant's motive was the sound one of trying to stop a breach of the peace is irrelevant.[25]

A further aspect of the *actus reus* of breach of the peace is that it also covers conduct which might provoke a disturbance. Clearly, shouting obscenities at opposing fans during football matches[26] and ordering an Orange band to play as it passed a Roman Catholic church[27] would both amount to conduct likely to cause a disturbance and are therefore classified as breach of the peace. Equally, it has been held that for a man to dress as a woman, wear make-up and loiter in a known "red light district" will amount to breach of the peace. It is conduct which is likely to cause a disturbance among men who might approach "her" and then discover that "she" was male.[28]

---

[22] 1995 SCCR 693.
[23] 1989 SCCR 262 at 264.
[24] 1976 JC 52.
[25] *Ibid* at 53. This affirms the established point that motive is of no concern to the criminal law.
[26] *Wilson* v *Brown* 1982 SLT 361.
[27] *McAvoy* v *Jessop* 1989 SCCR 301.
[28] *Stewart* v *Lockhart* 1991 SLT 835.

The *mens rea* of breach of the peace has been exposed to virtually no judicial comment over the years. It seems from *Hughes* v *Crowe*[29] that proof that the accused carried out actions which were objectively a breach of the peace (here, making excessive noise in an upstairs flat early on a Saturday morning) was sufficient to be able to infer *mens rea* on his part, although exactly what form of *mens rea* is required remains unclear. What is clear, however, is that motive is irrelevant, as was stated in *Palazzo* above.[30]

MISUSE OF DRUGS

This area of law is complex and subject to detailed statutory provisions. What follows is an overview of the core offences. There are a number of statutes which govern the misuse of drugs. The primary legislation is the Misuse of Drugs Act 1971, commonly referred to as "MODA". Under Sch 2, illicit drugs are separated into three broad classes, roughly in line with their potency and addictive qualities. The most serious drugs are grouped in Class A. These include, among others, the opiates (including heroin, morphine, diamorphine and methadone), cocaine and its derivatives, and the hallucinogens such as LSD and "Ecstasy". Class B includes amphetamines and cannabis, along with its derivatives. Class C includes the minor stimulants and tranquillisers such as temazepam and diazepam. In general terms, the severity of any sentence (whether for importing, supplying or possessing) will depend to some extent on the class of drug concerned.[31]

There are three main areas which are struck at by the various legislative provisions: importation; production and supply; and possession, with or without the intent to supply. Importation of drugs is covered by s 3(1) of MODA. Section 170(2) of the Customs and Excise Management Act 1979 also covers the accused who is knowingly concerned in the fraudulent evasion of a prohibition on importing drugs.[32] "Knowingly concerned" requires that the accused actually knows that the substance is an illegal drug. Under this section, ignorance is an automatic defence, as, if the accused does not know that the substance is a drug, he cannot be "knowingly" concerned in its importation. Conversely, if the accused imports an innocent substance, while believing it to be a drug, he has attempted to import an illegal narcotic and will be liable for that attempt on a subjective view of his actions. "Importation" in this context is held to take place not only at the port where the drugs are discovered, but also at any other port which has been entered *en route*, no matter what the reason.[33]

---

[29] 1993 SCCR 320.

[30] See also *Ralston* v *HM Advocate* (1989 SLT 474) where a roof-top protest by prisoners for the possibly laudable motive of drawing attention to poor prison conditions, was still classed as a breach of the peace, as motive is irrelevant.

[31] Clearly, other factors will also be considered by the sentencing judge, such as the quantities involved, the scale of the operation and other relevant issues.

[32] See *Montes* v *HM Advocate* 1990 SCCR 645.

[33] *MacNeill and ors* v *HM Advocate* 1986 SCCR 288.

Production, supply or the offer to supply an illegal drug are made offences under s 4 MODA. These are defined under s 37(1) to include both cultivation of natural narcotics, whether *au naturel* or in an artificial environment, and laboratory production of synthetic narcotics. "Cultivation" has been defined particularly widely, to cover anything which was designed to encourage growth. In *Tudhope* v *Robertson*[34] this was held to include placing a cannabis plant near to the window, and would also include any activity such as moving or watering a wild plant. Cultivation of cannabis plants is also illegal under s 6 unless authorised by the Secretary of State. "Supply" in this context refers to actual supply, being concerned in supply and offering to supply.[35] The essence is the direct transfer of the physical property in the drugs. Actual transfer of legal ownership is not an issue of concern. Section 4A applies where the accused is over 18 and the offence under s 4(3) took place near school gates or used a courier who was under 18. If either condition applies, then the court must classify the offence as one aggravated by these circumstances, and deal with the offender accordingly. Sections 4 and 5(3) (possession with intent to supply) can also be used to charge the accused in supply situations involving what is known as an impossible attempt. This would occur where someone offered to supply something which he thought was a drug, when in fact it was not. In *Docherty* v *Brown*[36] the accused had been supplying drugs to those attending a rave. He thought that he was supplying them with "Ecstasy" but, unbeknown to him, the tablets he was supplying did not contain the said drug. However, the court disregarded this and upheld his original conviction on the basis that he thought he was committing an offence and should therefore be convicted accordingly. Despite the physical impossibility of offering a real drug in these circumstances, the accused will still commit an offence under s 4 on the basis of what he thought he was doing. In general, drug offences are ones of strict liability and there is no need for the prosecution to prove that the accused knew the nature of the substances he imported, supplied, produced or possessed. However, s 28 provides a defence if the accused can show his genuine ignorance.[37]

Section 5 deals with possession and possession with intent to supply. There are two distinct aspects of possession for legal purposes. First, there must be physical possession, that is to say the exercise of some form of physical control over the drugs. The degree of control needed is determined according to the facts and circumstances of the case. It is a particular problem in shared properties where all the occupants may know of the existence of drugs on the premises. It has been held that mere knowledge that another member of the household has drugs in the

---

[34] 1980 JC 62.
[35] Section 4(3).
[36] 1996 SLT 325.
[37] *Salmon* v *HM Advocate, Moore* v *HM Advocate* 1999 SLT 169.

property is not sufficient. More has to be shown, and whether or not a particular occupier has access to the drugs will also be relevant.[38] Persons living in shared properties may also be liable under s 8. This imposes liability on the owner or manager of premises who knowingly allows specified activities to take place. These include producing, supplying, administering or using drugs. Secondly, and equally necessarily for a "possession" offence, the accused must show that he knows both the nature of the substance, and also that he knows he has it in his possession. Thus, if he does not know he has the drug in his possession, he is not guilty. However, if he does know he possesses a drug but is unsure of its precise nature, he will be guilty.

In the context of possession, the "container cases" have caused considerable difficulty. In *Salmon v HM Advocate; Moore v HM Advocate*,[39] Moore had been convicted of possession of "Ecstasy" with intent to supply under s 5(3), although he denied all knowledge of the existence of, or the nature of the contents of the plastic bag which contained the drugs. On appeal, it was held that if the charge was based on the possession of drugs in a container, then the Crown would succeed in securing a conviction if it could prove that the accused knew that he had possession of the container, and also knew that there was something in that container. Once that had been established, the accused would be deemed to be in possession of the drugs even though he did not know the nature of the contents. This fairly stringent approach requires the accused to be certain about the nature of the contents of any container or bag he has been given, but is mitigated by the effect of s 28(2) and (3). Under these provisions, the accused can prove, on the balance of probabilities, that he did not know, suspect or have reason to suspect that the contents were controlled drugs. Conversely, if he does know or suspect that the substance is an illegal narcotic, he has a defence under s 5(4) if he can show that he took the drug into his possession to prevent another from continuing to commit an offence in respect of that drug, so long as he took all reasonable steps as soon as possible either to destroy the drugs or to hand them in to the authorities.[40]

Further problems are raised when the accused is found to have a minute trace of a narcotic in, say, his pocket or a pipe. The question is whether this can amount to having possession of a drug. The issue used to be decided by reference to the amount found and whether or not it was a useable quantity. If not, there was no legally relevant possession.[41] This approach was rejected in *Keane v Gallacher*,[42] where the test expounded by the courts was whether the amount found was sufficiently large to allow it to be identified. This is considerably more restrictive. This makes it hard for someone to abandon use of a drug, as they may retain

---

[38] See *Allan v Milne* 1974 SLT (N) 76 where all the occupants knew about, and had access to the drugs.
[39] 1999 SLT 169.
[40] Section 5(4).
[41] See the English case of *Bocking v Roberts* [1974] QB 307.
[42] 1980 JC 77.

microscopic traces in equipment or a pocket long after they have renounced use of the substance. A particular problem arises when the accused has forgotten that he possesses a drug. In *Gill* v *Lockhart*[43] the accused had placed some cannabis in his golf bag years previously and had forgotten that it was still there. However, this does not operate as a defence, as possession does not require constant awareness of the object.

Possession with intent to supply is charged as a separate offence. The accused's conduct will be relevant if he has behaved in a way which shows that he has possession of drugs and will supply them to others. Likewise, the quantity of drugs which he holds may also be sufficient to infer an intent to supply, if that quantity far exceeds what one would expect for personal use. Convictions for supplying drugs can also be based on the existence of the requisite equipment for dealing in drugs, such as scales, bags or foil wraps.

OFFENSIVE WEAPONS

The Criminal Law (Consolidation) (Scotland) Act 1995, s 47 criminalises the carrying of offensive weapons or firearms in public. An offensive weapon is defined as one made or used in order to cause injury, or one which has been adapted from its lawful state in order to do so. It also covers weapons which can equally have an innocent purpose such as hunting or fishing knives, but which the accused intends to use to cause injury. If the weapon in question is one made or used to cause injury, or designed or adapted to cause injury, the prosecution simply need to prove that the accused was carrying such a weapon, and the accused bears the onus of proving that one of the two available defences applies to him. He can argue either that he had lawful authority to carry the weapon, or that he had a reasonable excuse.[44] If the weapon has an innocent purpose, it is for the prosecution to show that the accused's purpose was nefarious. Section 49 creates an offence of having an article with a bladed point in a public place. Pocket knives with blades under 3 inches are excluded. Again, the accused can raise good reason or lawful excuse as a defence, or that he had the article on him for work, religious reasons or as part of a national costume. Section 49A extends this offence to cover having such an article on school premises, and s 49C applies the same principles to a prison setting.

CRIME AND DISORDER ACT 1998

The Crime and Disorder Act 1998 allows for the imposition of orders which prevent socially undesirable conduct and provides alternative sanctions in areas such as drug offences and racially aggravated offences.

---

[43] 1987 SCCR 599.
[44] See *Frame* v *Kennedy* 2008 JC 317 where the accused had a justifiable reason for carrying police batons as they were part of his fairly realistic costume as a male stripper.

Racially aggravated offences

Section 33 of the 1998 Act amends the Criminal Law (Consolidation) (Scotland) Act 1995 by creating a new offence of racial harassment.[45] The accused must have pursued a racially aggravated course of conduct which amounts to harassment and have done so intentionally or in circumstances where a reasonable person would think it amounted to harassment. He will also be guilty if he acts in a manner which is racially aggravated and causes or intends to cause alarm or distress. The prosecution needs to show that, during or immediately before or after the incident, the offender showed malice and ill-will because of the victim's membership of a racial group or was engaged in a course of conduct which was motivated or partly motivated by that same malice or ill-will. A "racial group" is group defined by reference to race, colour, nationality or ethnic origins.

Sexual or violent offenders

The 1998 Act provides for extended sentences in cases of sexual or violent offences.[46] The section is limited to cases where the accused has either been convicted on indictment of a sexual offence deserving of imprisonment or has been convicted of a violent offence and the court intends to pass sentence exceeding 4 years. The court may, in certain circumstances, pass an extended sentence. An extended sentence is defined as the aggregate of the custodial sentence which would have been imposed anyway, and a further extension period where the offender is subject to a licence for as long as the court feels is necessary. The extension period is set at no more than 10 years for a sexual offence, and 5 years for a violent offence.

Drug treatment and testing orders (DTTOs)

DTTOs are now available under s 234B of the Criminal Procedure (Scotland) Act 1995.[47] The subject must be over 16, and have been convicted of an offence with a discretionary sentence. The DTTO will run for a specified period between 6 months and 3 years. However, the court must have received a report from the local authority that the offender is dependent on, or likely to misuse, drugs; needs and can respond to treatment; and is suitable for this type of order. The offender will be required to comply with some form of treatment and testing schedule. If he fails to comply with the order, s 93 of the 1998 Act entitles the court to vary or revoke the DTTO. If it is revoked, the court is then entitled to sentence the offender as they would have done had the order not been used initially.

---

[45] Under s 50A.

[46] Under s 86, inserting s 210A into the Criminal Procedure (Scotland) Act 1995.

[47] Inserted by s 89 of the Crime and Disorder Act 1998.

Antisocial Behaviour etc (Scotland) Act 2004

The 2004 Act repealed the measures originally introduced in this respect by the Crime and Disorder Act 1998 and instead set out provisions to deal with antisocial behaviour, including a revised version of the antisocial behaviour order (ASBO) and provisions relating to dispersal of groups and closure of premises.

ASBOs are dealt with in s 4 and are available on application to the sheriff by the local authority or registered social landlord. The application is made in the sheriff court sitting as a civil court, and ASBOs are civil orders requiring the subject of them to refrain from certain types of conduct for specified periods of time. However, if an ASBO is breached, then the breach of that order becomes a criminal matter. ASBOs apply where an individual over 12 years of age has acted in an antisocial manner towards a "relevant person" (that is, someone living within the local authority's area, or in or near housing provided by a registered social landlord). The ASBO must be necessary to protect the relevant person from further antisocial behaviour.[48] "Antisocial behaviour" is defined in s 143 in a way which is reminiscent of breach of the peace. It requires that the conduct in question is likely to cause alarm or distress to at least one person from another household. Once issued, the ASBO can be varied or revoked on the application of either the original applicant or the subject of the order.[49] However, given the nature of the conduct complained of in these cases, there is a recognised need for the law to be able to respond quickly to an application for a ASBO. It may well be that the local authority is faced with complaints from residents about extremely disruptive behaviour, which it would quite reasonably wish to have remedied as soon as possible. Under s 7, the court is therefore able to issue an interim ASBO. An application must have been made for an ASBO under s 4, but if the sheriff is convinced that the person whose conduct is complained of is over the age of 12, and that there is at least a *prima facie* case to be made that their conduct is antisocial, then he can grant an interim order if such an order is necessary to protect the other residents. Section 7(4) prevents the subject of the order from doing anything specified in it, while the case for imposing a "full" ASBO is being heard. Thus, fairly immediate relief can be given to those subjected to the alleged antisocial behaviour, while the case is in progress. If it is subsequently determined that the conduct was not antisocial, then the interim ASBO lapses. If it is found that there was sufficient antisocial behaviour to justify an order, then the interim ASBO lapses in favour of the "full" ASBO. Section 9 sets out the consequences of failing to adhere to an ASBO or interim ASBO. If the subject of the order carries out any activity specified in the order, without a reasonable excuse for doing so, then he will be liable to up to 6 months' imprisonment, a fine or both (summary cases); or up to 5 years' imprisonment, a fine or both (indictment cases). However, under s 9(3), if the conduct carried out in breach of the order itself

---

[48] Antisocial Behaviour etc (Scotland) Act 2004, s 4(2)(c).
[49] *Ibid*, s 5.

amounts to a separate criminal offence, and the subject of the order is charged with that offence, then they cannot also be charged with being in breach of their ASBO. Sentencing for that separate offence will, however, take account of the fact that it was done while subject to an ASBO.

Section 19 then moves on to deal with other measures designed to tackle antisocial behaviour. It covers the dispersal of groups where the police have reason to believe that the conduct or presence, in a particular location, of a group with two or more members has caused alarm or distress to the public. The section requires that the members of the group have behaved in an antisocial way which is significant, persistent and a serious problem in that locality. A senior police officer may then authorise constables in the area to disperse those groups, provided that the authorisation notice has been publicised. Section 21 requires the police constable who is considering using the power of dispersal to determine whether the alarm or distress caused by the group would be lessened if they were moved on. The section also allows for those who have been dispersed to be forbidden from returning to that locality for up to 24 hours, so long as they do not also live there. Further, if premises are used for antisocial purposes, then those premises can be made subject to a closure notice.[50] However, while dispersal and closure measures can be seen to have a potential immediate impact, they hardly represent a long-term solution as they merely serve to move those causing antisocial behaviour to other areas and/or premises.

MOBBING

Mobbing requires that a group of persons act together in a violent or intimidating fashion for a common illegal purpose. In this context, illegality refers to their joint activity and not to their aim. Thus, it would be illegal for a group to act in a violent and intimidating way, even if their aim was lawful. A definition is to be found in *Hancock v HM Advocate*:

> A mob is essentially a combination of persons, sharing a common criminal purpose, which proceeds to carry out that purpose by violence, or by intimidation by sheer force of numbers. A mob has, therefore, a will and purpose of its own, and all members of the mob contribute by their presence to the achievement of the mob's purpose.[51]

This clearly establishes art and part liability on members of the mob for its activities. Mobbing will often involve a breach of the peace, as the type of conduct required for mobbing will in many cases cause alarm and fear to the lieges. However, the two crimes are distinct and the accused can be charged with both.[52]

---

[50] Antisocial Behaviour etc (Scotland) Act 2004, ss 26 and 27.
[51] 1981 JC 74 at p 86
[52] *Idem.*

SUMMARY OF MAIN POINTS

Breach of the peace

- earlier cases establish a test of conduct likely to cause alarm, fear, annoyance, etc to the public
- *Smith* v *Donnelly* – conduct serious enough to alarm ordinary people *and* threaten to cause serious disturbance to the community
- breadth of definition potentially problematic with reference to Art 6(3)(a) ECHR
- huge range of conduct covered: peeping tom, begging, following wife
- no defence that no actual alarm caused
- also irrelevant that conduct aimed at preventing another breach of the peace

Misuse of drugs

- "production" (s 4) includes artificial laboratory production and natural cultivation
- "supply" refers to physical transfer of drugs
- also covers impossible attempts, where attempt to supply something which is not in fact a drug
- importing and being knowingly concerned in importation
- accused must know substance is an illegal drug, so ignorance is a defence
- possession requires physical control over drugs, but requires more than mere knowledge that, eg, fellow tenant has drugs in the premises
- must know nature of substance
- quantity must be sufficient to be identifiable
- possession does not require constant awareness so remain guilty even if forgotten about the drugs
- possession with intent to supply will be charged separately where conduct or amount involved suggests that acting as supplier

Offensive weapons

- something commonly used to cause injury or something adapted to do so
- defences – lawful authority or reasonable excuse
- offence to carry knife/blade in public which is more than 3 inches, unless it is a penknife or either of the two defences above applies

Crime and Disorder Act 1998

- racially aggravated offences dealt with under new offence of racial harassment

- requires intentional, racially aggravated course of conduct which amounts to harassment
- sexual or violent offenders can be subject to extended sentences
- drug treatment and testing orders apply to offenders over 16 serving a discretionary sentence where local authority reports that defender is dependent on or likely to misuse drugs and is a suitable candidate for treatment under such an order
- if fails to comply, court imposes original sentence

Antisocial behaviour
- ASBOs (s 4): civil order sought from sheriff by local authority etc
- where have evidence of antisocial conduct and that order needed to protect others
- becomes criminal when breach the ASBO conditions
- interim ASBOs (s 7)
- cannot simultaneously charge with breach of ASBO and the offence committed by virtue of that breach (s 9)

BREACH OF THE PEACE

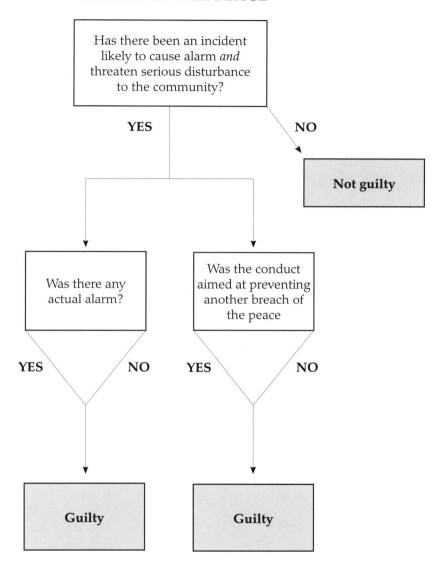

Note: Use of the word "guilty" is a convenient shorthand. There may be other issues to consider before the accused is convicted.

MISUSE OF DRUGS – PRODUCTION

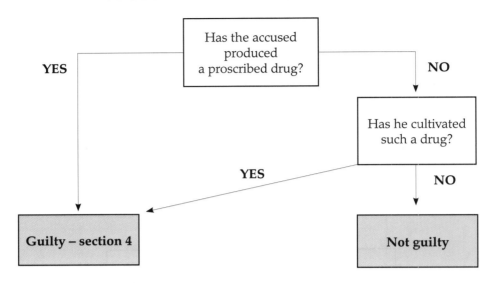

Note: Use of the word "guilty" is a convenient shorthand. There may be other issues to consider before the accused is convicted.

MISUSE OF DRUGS – POSSESSION

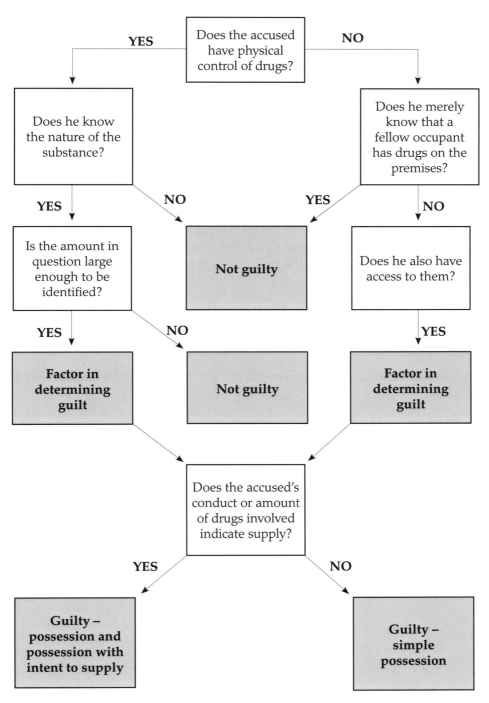

Note: Use of the word "guilty" is a convenient shorthand. There may be other issues to consider before the accused is convicted.

SELF-ASSESSMENT QUESTIONS (see Appendix for answers)

1   X is stopped in a routine random search at Heathrow Airport, having flown in from Bangkok. He is found to have a well-wrapped package in his suitcase. This turns out to be flour, although he was told it was heroin and asked to smuggle it into the UK. Would he be guilty of a s 170(2) offence?

2   X and his friend, Y, a notorious criminal, see policemen coming towards them. Before they get close, Y slips X a packet of a white substance and asks X to put it in his pocket. The police know Y well as a drug dealer and, suspecting that he might be carrying drugs, they stop and search him. They have no reason to suspect X, who stands aside and watches, but is not searched. The police then leave, having found nothing. X gives Y the packet back. Later that night, the police again stop both X and Y, and this time suspect that X may be part of Y's operation and search them both. The packet is found in Y's pocket and is identified as cocaine. However, the packet had leaked a minute quantity of the white substance into X's pocket which the police notice and take for testing. How many convictions will the police secure and why?

Further questions

1   Is the definition of breach of the peace too broad to be justifiable as part of Scots criminal law?

2   What would amount to a "reasonable excuse" for carrying an offensive weapon in public?

Further reading

Jones and Christie, *Criminal Law* (4th edn), pp 358–371.

McCall Smith and Sheldon, *Scots Criminal Law* (2nd edn), pp 210–221.

Gordon, *Criminal Law* (3rd edn), vol 2, pp 559–690.

Oliver, "Prosecutorial precision and the European Convention on Human Rights" 2000 *Scottish Law and Practice Quarterly* 111.

12 OFFENCES AGAINST PROPERTY

THEFT

A conviction for theft requires the wrongful taking of someone else's property with the intention permanently or, more recently, temporarily to deprive them of that property. Thus, it consists of an unauthorised infringement of the owner's rights over the property, no matter how long the duration. The types of property that can be stolen include both corporeal and moveable. This requirement comes from the traditional approach to theft which required the actual, physical removal of the property. Thus, corporeal property has a tangible, physical presence, and specifically excludes what is known as incorporeal property such as data and rights belonging to an individual.[1] Therefore, the accused can be charged with the theft of physical file containing data, but not of the information contained within it. However, it is possible to charge the accused with theft of electricity if, for example, he taps into the National Grid or into another individual's supply. The property must also be moveable, in other words, capable of being moved.[2] This means that land and buildings permanently attached to the land cannot be stolen. However, for the purposes of the law of theft, crops and anything else which is physically severable from the land are classed as moveable and so to dig them up, or otherwise remove them, is theft. The property must also belong to someone else and it is impossible to steal either one's own property or ownerless things such as wild animals. Wild, unconfined animals are classed as *ferae naturae* and are therefore *res nullius*.[3] There is thus no charge of theft if an individual catches such wild animals, unless they have already been confined in some way. In *Valentine* v *Kennedy*,[4] trout had been bought from a fish farm and transferred into a reservoir so that the owner could authorise and profit from permit fishing. Some of the trout escaped from the reservoir and were caught by several accused without any permit. However, despite the fact that the fish had escaped, they had not reverted to the status of wild and ownerless animals. Property in them still belonged to their owner and thus the accused

---

[1] Incorporeal property is instead protected by the appropriate area of intellectual property law.
[2] "Moveable" here is not used in the sense of the moveable/heritable distinction in property law.
[3] That is, something which has not previously belonged to anyone.
[4] 1985 SCCR 88.

were correctly charged with theft. Abandoned property reverts to the ownership of the Crown and can therefore be stolen. There remains an ancient common law crime of stealing children under the age of puberty, which is referred to as *plagium*. In *Hamilton* v *Mooney*,[5] a father had taken his legitimate child from his wife, who held an interim custody order, and was convicted of the theft of that child. In *Hamilton* v *Wilson*,[6] it was held that *plagium* amounts to the deliberate taking of a child from a party who has a parental right of custody at the relevant time. It is also possible to be convicted of removing human remains from their grave, but this is charged as violation of sepulchres rather than a form of theft.[7]

The cornerstone of the modern law on theft is the concept of appropriation. Historically, the law was more concerned with the unauthorised taking of another's property, but it is now clear that appropriation is the key. "Appropriation" denotes that the owner is unlawfully deprived of all or some of his rights in relation to that property, and that it is put to the thief's personal use. Thus, the owner will incur a loss of some sort. This can arise when the thief deprives the owner of his use and enjoyment of the property, or when the thief already has some degree of authorised control over the property, but abuses that to exercise control as if he were owner.[8] The law requires evidence of a deliberate and unauthorised deprivation of the rights associated with ownership.[9] Acts become theft at the point when the intention to carry out this appropriation is formed. The classic case here is *Herron* v *Diack and Newlands*.[10] The two accused, who were funeral directors, were charged with the theft of a steel coffin. They had taken the body out of the steel coffin and placed it in a chipboard version for burial at sea but were thwarted in their plans as the chipboard coffin took some time to sink. Almost immediately, the lid came away and floated to the surface and the next day, the rest of the coffin and the body were trawled to the surface by a prawn boat, re-committed, trawled up again by a second boat and, finally, returned to land. The accused then instructed that the body be returned to its original coffin for a further attempt at committal. The accused were charged, and Diack was convicted of theft because, at the point when they had taken the body out of the steel casket, they had formed what is known as "theftuous intent". From that point, they had intended permanently to deprive the owner of the coffin and appropriate it to their own use. This applied regardless of the fact that they had then returned the coffin to its rightful use as, by that time, they had already committed both the *actus reus* and the *mens rea* of theft.

---

[5] 1990 SLT (Sh Ct) 105.
[6] 1994 SLT 431.
[7] See *Dewar* v *HM Advocate* 1945 SLT 114 at 115.
[8] On this, see Gordon, vol 2, pp 5–6.
[9] *Ibid*, p 13.
[10] 1973 SLT (Sh Ct) 27.

The *actus reus* of theft

The acts required of the accused can be categorised under one of three headings – taking; finding; and appropriating. In order to commit theft by taking, the accused must actually take the property and move it away from its lawful location. This is referred to as *amotio*. The distance required here is a question of circumstances. What is essential is that the property is taken away from its proper place by the thief, and so unlawfully removing something from its shelf or container would amount to *amotio*. Similarly, removing the item from a room or moving to a point in the room from which it could more easily be stolen, such as a window ledge, would also found a charge of theft by taking. Theft by appropriation can still be committed by the person who is in lawful possession of the property but is not the owner. In *Dewar* v *HM Advocate*,[11] the manager of a crematorium was held guilty of theft by appropriating coffin lids for his own use. He argued that, once the coffins came under his control, they had been abandoned by the previous owners and therefore were his to do with as he wished. This argument was rejected, as the coffins were sent to him for one purpose only: destruction. By appropriating the lids for his own use, he was thereby stealing them even though there was no physical removal of the property. However, it would appear that theft by appropriation can also cover cases where the accused has simply denied the owner the use of his property. In *Black and Penrice* v *Carmichael*,[12] the use of a wheel clamp by a private security firm was held to amount to theft. The accused were employees who had fitted the clamp and then demanded a fee for removing it. The car had not been moved and the accused were not trying to appropriate it for their own use, but nonetheless their convictions for theft were upheld on appeal. The High Court justified this by viewing the essence of the *actus reus* of theft as removing control and possession of property from its owner. "It seems to me that the act of depriving the motorist of the use of his motor car by detaining it against his will can accurately be described as stealing something from him."[13] It was further noted by Lord Hope that, in holding this, he had not extended the definition of theft since, although it was clearly not theft by taking (there being no *amotio*), it was a case of theft by appropriation. Although the two accused had not personally benefited from their appropriation of the vehicle (they had not taken it away for their own use), the relevant point was the loss suffered by the owner, rather than the gain by the accused.[14] Thus, deliberately detaining the car and depriving the owner of its use was sufficient to amount to appropriation.

Theft by finding is, in reality, a form of theft by appropriation. If one was to come across lost property in the street, pick it up and take it home, it would not amount to theft at that point in time, as there could still be an intention on the part of the

---

[11] 1945 JC 5.
[12] 1992 SLT 897.
[13] *Ibid* at 902.
[14] *Idem*, citing both Hume and Gordon.

finder to return the property to the owner. Once a reasonable time had elapsed, it can no longer be said that the finder possesses the property with the intention of returning it to its true owner. Therefore, at this point, after the elapse of a reasonable time, the finder's conduct can be said to amount to theft. This is illustrated by *MacMillan* v *Lowe*,[15] where the accused had found a cheque book and bank card in a phone box. He was stopped and searched some 4 hours later, by which point he had still made no attempt to return them to either the owner (whose name was on the documents) or the relevant bank, and, further, he had tried to hide them from the police when he was being searched. This behaviour led the court to find him guilty of theft, as he had found property and kept it well beyond the time period during which it would be reasonable to expect him to return it.[16]

Consent and theft

In many areas of criminal law, such as assault and murder, the consent of the victim is wholly irrelevant. In theft cases the owner's consent is a defence, as theft requires appropriation *without* such consent. However, to avoid a charge of theft, the consent must be of a specific type: it must be to transfer ownership of the property. If the owner were simply to transfer mere possession of the property, the possessor could still be liable for theft if he appropriated the property to his own use.[17]

Mens rea of theft

Previously, the prosecution had to establish that the accused had the intention *permanently* to deprive the victim of his property. This is emphasised by the decision in *Herron* v *Best*,[18] where the accused had repaired a van and found subsequently that the cheque covering those repairs had been dishonoured. He located the van in question and drove it away, intending to return it when payment had been made in full. He was charged with theft but it was held that, as he had only a conditional intention to appropriate the van, he could not be convicted. However, although this is a serviceable general definition and would previously have been entirely accurate, it must now be read in conjunction with *Milne* v *Tudhope*[19] which established the rule that, in exceptional circumstances, temporary appropriation would suffice. The case related to a dispute between an owner and a builder about remedial work which was to be carried out following defects in the initial and contracted construction work. The builder, Milne, refused to do further work unless he was paid for the

---

[15] 1991 SCCR 113.

[16] The finder of lost property is also subject to statutory provisions under the Civic Government (Scotland) Act 1982, s 67 *et seq.*

[17] Gordon, vol 2, pp 45–48.

[18] 1976 SLT (Sh Ct) 80.

[19] 1981 JC 53.

contracted work and, when the owner refused to pay him any more money until the defects were remedied, Milne removed a quantity of materials from the house. He then told the owner that if he was allowed to do the extra work and receive payment for it, the materials would be returned.[20] Milne was then convicted of theft on the basis of temporary appropriation of another's property. The sheriff held that clandestine taking of another's property for a nefarious purpose amounted to theft, even if the taker's intention was only to remove the property temporarily. The High Court upheld this, in effect denying that permanent appropriation was an absolute necessity for conviction in all cases. It was noted that the property must be taken secretly so far as the owner was concerned, but that, so long as the owner was not aware that the property had been taken, it did not matter if other people had observed the activities.[21] In Milne's case, it was further clear that the goods had been taken for a nefarious purpose, namely that they were being held in order to force payment of extra money. However, it is also clear that this definition of theft should apply only in exceptional cases where the appropriation forms part of some other nefarious purpose, such as, in this case, extortion. It was also argued for Milne that, following *Herron*, there was here a conditional intention to return the items after full payment had been made and that therefore the *mens rea* of theft had not been made out fully, but this argument was unsuccessful.

In *Kidston* v *Annan*,[22] the accused had collected a television set in order to give an estimate for repairs, and had then proceeded to carry out the repairs, to the value of £12.65, without the owner's instruction. He then held the set to ransom, demanding payment of the outstanding sum. He was convicted of theft, following the temporary appropriation argument from *Milne* and appealed. The appeal was refused on the basis that the case in hand was on all fours with *Milne* and that therefore the *mens rea* of theft was present. The issue of temporary appropriation was examined again in *Fowler* v *O'Brien*.[23] Here, the accused had taken a bicycle without permission and had been quite open about doing so. Further, he had given no indication of when, or if, he would return it. He was convicted of theft on the basis of temporary appropriation, and appealed to the High Court. On appeal it was held that, although there was clearly no evidence of permanent appropriation, neither was it a case of temporary appropriation since it was clear that the appellant had given no indication of when, if ever, he would return the bicycle. This sets *Fowler* apart from cases such as *Milne* and *Kidston* which both involved holding the property to ransom in order to force a particular action from the owner. The High Court in *Fowler* held that, more strictly, it could be described as a case of indefinite deprivation of property, and so there was no need to prove the clandestine, nefarious purpose referred to in *Milne*, or any exceptional circumstances, and the

---

[20] In effect, he held the property to ransom.
[21] 1981 JC 53 at 57.
[22] 1984 SLT 279.
[23] 1994 SCCR 112.

appeal was refused. Thus, the courts have establish several variants of the *mens rea* of theft: an intention permanently to deprive, an intention temporarily to deprive and, as a separate issue, an intention indefinitely to deprive.

AGGRAVATED THEFT

Aggravated theft can be committed in a number of ways, all of which show a more serious act on the part of the accused. Housebreaking, forcing entry and opening lockfast places all amount to aggravations of a charge of theft, which will be reflected in sentencing. As regards housebreaking, it amounts to an offence if teamed with an intent to steal property from the premises. It has been held, in *HM Advocate* v *Forbes*,[24] that there is no such crime as "housebreaking with intent to commit rape", or indeed with intent to commit any other offence. The intention following on from the housebreaking must be to commit theft, and the theft must be shown to have taken place after the housebreaking. Thus, as noted in Gordon, the accused who enters a building, steals property and then breaks out does not commit theft by housebreaking.[25] "Housebreaking" is something of a misnomer in this context, as it applies equally to houses and any other roofed building. It is also necessary to show that the thief actually broke into the premises in order to carry out the theft. If he did not need to break in (for example, if the door was not locked or barred in some way), then he should be charged with theft only. However, if he used a skeleton, stolen or found key to gain otherwise unauthorised entry, that would amount to housebreaking. It is further the case that the thief need not wholly enter the premises in order to carry out theft by housebreaking. He may simply reach into the premises through, for example, an open window and reach in to steal property by pulling it through the opening.[26]

Most cases involving convictions for opening lockfast places centre on thefts from motor vehicles, but the charge applies equally to the opening of anything which is locked and is not a building.[27] However, it is proper to charge the accused with opening lockfast places if he has forced entry to a locked room within a house. It also includes, for example, the theft of money by opening the cash box in public phone boxes,[28] or opening locked drawers, a safe or anything else secured by a lock. In *Gillan* v *Vannet*,[29] the court made it clear that there is an important distinction to be drawn between opening lockfast places and attempted theft. In this case, the accused had been found guilty of forcing open a lockfast place, namely a car, with the intention of stealing it, and, in consequence, had been disqualified from driving.

---

[24] 1994 SLT 861.
[25] Gordon, vol 2, p 57.
[26] See *O'Neill* 1845 2 Broun 394.
[27] This is covered by housebreaking.
[28] *Maxwell* v *HM Advocate* 1999 GWD 13-614.
[29] 1997 SLT 1299.

It was held on appeal[30] that a conviction for attempted theft of a car required that the court endorse the accused's licence, and allowed the court, at its discretion, to disqualify him as a driver. However, as opening a lockfast place was a lesser offence than attempted theft, neither of these disposals was appropriate as they were both dependent on a charge of attempted theft.

It is possible to infer an intention to commit an aggravated theft. Under s 57(1) of the Civic Government (Scotland) Act 1982, anyone who is found in or on any premises, vessel or vehicle without lawful authority and in circumstances which point to an intention to steal, is guilty of an offence and liable to a fine, imprisonment or both. However, it must be possible to draw an inference that the accused was unlawfully on the premises with the intent to *steal* and this inference will often be drawn from factors such as the accused's behaviour or the time of day. In *Glancy* v *Lees*,[31] the accused had been seen by the police and had run into a garden to hide. He was convicted under s 57(1) and appealed on the ground that it was not possible to draw the inference that he was there to steal. The High Court allowed his appeal, stating that the charge required the Crown to show that it could be inferred from his presence and the circumstances that he was intent on theft. It was clear in this case that he was in the garden to hide from the police. This hardly suggested that he was innocent in all respects, but it certainly did not give the Crown sufficient evidence to draw the required inference of theftuous intent.

ROBBERY

Robbery and theft are related, but distinct, crimes. As a charge against the accused, robbery is competent only once the accused has already committed a theft in a particular way. Thus, he must first be shown to have met all the requisites for a charge of theft. In order to be charged with robbery, the accused must then also be shown to have committed a theft by means of actual violence against the person of the victim, or by threats of immediate violence. In *O'Neill* v *HM Advocate*[32] it was noted that robbery requires violence, but does not actually require that there be an assault. This has been upheld in the case of *MacKay* v *HM Advocate*,[33] where the court held that conviction for robbery was possible on the basis of theft committed either by violence or by intimidation. In *Harrison* v *Jessop*,[34] personal violence was established on the basis of a threat to detain the victims until arrears of rent were collected. It seems, however, that relatively little "violence" will be sufficient to satisfy the personal violence requirement of a charge of robbery. In *Cromar* v *HM Advocate*,[35] the accused had come up behind the victim, grabbed a plastic bag he

---

[30] Following *McLeod* v *Mason* 1981 SCCR 78.
[31] 1999 SCCR 726.
[32] 1934 SLT 432.
[33] 1998 SLT 751.
[34] 1992 SLT 465.
[35] 1987 SCCR 635.

was holding and pulled it until the handles broke, allowing him to run off with it. This was held, refusing the appeal, to be sufficient to amount to robbery rather than simple theft. If there has been a distinct assault prior to commission of the robbery, then the accused can be charged with robbery, aggravated by the presence of an assault.

RESET OF STOLEN GOODS

The essence of the crime of reset is found in the knowing receipt, by someone other than the thief, of stolen goods. Section 51 of the Criminal Law (Consolidation) (Scotland) Act 1995 extends the crime of reset so that it now covers property taken by theft, and also property taken by means of embezzlement and fraud. Thus, the resetter must first take possession of the goods in question. This is what is commonly referred to as "handling" stolen goods. However, it will also be sufficient if the goods are delivered and taken into the accused's house, as these will also be "possessed" by the accused for these purposes. It does not matter if the accused takes possession of these goods fleetingly or for a longer period of time. It does not matter, therefore, if the accused's possession of the goods is limited to taking them for a few minutes before passing them on to someone else, or giving them back to the thief. It is not a prerequisite that the accused receive the goods from the actual thief, so long as he knows that the goods are stolen. Equally, it is not necessary for the resetter to have actual possession of the stolen goods if he knows of their theft and retention from their owner. In *Girdwood* v *Houston*,[36] the accused denied all knowledge of the theft of the goods but later admitted that he knew they had been stolen, by whom, and where they were hidden. On appeal, his conviction was upheld, as reset does not require that the accused be in actual possession of the goods so long as he is privy to their retention.

Secondly, the accused must know that the goods are stolen: he must have guilty knowledge.[37] It is not sufficient that he is merely suspicious of their heritage. However, the accused can be convicted on the basis of wilful blindness; if the circumstances are such that he should have known the goods were stolen, but he turns a "blind eye" to this. In *Friel* v *Docherty*,[38] the accused had obtained HGV certificates for six vehicles from a travelling person who took the vehicles away for repairs and to obtain the necessary certificate. All the vehicles were returned with stolen HGV certificates, and the accused's conviction was upheld on appeal as he must either have known or at least accepted the possibility that

---

[36] 1989 SCCR 578.

[37] This is clear from *Gillespie* v *Brown* 1999 SLT 1115, where the accused was convicted of reset due to his presence in a car which had obviously been stolen. The covering over the steering column and the dashboard were damaged to such an extent that it must have been obvious to the accused that the car had been stolen.

[38] 1990 SCCR 351.

the certificates had not been properly issued. In *Boyd* v *Vannet*,[39] a conviction for reset was upheld on appeal, given evidence of the appellant's clear knowledge that the car was stolen. He was in possession of a car which he had helped to disguise, and had lied to the police about having the car resprayed. He also recounted an unbelievable story to explain his possession of the stolen vehicle. If the circumstances of the accused's possession of the goods are suspicious (what is termed "criminative circumstances") then his inability to enter an innocent explanation may be sufficient evidence of his guilt. In *Nisbet* v *HM Advocate*,[40] the accused gave an "awkward" explanation for his possession of the stolen goods (that he had bought a cement mixer and heater from a stranger who knocked at his door). The implausibility of this explanation was sufficient to infer that he knew the goods were stolen. Likewise, an explanation for possession of goods which was viewed as "incredible" contributed to an inference of guilty knowledge in *Murray* v *O'Brien*.[41] However, in *Shannon* v *HM Advocate*,[42] the accused was in possession of a stolen firearm which had also been shortened illegally. He kept the gun hidden in his house and disappeared when the police came to search the premises. His actings were held to be sufficient to infer that he knew he was in possession of an illegally shortened firearm, but not sufficient to infer that he also knew it was stolen. As a further aspect of the *mens rea* of the offence, it is necessary that the accused takes possession of goods which he knows to be stolen, with the intent of concealing and withholding those goods from the true owner. There is no requirement that he keeps the goods for himself, so long as it can be established that he intends to keep them from the true owner.[43]

There is, however, one exception whereby a wife who receives stolen property from her husband, and retains it simply to protect him, is not guilty of reset. However, the goods must be brought into the house by the husband and thus, in *Smith* v *Watson*,[44] the wife could not benefit from the spousal exception. She had received and kept money from a robbery committed by her husband. The money had been posted through her letterbox by someone else while her husband was serving his sentence for the robbery and had therefore not been brought into the house by the husband. Further, the doctrine requires that the wife keep the stolen goods in order to protect her husband from detection and punishment for the theft. As he was already in prison, it was clear that she had some other reason for keeping the money. It should be noted that the exception protects only the wife of a thief, and cannot be used by the husband whose wife has brought stolen goods into the matrimonial home.

---

[39] 2000 GWD 26-974.
[40] 1983 SCCR 13. See also *Forbes* v *HM Advocate* 1995 SLT 627 and, allowing the appeal, *Hamilton* v *Friel* 1994 SCCR 748.
[41] 1993 SCCR 90.
[42] 1985 SCCR 14.
[43] Gordon, vol 2, p 239.
[44] 1982 JC 34.

FRAUD

Fraud exists as a statutory offence[45] and as a common law crime in Scotland, requiring dishonesty which can be proved to have caused some practical result. This was clearly demonstrated by the High Court in *MacDonald* v *HM Advocate*.[46] In this case the sheriff had instructed the jury members that they should look for dishonest conduct leading to a practical result and he made reference to "cheating" and "fiddling". Crucially, he did not make any reference to the need for a false pretence and thus the High Court quashed the accused's conviction. The jury would not, in the appeal court's view, have been aware that fraud required a false pretence to be made and, further, it would not have been aware that the false pretence would need to be corroborated (that is, supported by two independent pieces of evidence). Thus, the original conviction rested on a misdirection.

There are three prerequisites for a conviction for fraud: a false pretence; some result which is prejudicial to the victim; and a causal connection between the two The false pretence required for fraud can take the form of either a misleading statement, or an act which creates the relevant false impression in the mind of the victim (whether this false impression relates to the identity of a person, the nature of goods, or is of some other type). This conduct would amount to an implied representation. Likewise, fraud can be committed by remaining silent about specific facts about which the accused has knowledge, where he is under a duty to disclose certain information and fails to do so. Thus, the accused can be found guilty by omission. If the victim was not induced to act as he did because of the false pretence (if he did so for some other unrelated reason, or would have done so anyway), then there is no basis for a fraud charge. So long as some false pretence has been made relating to any relevant matter, and that false pretence can be shown to have led to a prejudicial result for the victim, that will be sufficient for conviction. Thus, it is not necessary to prove that any individual was actually deceived by the pretence. In *McKenzie* v *HM Advocate*,[47] the accused had made false representations to solicitors, inducing them to raise an unfounded claim against a company. The scheme did not succeed and therefore the charge was one of attempted fraud, but the High Court on appeal affirmed that, since a false pretence had been made, which had led to the lodging of an unfounded claim against the company, there was sufficient evidence to charge the accused with attempted fraud. The accused must make the false pretence knowing that it is false and intending that the result should follow. Thus, in *MacKenzie* v *Skeen*,[48] a charge of fraud failed as it could not be proved that the accused had intended to defraud his employer. The result envisaged in a charge of fraud is often that the accused has benefited by obtaining some property

---

[45] Statutory frauds include offences under the trade descriptions legislation and weights and measures offences.
[46] 1996 SLT 723.
[47] 1988 SLT 487.
[48] 1971 JC 43.

belonging to the victim. However, it is clear that this is not a requirement of the charge. In *Adcock* v *Achibald*,[49] the accused had marked a hutch of coal dug by another miner as one dug by himself. Clearly, he had made a false pretence with the intention of defrauding his employers, although the result did not cause any loss or gain. Both the accused and the victim received the miners' minimum wage that week, as neither had dug enough coal to merit any bonus. Thus, there was no loss to the employers or the other miner, or gain to the accused. However, it was stated that any definite practical result would be sufficient, regardless of whether the accused had gained anything, or the victim suffered any loss, and thus the accused's conviction was upheld.

FORGERY

Forgery *per se* is not a crime.[50] For the accused to be convicted of forgery, it must first be shown that he has forged a document, which can be established by evidence of a forged signature or by evidence that material parts of the document have been altered. Thus, the signature at the foot of the document may be a forgery, or the signature may be genuine and the forgery consists of the addition of a document which is appended above the genuine signature. Secondly, it must be shown that the accused has intentionally "uttered" that document (displayed, presented or placed it outwith his control) as though it were genuine, with the intention of deceiving its recipient while knowing that it is false. The uttered document must also be to the prejudice, or potential prejudice, of the recipient, as was made clear in *MacDonald* v *Tudhope*.[51] It does not matter whether the document was forged by the person uttering it, or by someone else.

EMBEZZLEMENT AND EXTORTION

In *HM Advocate* v *Scott*,[52] Lord Young identified the distinction between theft and embezzlement. In cases of theft, the property has been stolen by being wrongfully removed from the possession of the owner or lawful possessor. However, in embezzlement, the property has been handed over by the real owner to the embezzler, who has already achieved lawful possession of the property on behalf of the true owner, often with a mandate to deal with the property in some specified way. Although cases arise in many areas, common examples involve those who administer goods or funds for others and include accountants, stockbrokers and solicitors. Monies will be received from, for example, from the buyer of a house and will initially be held by the seller's solicitor in a client account. Embezzlement will

---

[49] 1925 JC 58.
[50] *Barr* v *HM Advocate* 1927 JC 51.
[51] 1984 SLT 23.
[52] (1879) 4 Coup 227.

take place when the solicitor dishonestly appropriates that property to himself. Thus, theft and embezzlement share the common factor of appropriation, but differ with regard to the location of the property so appropriated. Therefore, in *Allenby* v *HM Advocate*,[53] a prosecution for embezzlement failed for lack of proof of dishonesty. The rationale for treating embezzlement as a serious crime is the element of breach of trust involved on the part of someone who stands in a fiduciary relationship to the victim. This was highlighted in *HM Advocate* v *Carpenter*,[54] where a solicitor had embezzled over £34,000 in the process of conducting executry work for a client. The sheriff had imposed a fine of £10,000 which was appealed by the prosecution on the ground of undue leniency. The appeal failed in the light of the mitigating circumstances, but the High Court noted that the public were usually entitled to expect a custodial sentence in such cases, and that they themselves might well have imposed one had they been the first Bench to try the case. Equally, successful prosecution was secured in *Guild* v *Lees*,[55] when a club secretary used the club cheque book to pay his own electricity bill. It was argued for him that this did not amount to embezzlement as it simply involved the transfer of incorporeal property rather than the transfer of money as such. This argument failed as the appellant had transacted in respect of money held in his club's account and that therefore embezzlement was an appropriate charge.

A definition of extortion can be found in *Crawford*,[56] where it was stated that "(t)he crime consists in using threats to concuss a person into paying a demand which he intends to resist; and the crime, the use of threat for that purpose, is the same, whether the party using the threat thinks his demand good or bad".[57] The modern definition looks for a demand for money to which the accused is not entitled, or an illegitimate demand for money which is legitimately due. Such a demand can be made either verbally or in writing[58] and will often encompass threats to expose some secret, such as an affair, or threats that the victim will lose their job or be dispossessed, to name but a few. One of the most cited cases dealing with extortion and theft is *Black and Penrice* v *Carmichael*.[59] The two accused were charged with extortion and, as an alternative, theft, for wheel clamping and immobilising a car, and extorting money from the owner for its release. On appeal, it was held that the case was clearly one of extortion, since the accused had set out to obtain money from the owner as a condition of freeing the car. However, it was also held that the facts made out a charge of theft, as the accused had deprived the owner of the use of his car without his consent and therefore had stolen it

---

[53] 1938 JC 55.
[54] 1999 SLT 1274.
[55] 1995 SLT 68.
[56] (1850) J Shaw 309.
[57] *Ibid* at 322.
[58] *Hopes and anr* v *HM Advocate* 1960 SLT 264 (verbal) and *Hogg* v *HM Advocate* 1954 SLT 82 (written).
[59] 1992 SLT 897.

from him. With reference to the charge of extortion, it was noted that, although the car owner had no right to park on that particular piece of private land, this was no defence to a charge of extortion. The Crown argument was based on the distinction between wheel clamping by the police in authorised circumstances, and private wheel clamping. The Lord Justice-General took his discussion of the issues back to first principles, namely that the accused cannot argue that he was entitled to take the law into his own hands: "The result or motive cannot justify the means, if what is done constitutes an offence."[60] Thus, while he sympathised with the landowner's outrage at finding cars parked without his permission on his land, it could not be said that the subsequent actions were legitimate. Instead, they clearly amounted to the crime of extortion.

MALICIOUS MISCHIEF

Malicious mischief will be charged where there has been wilful destruction of or damage to someone else's property. The essence of the crime is that the accused has shown deliberate disregard for or indifference to the property rights of another.[61] However, direct physical damage is not necessarily required. In *HM Advocate* v *Wilson*,[62] the appellant had activated the stop button on the turbines in an electricity generating station, halting its output into the National Grid for 28 hours and causing a loss of £147,000. It was argued for him that, since there was no direct physical damage and only pure economic loss, the indictment did not set forth a relevant charge. The High Court rejected his appeal, stating that there had been deliberate, malicious damage caused to another's property which, although usually shown through physical damage, could also be proved by economic loss as in this case. However, the decision was not unanimous and Lord Stewart felt that the charge was irrelevant as it failed to specify any physical damage to property.

A recent case investigating the extent of the crime of malicious mischief is *Bett* v *Hamilton*.[63] Bett was convicted of malicious mischief by moving a video camera so that it did not record activity in the area it was originally set to survey. The bank (whose building was covered by the camera) thereby wasted money on its inefficient use and were exposed to a greater risk of crime. The sheriff found this sufficient to impose liability for malicious mischief, as there had been financial loss. On appeal, it was held that it was necessary to show wilful intent to cause injury (in the form of either physical damage or patrimonial loss) to the owner of the property. In this case, the running costs of the camera would have been incurred regardless of the direction of the camera and the court declined to describe any such loss as patrimonial. Therefore the appeal was allowed.

---

[60] 1992 SLT 897 at 899.
[61] *Ward* v *Robertson* 1938 SLT 165, citing Hume.
[62] 1984 SLT 117.
[63] 1997 JC 1.

VANDALISM

Under s 52(1) of the Criminal Law (Consolidation) (Scotland) Act 1995, vandalism is charged where the accused has wilfully or recklessly destroyed or damaged someone else's property. The offence is separate from that of malicious mischief. There is, however, a defence of reasonable excuse. In *Murray* v *O'Brien*,[64] the accused had raised the issue of reasonable excuse in response to a charge of vandalism. She had witnessed an incident in her home during which her husband had been assaulted. As the third party tried to drive away, she vandalised his car in an attempt to stop him from leaving, by breaking a headlight and the windscreen. She had been convicted on the ground that this did not amount to a reasonable excuse. Her appeal against conviction failed, as it was clear that the justice had taken into consideration whether or not she had a reasonable excuse for her actions. The High Court held that it was for the justice to decide this issue and, in this particular case, the justice's decision was not an unreasonable one, and her appeal was rejected. In *John* v *Donnelly*,[65] the accused had cut a hole in part of a fence surrounding a nuclear base. She argued that her sincere belief in the illegality and "genocidal nature" of nuclear weapons was sufficient to provide her with a reasonable excuse which would prevent her conviction for vandalism. The High Court held that a reasonable excuse would cover situations where the accused had responded to an immediate situation (such as witnessing those who had just committed a crime in the process of escaping), but that it did not cover cases of deliberate action such as this, and her appeal was refused.

WILFUL FIRERAISING

Charges of fireraising can be brought under one of two headings: either wilful fireraising or culpable and reckless fireraising. The extent to which they differ is purely in terms of *mens rea*. In wilful fireraising, it is clear, and was reaffirmed in *Byrne* v *HM Advocate*,[66] that the prosecution must show that the accused intended to set fire to the property which is specified in the charge. There is no room in this offence for what is known as "transferred intent". If this doctrine were to apply in these cases, then the accused who intended to set fire to one piece of property would then be guilty of wilful fireraising in relation to all other pieces of property to which the fire then spread. Having intended to burn one item, his intention would then be transferred to the other items which were subsequently caught in the blaze. This is not the case. The authority of *Byrne* can also be used to show that, if the accused was reckless as to the consequences of his initial actions (if he set fire to items of property with utter disregard for the possibility that the fire

---

[64] 1994 SLT 1051.
[65] 2000 SLT 11.
[66] 2000 JC 155.

might spread to the property in question), then he should instead be convicted of culpable and reckless fireraising.[67] However, it was also stated in *Byrne* that wilful fireraising did not include any implied alternative charge of culpable and reckless fireraising and thus, if intention was not found, the jury could not be directed to return an alternative and lesser verdict unless the accused had been charged in the alternative.[68] The *actus reus* of these offences is satisfied by setting fire to property, whether that is moveable property[69] or heritable.[70] However, it will apply only where the article set alight is inanimate. This was made clear in *Wither* v *Adie*,[71] where the accused had set light to another person's shoelaces, causing the fire to spread to their trousers and injure their leg. It was argued for the accused that there could be no charge of wilful fireraising where the "article" set alight was a person. The High Court rejected this argument, stating that the reality of the case showed that the accused had set light to inanimate objects (the shoelaces). This was sufficient to found a charge of wilful fireraising, and the injuries caused to the victim were an aggravation of that charge.

COMPUTER CRIME

The area of computer crime is a vast and fast-evolving one, and thus one which it is impossible to discuss in any depth in a text of this sort. The field of computer crime encompasses issues such as hacking, pornography, obscenity, defamation, dissemination of viruses, privacy issues and fraud – to name but a few. Such issues require a depth of focus which cannot be provided here, and students should refer to more specialised texts.[72] However, there is one piece of legislation which can effectively be commented upon within the scope of this text. The Computer Misuse Act 1990 was enacted as the first major attempt to combat some, although by no means all, of the issues in computer crime. There is considerable theoretical difficulty in finding a home for this section within the chapter headings of this text. Whether or not pure information is "property", and therefore whether crimes relating to such information are "offences against property" for the purposes of this chapter, are difficult questions. However, without devoting an entire chapter to the issues involved in cyber-crime, this seems as good a chapter as any in which to discuss computer misuse.

The Computer Misuse Act 1990 takes as its starting point the problem of unauthorised access to a computer, which is covered both as an offence in itself and

---

[67] In this respect, *Byrne* overrules *Blane* v *HM Advocate* 1991 SCCR 576, in which it was held that a conviction for wilful fireraising was appropriate in cases where the accused exhibited recklessness alone.

[68] This overrules the position taken in *McKelvie* v *HM Advocate* 1997 SLT 758.

[69] *Thomson* v *HM Advocate* 1995 SLT 827, where the accused set fire to papers and office furniture.

[70] *Carr* v *HM Advocate* 1995 SLT 800, where the accused set fire to interior furnishings and ultimately the whole building.

[71] 1986 SLT (Sh Ct) 32.

[72] Akdeniz, Walker and Wall, *The Internet, Law and Society* (Longman, Harlow, 2000). See also chapters in Bainbridge, *Introduction to Computer Law* (5th edn, *Financial Times*/Prentice Hall, 2004).

as an offence preparatory to the commission of a further offence. Section 1 applies to persons who have caused a computer to perform a function with the intent of securing access to any data or program held on any computer. The *mens rea* is firmly rooted in intention. So far as the *actus reus* is concerned, causing a computer to perform a function can be satisfied by as little as turning the machine on, or by accessing it remotely and triggering display of a log-on menu or activating a security device. The offence requires that the intended access was unauthorised and the accused knew that his access was unauthorised. The type of data or program attacked is irrelevant, as is the location of the computer holding that information. Thus, it is competent to charge someone with performing a function on computer A in order to access data or programs stored on computer A, or on computer B. The section provides for a sentence, on summary conviction, of up to 6 months, or a fine, or both. This increases on indictment to up to 2 years' imprisonment, a fine, or both.

Section 2 penalises unauthorised access with the intent to commit or facilitate the commission of a further crime which has a sentence fixed by law, or which could lead to imprisonment for more than 5 years. It does not matter whether the further offence is to be committed by the accused or another, or whether it is to be committed contemporaneously with the unauthorised access offence, or is envisaged for some time in the future. The offence under s 2 will also still apply even if the further offence in question is not possible. If the accused is convicted on summary complaint, he faces a fine or up to 6 months' imprisonment, or both. If the charge is brought on indictment, he faces up to 5 years' imprisonment, a fine, or both. Section 3 applies to any intentional and unauthorised act which causes unauthorised modification to the contents of any computer. The unauthorised modification can be temporary or permanent, and includes alteration, deletion or addition to any program or data. The accused must have intended to cause such a modification, and that modification must have impaired the operation of the computer, program or reliability of data, or prevented or hindered access to programs and data. If convicted on a summary complaint, the accused faces up to 6 months' imprisonment, a fine, or both. If on indictment, he faces up to 10 years' imprisonment, a fine, or both.

SUMMARY OF MAIN POINTS

Theft
- wrongful appropriation of another's property
- intention permanently or temporarily to deprive
- corporeal and moveable property
- *appropriation*
  - unlawful deprivation of rights of ownership
  - thief puts property to his own use
- *by taking*
  - *amotio*
  - can be committed by lawful possessor
- *by finding*
  - if keep property beyond a reasonable time without returning
- consent is a defence
- *mens rea*
  - intention permanently to deprive
  - or temporarily deprive if coupled with a nefarious purpose
- aggravations
  - housebreaking with intent to steal
  - opening lockfast places
  - being found on premises in criminative circumstances

Robbery
- theft by means of personal violence or immediate threats of the same

Reset
- handling goods known to be stolen
- retaining them from true owner
- spousal exception

Fraud
- dishonesty which cause a practical result
- false pretence, prejudicial result, causal connection

Forgery
- forged documents must be intentionally uttered
- uttering amounts to displaying, presenting or putting out of one's control

Embezzlement
- accused is already in lawful possession of the property
- dishonestly appropriates it to himself
- abuse of trust

Extortion

- use of threats to force payment of money
- verbal or written threats

Malicious mischief

- wilful destruction of, or damage to, another's property
- not necessarily physical damage

Vandalism

- s 52(1) Criminal Law (Consolidation) (Scotland) Act 1995
- wilful or reckless destruction or damage to property
- defence of reasonable excuse

Fireraising

- either wilfully or culpably and recklessly
- setting fire to any inanimate property

Computer crime

- Computer Misuse Act 1990
- unauthorised access
- unauthorised access with intent to commit another offence
- unauthorised modification

THEFT

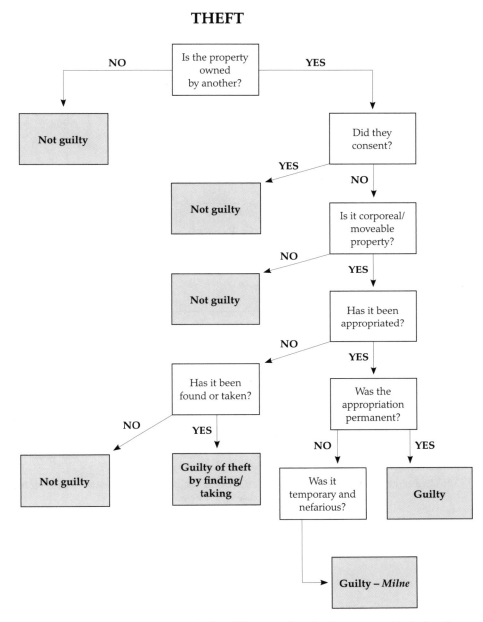

Note: Use of the word "guilty" is a convenient shorthand. There may be other issues to consider before the accused is convicted.

RESET

Is the accused in possession of stolen property?

NO

Was it stolen by someone else?

YES

Not guilty

NO

Guilty – theft

YES

Does he know it is stolen?

NO

YES

Was he wilfully blind?

Was the property brought into the house by the husband?

NO

YES

NO

YES

Not guilty

Guilty

Guilty

Not guilty – spousal exemption

Note: Use of the word "guilty" is a convenient shorthand. There may be other issues to consider before the accused is convicted.

FRAUD

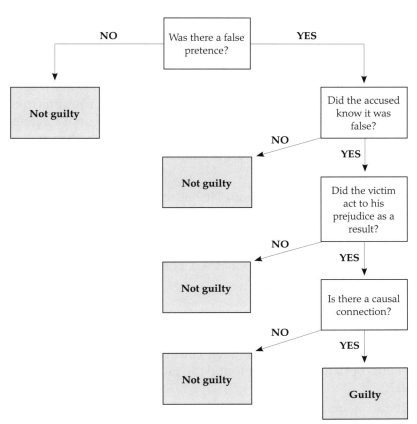

Note: Use of the word "guilty" is a convenient shorthand. There may be other issues to consider before the accused is convicted.

SELF-ASSESSMENT QUESTIONS (see Appendix for answers)

1   X had been in a long-running and bitter dispute with Y over Y's fondness for garden gnomes. Y currently has 50 gnomes in his front garden and X decides that the only way to force Y to remove the offending gnomes is to steal one and hold it to ransom. He waits until Y is out at work and then marches into Y's front garden and carries off Y's most precious gnome. Y's other neighbours are in their front garden and see what has happened. When Y returns from work, X confronts him, saying that he will not return the gnome until Y agrees to move all the gnomes to the back garden. What charge could be brought against X? Will the fact that the neighbours saw what X was doing have any effect on the charge brought?

2   X is involved in forging documents. He has several such documents on his desk when the police arrive with a warrant to search his premises. One document is genuine but has a false signature, and the other two are entirely forged. Of these documents, the first two are copies retained by X, the originals having been sent to a newspaper and published. The last document has yet to be sent. How many charges will X face?

Further questions

1   Should Black and Penrice have been convicted of theft, given that they had neither appropriated, taken nor found the property under the traditional heads of theft?

2   Is there any justification for the retention of the spousal exemption in reset?

Further reading

Jones and Christie, *Criminal Law* (4th edn), pp 283–332 and 338–357.
McCall Smith and Sheldon, *Scots Criminal Law* (2nd edn), pp 240–318.
Gordon, *Criminal Law* (3rd edn), vol 2, pp 5–281.

APPENDIX

Answers to self-assessment questions

Chapter 1

1   The case will be heard in the district court in Edinburgh by a justice of the peace. The maximum fine which could be imposed on the accused would be £2,500.

2   The jury is only used in solemn procedure. Its function is to determine matters of fact based on the evidence presented during the case, and following a direction on the law given by the sheriff. The jury will then determine the verdict (guilty, not guilty or not proven).

3   The sheriff's maximum sentencing powers differ depending on the type of procedure used. In summary procedure, he can sentence the accused to 3 months' imprisonment (6 months' imprisonment for a second or subsequent conviction) or fine him up to £5,000. Under solemn procedure, the sentence can be increased to 3 years or an unlimited fine. If this is felt to be insufficient for the severity of the crime, the sheriff can remit the case to the High Court of Justiciary, for sentencing purposes only.

4   Rape is one of the pleas of the Crown, and is therefore under the sole jurisdiction of the High Court of Justiciary.

Chapter 2

1   X's defence would raise the question of uninduced automatism, following *Ross*. His defence would argue that he was unaware and incapable of controlling his responses, because of his unintentional ingestion of amphetamines. Since he did not know that he had taken them, he could not be held responsible for their effects. This shows the leniency brought into the law by *Ross* which significantly mitigates the harshness of *Cunningham* in this type of case. Question: should he have been more suspicious when he realised that his pint tasted slightly odd? If he had consumed the amphetamines voluntarily, this line of argument would be closed to him as his automatistic state would be self-induced, and therefore would be something for which he should be held responsible.

2   X will be liable for murder. Although the wound he inflicted would have resulted in nothing more than a charge of aggravated assault in the normal

course of events, Y's pre-existing condition brings the "thin skull" rule into play. Thus, although X has no reason to be aware of Y's condition, he remains fully responsible for the full range of results caused by his criminal act, even though the result is well beyond what one would normally expect in such a situation.

Chapter 3

1   X's defence could try to argue that there was no *mens rea* for assault. Assault requires evidence of intent (specifically, evil intent). In cases such as *Lord Advocate's Reference (No 2 of 1992)* and *Baxter* v *HM Advocate*, the defence argument relied on a lack of *mens rea* given that the accused was joking. In both cases, these arguments failed. It is clear that the courts distinguish between the intention which allows the accused to commit deliberate and considered acts, and the motive which drives him to undertake the course of action. Playing a joke is an aspect of the motive for action. The acts themselves remain intentional and thus X would be convicted. It might be worth considering whether the charge should be lowered to simple assault, given that aggravated assault requires the accused to have a weapon and, arguably, X did not.

2   "He who wills the end wills the means." If the accused intends to steal property which is within some form of premises or container, he must, logically, also intend to force entry in order to carry out his theft. Thus, by intending to steal the diamonds, X must also intend to carry out such acts as are necessary to commit his intended crime. This clearly includes breaking into the premises and the display case.

Chapter 4

1   Y's argument would probably fail. Before a due diligence defence can succeed, it is necessary to show that the employer has relevant policies and procedures, and that they are enforced and monitored in order to ensure that they are working effectively. See *First Quench Retailing Ltd* v *MacLeod.* Here, although Y has maintained that there are such procedures, they are not physically available to X and his request for training has been ignored. This does not show an exercise of due diligence on the part of Y.

2   There is a strong presumption in favour of *mens rea*. It is assumed that Parliament will have intended to draft legislation so as to require both a criminal act and a criminal state of mind, although this presumption is rebuttable. Even if there is no mention of *mens rea* in the section itself, it is still necessary to consider the surrounding context so as to be sure that Parliament did intend strict liability. The fact that the rest of the statute specifies the required *mens rea* does not mean that its omission in this section denotes strict liability. If it is clear that the

section can only be applied effectively without any *mens rea* requirement, then the presumption is set aside.

Chapter 5

1   The knife-wielding accused will be convicted. The accused who stopped his part in the attack immediately will be able to dissociate himself from subsequent events, although he will be liable for the assault prior to that point. The other accused will be fully liable with the knife-wielding accused, as he has taken on responsibility for the foreseeable consequences of this new turn of events by continuing with his attack. See *Mathieson and Murray* v *HM Advocate*.

2   Yes, he will be liable art and part, as he is a public officer and thus under a duty to prevent the commission of a crime. By standing by and not acting to prevent the crime, he will automatically be liable art and part.

Chapter 6

1   The *actus reus* of incitement requires the accused to encourage another to commit a crime (by persuasion, suggestion etc). There is no need for incitee to respond to the incitement: *HM Advocate* v *Tannahill and Neilson*. Likewise, there is no need for any definite instruction by the inciter: *Baxter* v *HM Advocate*.

2   The accused would not be guilty of inciting the illegal fight, as his mere presence is not enough. He must show intentional encouragement of the crime.

3   Impossibility is not a defence to a charge of conspiracy: *Maxwell* v *HM Advocate*. Once the prosecution has established the fact of agreement along with intention, the accused is guilty regardless of whether the conspiracy could be carried out. Impossibility is a fortuitous event which has no bearing on their guilt, as they have subjectively carried out what was necessary to commit the crime and should therefore be convicted on that basis.

4   The Scottish approach is to impose liability on the basis of the preparation–perpetration test. This requires the accused to have carried out acts that go beyond simple preparation for the intended crime, and amount to perpetration: *HM Advocate* v *Camerons, Barrett* v *Allan, Guthrie* v *Friel*.

5   Impossibility is irrelevant to conviction for an attempt: *Docherty* v *Brown*. The accused thought he had possession of "Ecstasy" and intended to supply it, therefore he was guilty of the attempt even though the tablets did not contain the drug. Conviction is based on a subjective assessment – what did the accused think he was doing? Would he have committed a crime if he had succeeded in carrying out his (misconceived) plan? Therefore the accused here would be guilty of attempting to import cocaine even though he actually imported a harmless substance.

Chapter 7

1   No. The accused is under a duty to retreat so long as that will not expose him to any further risk or danger. Here he has an escape route through the open door which he should have used, unless that escape route itself would lead him into further danger. See *HM Advocate* v *Doherty*.

2   No. Intoxication is the only option available to the accused under the topics covered in this chapter. However, his intoxication is voluntary and so the defence is not open to him. See *Brennan* v *HM Advocate* and *Ebsworth* v *HM Advocate*.

3   No. *Ignorantia iuris neminem excusat*. He is in error as to the general criminal law and this is not a defence.

Chapter 8

1   Yes. X will be guilty of culpable homicide for assaulting Y and causing his death. The fact that Y suffers from a peculiar weakness will not be a defence, relying on the "thin skull" rule.

2   *Galbraith* overrules *Connelly*, which had wrongly interpreted the *Savage* criteria as joint pre-requisites. *Galbraith* also established the revised test for diminished responsibility – an abnormality of mind which had a substantial effect on the accused's actions. This includes abnormalities arising because of congenital, organic or psychological factors, or severe psychological trauma induced by abuse.

3   Provocation requires an attack on the accused by the victim or a confession of adultery. It is further necessary to show a loss of self-control in circumstances where the reasonable person would lose control, an immediate response (but note cumulative provocation) and a proportionate response.

Chapter 9

1   In the past, it was restricted to situations where the citizen had actually seen the accused commit the crime. However, modern authority would tend to suggest that this strict requirement is applied less rigidly than once it was.

2   Consent will operate as a defence in a case of assault if the context is one of consensual sporting activity within the rules of the game, or if informed consent has been acquired prior to medical intervention.

3   There is no requirement that the victim should suffer any physical injury as a result of the assault.

Chapter 10

1 Public indecency requires that the accused has committed an act which is objectively indecent by the standards of the day, and done so in a way in which the public would be able to see it or otherwise be exposed to it

2 Under the previous definition of shameless indecency (with which he was charged), his conduct was found to be criminal. Were such conduct brought to trial on a charge of shameless indecency more recently (but still prior to 2003), it may be that his conduct would have been viewed as less socially abhorrent and his conviction may have been harder to secure. However, post-2003, the ruling in *Webster* v *Dominick* precludes conviction in this type of case as there is no element of public exposure to the indecent conduct.

3 The 2007 Act has brought in an offence aimed specifically at the client rather than the prostitute (which is in itself relatively novel). It criminalises behaviour which would amount to what is known as "kerb crawling".

Chapter 11

1 He will be guilty of a criminal attempt since he subjectively believes that he is importing a prohibited narcotic. The modern approach, following *Docherty* v *Brown*, is to ignore the objective impossibility and convict him on the basis of his subjective conduct because it shows his potential criminality.

2 Y will clearly be convicted of possession of the packet of drugs which was found in his pocket. However, X will also be convicted, provided that the minute quantity is identifiable as a drug. Prior to *Keane* v *Gallacher*, X would not have been convicted because the tiny amount in his pocket would not have been useable.

Chapter 12

1 X will be charged with theft. Under *Milne* v *Tudhope*, he has exhibited an intention temporarily to deprive Y of the gnome, clandestinely and for a nefarious purpose. The fact that the neighbours saw what X was doing is not important. "Clandestinely" in this context simply refers to Y. The question to be asked is whether X acted secretly so far as Y was concerned.

2 X will face two charges of forgery. The fact that part of the first document is genuine is irrelevant. However, uttering is required before forgery becomes criminal and so he will face no charges in relation to the last document as it has not been uttered.

INDEX

Note: Summaries and self-assessment questionnaires have not been indexed.

Abbreviations used in the index

ASBO (antisocial behaviour order)
CEMA (Customs and Excise Management Act 1979)
DTTO (drug treatment and testing order)
ECHR (European Convention on Human Rights (1950))
High Court (High Court of Justiciary)
HRA (Human Rights Act 1998)
Hume (*Commentaries on the Law of Scotland Respecting Crimes*) (1797)
MODA (Misuse of Drugs Act 1971)